CU00766408

H.S.E.
JOSEPHUS WARTON S.T.P.
HUJUS ECCLESIÆ
PRÆBENDARIUS
SCHOLÆ WINTONIENSIS
PER ANNOS FERE TRIGINTA
INFORMATOR
POETA FERVIDUS FACILIS EXPOLITUS
CRITICUS ERUDITUS PERSPICAX ELEGANS
OBIIT XXIII FEB. M·DCCC
ÆTAT LXXVIII.
HOC QUALECUNQUE
PIETATIS MONUMENTUM
PRÆCEPTORI OPTIMO
DESIDERATISSIMO
WICCAMICI SUI
P·C·

CLASSICAL
EDUCATION IN
BRITAIN
1500–1900

BY THE SAME AUTHOR

Richard Porson
Greek Studies in England 1700–1830

CLASSICAL
EDUCATION
IN
BRITAIN
1500–1900

BY

M. L. CLARKE

Professor of Latin
University College of North Wales, Bangor

CAMBRIDGE

AT THE UNIVERSITY PRESS

1959

CAMBRIDGE
UNIVERSITY PRESS

University Printing House, Cambridge CB2 8BS, United Kingdom

Published in the United States of America by Cambridge University Press, New York

Cambridge University Press is part of the University of Cambridge.

It furthers the University's mission by disseminating knowledge in the pursuit of education, learning and research at the highest international levels of excellence.

www.cambridge.org
Information on this title: www.cambridge.org/9781107622067

© Cambridge University Press 1959

This publication is in copyright. Subject to statutory exception and to the provisions of relevant collective licensing agreements, no reproduction of any part may take place without the written permission of Cambridge University Press.

First published 1959
First paperback edition 2014

A catalogue record for this publication is available from the British Library

ISBN 978-1-107-62206-7 Paperback

Cambridge University Press has no responsibility for the persistence or accuracy of URLs for external or third-party internet websites referred to in this publication, and does not guarantee that any content on such websites is, or will remain, accurate or appropriate.

CONTENTS

CONTENTS

PREFACE

'Not to name the school', wrote Samuel Johnson, 'or the masters of men illustrious for literature, is a kind of historical fraud by which honest fame is injuriously diminished.' If their place of education deserves to be mentioned, no less do the studies they followed, and since in the past most of those illustrious for literature, and for other things as well, have studied the classics, a special importance attaches to this subject, to the part it has played in our education and the way in which it has been taught. This, together with the interest which teachers of the classics will naturally feel in the history of their trade, is my excuse for adding to the already large number of books on education.

I have ended with the end of the last century, since the historian shrinks from what he cannot see in perspective, and I do not feel competent to survey the present-day educational scene, much less to suggest solutions for its problems. But if a knowledge of the past can assist towards an understanding of the present, my book may be of some value to those who are concerned with shaping our educational policy.

While I have been mainly concerned with England I have tried to do justice to Scotland, whose educational history presents an interesting and instructive contrast to that of England. As regards Ireland I have compromised. I felt it was beyond my capacity to treat that country with the same detail as England and Scotland, and decided to confine myself to Trinity College Dublin, the materials for whose history are readily accessible.

To a small extent the present work overlaps with my earlier book *Greek Studies in England 1700–1830*, published in 1945, and a little material from that work has been repeated here.

I am grateful to Professor W. B. Stanford and Dr R. G. Cant for answering questions relating to Trinity College Dublin and St Andrews University respectively, and to Mr R. N. Quirk for criticism and encouragement. Among published works I owe a special debt to T. W. Baldwin's *William Shakspere's small Latine & lesse Greeke*, which was my guide when I first began to study the sixteenth-century grammar school.

M.L.C.

BANGOR

June 1958

Superior figures in the text refer to notes, which begin on p. 180

INTRODUCTION

The history of classical education in Britain may be said to begin in the year 78, when the Roman governor Agricola, after the spectacular military successes with which his governorship began, took measures to bind his subjects more closely to Rome. He encouraged the Britons to adopt the Roman way of life, and provided a liberal education for the sons of the local chieftains, 'so that those who had lately rejected the language of Rome now wished to acquire eloquence'. The words of Tacitus make it clear that the Britons were not only taught the Latin language; they were taught, as were the Romans themselves, to study literature in the school of the *grammaticus* and to practise the art of self-expression in the school of rhetoric.

Britain produced no Ausonius to celebrate her teachers, and evidence for the further history of education in Roman Britain is all but non-existent. None the less it is fitting that we should turn to the ancient world by way of prelude to this study, for it is there that we must seek the origins of the type of education we know as classical. Under the Roman Empire the established system of education was one based on the study and imitation of the best models of literature, one moreover in which a foreign language and literature, that of Greece, was regarded as having a claim on the schoolboy no less strong than that of his own language and literature.

The main function of the ancient *grammaticus* was to expound the poets. He would explain allusions and difficult words, expound the metre and insist on correct reading aloud. The Greek *grammaticus* would begin with Homer and proceed to the dramatists, Menander in particular; the Roman *grammaticus*, closely following the Greek example, concentrated on Virgil and on the Roman Menander, Terence. Sallust was read in the schools of the later Empire, but otherwise prose writers were generally ignored.

Grammar in the modern sense of the word had a place in the ancient grammar-school course, but the part it played was somewhat different from that which it plays in modern classical teaching. It was not the means of acquiring a knowledge of the language, but part of a course in language and literature for those who could already read and write. The Roman did not have to learn his own language by means of the grammar book, and the same may be said of Greek too; the Greek world and the Roman were so closely intermingled that Greek was hardly a foreign language to the Roman.

Closely connected with the school of the *grammaticus* was that of the rhetorician, to which the boy passed after completing his grammar-school course. In theory the functions of the *grammaticus* and the rhetorician remained distinct, and the teaching of composition belonged to the latter, but in practice it was usual, at any rate in the Latin schools of Quintilian's day, for *grammatici* to prepare their pupils for the rhetoric school by starting them on the preliminary exercises known as *progymnasmata*. Once under the rhetoric master the boy would concentrate on learning the theory of rhetoric and practising declamation, and would emerge from his training a thorough master of words, able to express himself elegantly and eloquently on any theme.

The tradition of the Roman schools, though it survived faintly, was very much weakened in the Middle Ages. The idea of an education based on literature and rhetoric, on the lies of the poet and the vanities of the orator, came under heavy fire from the fathers of the Church, who preferred to take from paganism only what was useful, and to subordinate this to sacred learning. The seven liberal arts handed down by the encyclopaedists of later antiquity became the trivium and quadrivium of medieval education, and though the study of the poets might creep in under the head of grammar and rhetoric, the first two stages of the trivium, it was at most periods of the Middle Ages very much in the background. It showed signs of returning in the eleventh and twelfth centuries, but was once more thrust out by the rediscovery of Aristotle in the thirteenth century and the new interest thereby aroused in philosophy, moral and natural.

There was no lack of grammar schools in England of the later Middle Ages, and, though evidence about their curriculum is scanty, it appears that in them the schoolboy might read some Ovid and Virgil and even compose Latin verses. But the level of scholarship was low, the elegances of classical Latin were little appreciated and there was no Greek. The student soon put grammar behind him and proceeded to the disputations of the universities.

In the early sixteenth century a new spirit came into the English schools, the spirit of humanism. The humanists spurned as barbarous the utilitarian Latin of the Middle Ages, and cultivated the classical elegances of Cicero and the Augustan poets. The study of Latin meant for them the study of the classics and the reading and imitation of the best classical models. It was not enough to be able to speak and write Latin; the student must learn to speak and write the best Latin, and to do this he must undergo a course of reading the best authors. And as the Romans had studied the classics of Greece as well as those of their own literature, so the second great language of antiquity was added to the programme of school studies.

This change in education was a part of the movement we know as the Renaissance. The revival of learning involved not only the reading and study of the classics but also the attempt to recover the ancient way of life, and the ancient way of life included the educational methods of antiquity. Quintilian's *Institutio Oratoria*, the full text of which was discovered by Poggio in 1416, became the acknowledged authority on education, and the ancient schools were revived with such modifications as changed conditions made necessary. The English grammar school as it was established in the sixteenth century, and continued for some three centuries after, was essentially the grammar school of the ancient world, or, to be

I-2

more precise, a combination of the ancient schools of grammar and of rhetoric, with the former predominating. Its curriculum and methods were not very different from those of the Roman Empire, and an Etonian under Keate would have felt quite at home in the schools of the time of Quintilian or Ausonius.

The year 1509, in which St Paul's school was founded by Colet, may be taken as the date of the introduction of humanism to English education. During the preceding century there had been a number of individual humanists in England, men who had visited Italy and learnt from Italian scholars, who read the classics and collected manuscripts and who could write respectable classical Latin. But they had little effect on education. They were noblemen and churchmen and men of affairs, not teachers or educational reformers. The main impulse to reform in education came from Erasmus, who first visited England in 1499 and made the acquaintance of English humanists such as Colet, More, Grocyn and Linacre. Of all humanist scholars Erasmus devoted most thought to education, and not only to theory but also to details of curriculum and method; and he found in Colet one who was ready to put his ideas into practice. St Paul's owed much to Erasmus; he took a keen interest in the school, helped in the compiling of a grammar book for it and wrote his *De Copia* for use there. It was here too that for the first time it was specifically laid down that Greek was to be taught.

The humanist ideas embodied in St Paul's soon spread to other schools, whether old foundations such as Winchester and Eton or the numerous schools founded or refounded under the Tudors. A regular system of grammar-school education was established, was embodied in statutes and ordinances, and, aided by the multiplication of school-books which the invention of printing made possible, long outlived those who initiated this reform in education. The English tradition of classical education goes back to the grammar schools of the sixteenth century, and it is with them that we begin our survey.

4

CHAPTER I

THE SIXTEENTH-CENTURY GRAMMAR SCHOOL

In 1518, a few years after the establishment of St Paul's school, Colet provided it with statutes.[1] The directions which he gave with regard to the curriculum are curious and a little puzzling. We might expect a kind of manifesto of humanism; what we find is in some respects out of keeping with what humanism normally involved and suggests that Colet's belief in the virtues of the classics was somewhat half-hearted.

As towchyng in this scole what shalbe taught of the Maisters and lernyd of the scolers it passith my wit to devyse and determyn in particuler but in generall to speke and sum what to saye my mynde, I wolde they were taught all way in good litterature both laten and greke, and goode auctors suych as have the veray Romayne eliquence joyned withe wisdome specially Cristyn auctours that wrote theyre wysdome with clene and chast laten other in verse or in prose. [He goes on to express the wish that after the Catechism in English and the Latin Accidence, the boys should read Erasmus's *Institutum Christiani Hominis* and his *Copia*.] And thenne other auctours Christian as lactanicus prudentius and proba and sedulius and Juvencus and Baptista Mantuanus and suche other as shalbe tought convenyent and moste to purpose unto the true laten spech all barbary all corrupcion all laten adulterate which ignorant blynde folis brought into this worlde and with the same have distayned and poysenyd the olde laten spech and the varay Romayne tong which in the tyme of Tully and Salust and Virgill and Terence was usid, whiche also seint Jerome and seint ambrose and seint Austen and many hooly doctors lernyd in theyr tymes. I say that ffylthynesse and all such abusyon which the later blynde worlde brought in which more ratheyr may be callid blotterature thenne litterature I utterly abbanysh and Exclude oute of this scole and charge the Maisters that they teche all way that is the best and instruct the chyldren in greke and laten in Redyng unto them suych auctors that hathe with wisdome joyned the pure chaste eloquence.[2]

While these directions show the true humanist scorn for un-classical Latin, they appear to propose that the authors studied in school should be not the recognised classics of the ancient world, but those Christian poets, whether belonging to late antiquity or to the period of revived classicism, who imitated their style. 'No more deadly or irrational scheme could have been propounded', is C. S. Lewis's comment.[1] It is indeed so strange that Colet has been suspected of disingenuousness.[2] It is true that elsewhere he shows himself highly suspicious of pagan writings,[3] but he had expressed admiration and approval of Erasmus's *De Ratione Studii* (1511), in which it was proposed that the authors read in school should be Plautus and Terence, Virgil and Horace, Cicero, Caesar and Sallust. Moreover, in a letter to Erasmus of 1512 he refers to the criticisms of a certain bishop who had described St Paul's as a house of idolatry, 'because the poets are read there'; no doubt it was the pagan poets who gave offence, and Colet here shows no signs of uneasiness.[4] There is in fact little doubt that the pagan authors formed the staple of the curriculum at St Paul's from the beginning. William Lily, the first High Master, in the *Carmen de Moribus* prefixed to his Latin grammar, mentions Virgil, Terence and Cicero as the authors whom the schoolboy will read, and in the curriculum designed by Cardinal Wolsey in 1528 for his school at Ipswich, which is probably derived from St Paul's, we find an exclusively pagan course of reading.[5] In the third form Aesop and Terence are to be read, in the fourth Virgil, and in the fifth Cicero's letters; the sixth form reads Sallust or Caesar, the seventh Horace's *Epistles* and the *Metamorphoses* or *Fasti* of Ovid, while the eighth and highest form is to read 'any ancient authors'.

Whether Colet's statutes represent a genuine desire to chris-tianise the grammar-school curriculum, or were merely designed to appease his critics, they had little influence on school practice, either at St Paul's or elsewhere. Christian Latin poets were occasion-ally prescribed, probably in deference to Colet, in the statutes of other schools,[6] but the only such author who seems to have been regularly used was Mantuanus, the 'old Mantuan' of *Love's Labour's Lost*.[1] Grammar-school reading was in the main pagan, and the English schoolboy was brought up on the same classics as his counterpart in ancient Rome.

The foundation of grammar-school education was the Latin grammar. Among the modest but not unimportant services of the humanists to education was the rescuing of Latin grammar from the mystifications with which it had been surrounded in the Middle Ages, so that it might be a useful instrument for learning the language. A beginning in this direction was made by John Stanbridge and his pupil Richard Whittington,[2] but their work was superseded by that of Lily of St Paul's. In the early years of Colet's foundation Lily, with some help from Colet and Erasmus, compiled the grammar which became the standard text-book for the English schools. Henry VIII ordained in 1540 that it should be used throughout the kingdom, and the mandate was confirmed by Elizabeth I.

This old grammar book will probably suggest to many a dismal picture of a class of boys chanting ill-understood rules before a dull pedant armed with the birch. But by no means all Tudor schoolmasters were dull or pedantic. Roger Ascham makes much of his idea of teaching syntax through retranslation of Cicero instead of what he calls 'the common waie used in common scholes, to read the Grammer alone by it selfe',[3] but his method is not very different from that advocated in the address to the reader prefixed, from 1546, to Lily's Grammar, which must have had a considerable influence on school practice. Here it is suggested that after learning the declensions and conjugations, with numerous examples, so that they may 'best understand and soonest conceive the Reason of the Rules', the schoolboys should accompany the learning of syntax by the reading of 'some pretty Book, wherein is contained not only the Eloquence of the Tongue, but also a good plain Lesson of Honesty and Godliness'. Sentences from this should be turned from an English version into the original

7

Latin, and the rules of syntax learned as they arose in connection with these sentences.

In some sixteenth-century schools the boys were encouraged to teach one another grammar by 'appositions', that is by asking each other questions. The statutes of Bury St Edmund's school lay down that half an hour before leaving school for dinner or supper the scholars should ask each other the inflections, cases, conjugations, tenses and moods, and a similar provision is found at Friars School, Bangor, whose statutes are closely copied from those of Bury, and at Harrow. In London grammatical disputations were conducted in public. The practice, which went back to the Middle Ages, was still in use at the end of the sixteenth century. Each year on the eve of St Bartholomew the boys of the City grammar schools went to the churchyard of St Bartholomew the Great, 'where,' says Stow, 'upon a bank boarded about under a Tree, some one Scholar hath stepped up, and there hath apposed and answered, till he were by some better Scholar overcome and put down: And then the Overcomer taking the Place did like as the first'. When this practice came to an end the City schoolboys 'did for a long Season disorderly in the open Street provoke one another with *Salve; Salve tu quoque. Placet tibi mecum disputare? Placet.* And so proceeding from this to Questions in Grammar, they usually fell from Words to Blows, with their Satchels full of Books, many times in so great Heaps, that they troubled the Streets and Passengers.'[1]

From the grammar book the schoolboy passed to his first reading-books. These were of an improving character. That old favourite of the Middle Ages, the 'Distichs of Cato', a collection of maxims in verse, which was re-edited by Erasmus along with other moral maxims such as those of Publilius Syrus, was regularly used in the schools of the sixteenth century, and with it usually went the Fables of Aesop, in a Humanist Latin version.[2] These well-established works were supplemented by books of dialogues devised by humanist scholars to help the young to acquire a command of conversational Latin. Of these the most popular was Erasmus's *Colloquies*, first published in 1519, which was being used at Eton by 1528, and is attested for a number of schools after that date.[1] A similar work was the *Colloquies* of the famous Spanish scholar Vives, otherwise known as *Exercitatio Linguae Latinae*, first published in 1532.[2] Second only in popularity to the *Colloquies* of Erasmus were those of Maturin Cordier, or Corderius (1479–1563), which were in use at Westminster in the 1570's and had a long life in the grammar schools after that date. Religious instruction was conveyed in dialogue form in the *Colloquia Sacra* of Castalion (1545), which was used in a few schools in the second half of the sixteenth century.[3] Latin poems of an improving nature prescribed for use in the lower forms include Lily's *Carmen de Moribus*, printed with his Latin grammar; Erasmus's *Christiani Hominis Institutum*, which, in view of its references to Catholic practice, presumably did not survive the Reformation; the elegiac poem *De Moribus in Mensa* of Sulpitius Verulanus (Sulpizio of Veroli) and that of Mancinus (Dominic Mancini) *De Quattuor Virtutibus* (1516).[4]

Among the classical authors to be read at school Erasmus had given first place to Terence as being the best author for teaching colloquial Latin.[5] His usefulness for this purpose gave him a place in almost every grammar-school curriculum. As Wolsey put it in his directions for Ipswich school, 'of those authors who contribute much towards a pure, terse and finished conversational speech is any wittier than Aesop or more useful than Terence?' Each of these authors, he goes on, is by the very nature of his subject not unpleasing to the young. That the subject-matter of Terence was largely illicit love did not worry the educationalists of the Tudor period; indeed Erasmus thinks of his plays as providing lessons in philosophy, and in the statutes of one sixteenth-century school we find him included among those authors 'which may induce and teach them to vertue to godliness and to honest Behaviour'.[6] Erasmus had suggested that some of Plautus's plays might be added to those of Terence, but in the English schools Terence was generally found sufficient.[1] At one school, Rivington in Lancashire, we find the *Adelphi* specified, but normally, we may surmise, the English schoolboy, like his Roman counterpart, began with the first play, the *Andria*, and in most cases perhaps this was the only play read.[2]

School reading was sometimes supplemented by the acting of the whole or part of a play. The Shrewsbury ordinances lay down that the first form, in this case the highest, 'shall for exercise declame and plaie one acte of a comedie', and there is a similar provision at the North Wales school of Ruthin. Where a whole play was acted it was normally done at Christmas. At Eton plays either Latin or English were performed at this season.[3] At Sandwich there was a statutory provision that every Christmas, if the Master thought fit, a 'comedy or tragedy of chaste matter' in Latin was to be played. So too in the Westminster statutes we read:

That the boys may with greater profit spend the season of Christmas and become better accustomed to a proper delivery and pronunciation, we ordain that each year within twelve days after Christmas day, or later at the discretion of the Dean, the master and usher shall cause their pupils to perform in the hall, in private or public, a Latin comedy or tragedy, and the master of the choristers an English one. And if they do not each do this, those whose negligence is responsible for the omission shall be fined ten shillings.

The explicit nature of the statute was no doubt the reason why the Westminster Latin play survived when similar productions at other schools had fallen into disuse.[4]

From Terence the schoolboy passed on through Ovid to Virgil and Horace. Of Ovid's works the *Metamorphoses* and *Tristia* were about equally popular; the former is found in Wolsey's Ipswich curriculum of 1528, the latter not until the middle of the century. Other works of Ovid occasionally used in schools of this period are the *Epistolae* (*Heroides*), the *Fasti* and the *Letters from Pontus*.[5]

Virgil probably had a place in every grammar-school curriculum. Usually the documents mention only the name of the author, and it is impossible to say which works were read. The intention perhaps was that all the works should be read, in the order in which they were written, but this was not always accomplished. If any work was omitted it would probably be the *Georgics*; thus at Eton in 1530 and Sandwich in 1580 only the *Eclogues* and the *Aeneid* are specified.[1] Horace, if not so universally read as Virgil, had a place in the curriculum of most schools. Here again we are usually given only the name of the author. At one school, Rivington, the *Odes* are specified, and in view of later school practice one would be inclined to interpret 'Horace' as meaning this work; but Wolsey mentions only the *Epistles* in his Ipswich curriculum, and it may well be that they were preferred in some other schools.

Other verse authors were seldom read. At Eton, however, in 1560 Martial and Lucan were included in the curriculum; the Westminster curriculum, which is based on that of Eton, included the same authors, as did that of Ruthin, which in turn was derived from Westminster. Westminster adds Silius Italicus and Ruthin Seneca's tragedies.[2] Juvenal and Persius are also occasionally found.[3]

In 1582 a curious attempt was made to oust some of the accepted classical texts in favour of a modern Latin poem. In that year a historical work in verse, *Anglorum Proelia*, by Christopher Ocland, was reissued together with a loyal and patriotic poem entitled Εἰρηναρχία, on the peaceful state of the country under Elizabeth's rule. The Privy Council directed the Commissioners for Causes Ecclesiastical to instruct the bishops to see that this work was introduced to grammar schools 'in place of some of the heathen poets nowe read among them, as *Ovide de arte amandi, de tristibus* or such lyke'. The commissioners did as they were directed, but fortunately either the bishops took no action or the schoolmasters ignored them.[4] There is no evidence that Ocland's work was ever read in schools.

As regards prose writers, the book most commonly read in the lower forms was a selection of Cicero's letters, no doubt that of Sturm, which is specified in some of the documents and may be assumed to have been generally used. In an age in which Latin letter-writing was an important accomplishment Cicero was a useful model. As Wolsey put it, 'no other letters in my opinion are easier or more fruitful for the acquiring of a rich store of language'.[1] Speeches of Cicero are first mentioned in the statutes of Norwich school (1566), though there are documents before that date which mention Cicero without specifying any particular work. But the speeches were probably less read than the philosophical works, in particular *De Officiis*, which is frequently found in school curricula from the middle of the century onwards. *De Amicitia* and *De Senectute* were also known to the schools, and there are occasional references to the *Tusculans*, *De Finibus* and *De Natura Deorum*. At Winchester in 1530 the *Paradoxa* was read on Sundays.

Of the historical writers both Caesar and Sallust are mentioned in the Ipswich curriculum, and are found in those of numerous later foundations, Sallust being the more popular of the two. In preferring Sallust school practice reversed the judgment of Erasmus,[2] and returned to that of antiquity; Sallust, as has already been said, was read in the Roman grammar schools, and Quintilian, who gives Sallust high praise, did not think Caesar's *Commentaries* worthy of mention. Livy entered the school curriculum comparatively late; there appears to be no mention of him before the Elizabethan statutes of Westminster. At Ruthin towards the end of the sixteenth century we find speeches from Livy prescribed, and it may be surmised that elsewhere where Livy was read he owed his place more to his rhetorical gifts than to his importance as a historical authority. Indeed at this period there was scarcely any interest in ancient history for its own sake, and the historical writers were read partly for their style and partly as a source of moral tales and examples. Hence we find authors such as Justin and Valerius Maximus, who are commonly neglected today, included now and again in sixteenth-century curricula.[1]

The word used in Latin statutes for the reading of authors in class is *praelectio*. The word and the method were derived from the Roman grammar school, and a prelection on Terence as described by Cardinal Wolsey must have been very like that of a Roman *grammaticus*. The master begins with a brief account of the author's circumstances, character and stylistic virtues; then he explains how pleasant and useful is the reading of comedies and what is the meaning and derivation of the word 'comedy'. He summarises the plot and explains the metre, reads the lines in grammatical order, and points out archaisms, coinages, Greek words and various grammatical and rhetorical figures, calling attention to beauties of style and features worthy of imitation. But the Roman *grammaticus* taught his boys the literature of their own language, whereas the English schoolmaster did not; Roman methods had to be modified, and the first task was to see that the boys understood what they were reading. Reading an author in school meant primarily construing, or 'construction' as it was often called. John Brinsley, master of Ashby-de-la-Zouch school and author of the dialogue on education *Ludus Literarius*, describes the usual method as 'to give lectures (i.e. readings) to the severall formes or cause some Scholler to do it. And therein first to reade them over their Lecture, then to construe them and in the lower formes to parse them. So when they come to say; to heare them whether they can reade, say without booke, construe and parse.'[2] The statutes of Sandwich school add translation into continuous English to word-for-word construing: 'Everie lesson shall be said without booke and construed into Englishe by every scholler reading that author; the words shall first be Englished severallie as the grammaticall construccion lieth and afterwards the hole sentence or lesson rehersed in English as it lieth together.' It will be seen that in addition to construing and translating the schoolboy had to learn by heart the passages read. The evening was the time for memorising and the morning for repetition. Thus the statutes of Westminster lay down that at seven o'clock in the morning all the classes shall recite from memory the passages read the previous day.

The main purpose of school reading was to acquire a good command of spoken and written Latin. In the sixteenth century the language was still living, and would be required by the educated man for speaking and writing as well as for reading. The first aim of the grammar school was to teach the boys to speak Latin, and consequently it was the rule that the language should be spoken in school.[1] That this practice did not necessarily produce good results is shown by the remarks of Ascham, according to whom even in the best schools 'for wordes, right choice is smallie regarded, true proprietrie whollie neglected, confusion is brought in, barbariousnesse is bred up so in yong wittes, as afterward they be, not onelie marde for speaking, but also corrupted in judgement: as with much adoe, or never at all, they be brought to right frame againe'.[2]

Some school statutes show a desire to give the boys a wide vocabulary for everyday use at an early stage. At Rivington, for example, the usher is to begin with the Latin words 'for every part of a man and his apparel; of a house and all household stuff, as in bedding, kitchen, buttery, meats, beasts, herbs, trees, flowers, birds, fishes with all parts of them; virtues, vices, merchandise and all occupations; as weavers, tanners, carpenters, ploughers, wheelwrights, tailors, tilers and shoemakers'.[3] But even apart from such lessons the schoolboy who read Erasmus's *Colloquies* would acquire from them a far wider vocabulary than the schoolboy of today acquires, while Terence would supplement the *Colloquies* in supplying conversational phrases and idioms.

In addition to learning to speak Latin the schoolboy would be required to do a number of written exercises. First came 'the making of Latins', that is translating English sentences or 'Vulgars'. Thus at Eton in 1560 the usher gives his three classes a sentence for translation (a very short one for the first form); the boys write out their version, learn it by heart and say it the next day. Schoolmasters devised their own 'vulgars', or used published books, such as the *Vulgaria* of William Horman of Eton (1519), a collection of English sentences with the Latin equivalents. Horman's work, along with that of Whittington, is unfavourably mentioned by Ascham, who considered that 'Latins' only taught the young a Latin which they would have to unlearn later and dulled their wits by encouraging them to produce the version that their master expected.[1]

Apart from this elementary exercise translation of English into Latin was not practised, and the schoolboy soon passed to exercises in original composition. Important among these was letter-writing. As the statutes of Rivington put it,

the elder sort must be exercised in devising and writing sundry epistles to sundry men, of sundry matters, as of chiding, exhorting, comforting, counselling, praying, lamenting, some to friends, some to foes, some to strangers; of weighty matters, or merry, as shooting, hunting etc., of adversity, or prosperity, of war, and peace, divine and profane, of all sciences and occupations, some long and some short.

Cicero's letters, as we have seen, provided a model, but they were supplemented by treatises on epistolary composition such as Erasmus's *De Conscribendis Epistolis*,[2] in which could be found an elaborate classification of the different types of letters and directions on the appropriate manner of treating each type, together with formulae for beginning and ending a letter. The influence of rhetoric lay heavy on the letter-writing of the Renaissance. The simple letters of Cicero in Sturm's selection were embedded in an elaborate rhetorical commentary. As Erasmus said, some kinds of letters might be called declamations or orations,[3] and the Latin letters composed in school were probably not much different from the other prose exercises, themes and declamations.

The theme was a written essay, corresponding to the *pro-gymnasmata* which under the Roman Empire had formed part of the grammar-school course. The declamation was distinguished from the theme in being concerned with some controversial subject which could be handled in the affirmative or the negative; it was delivered orally, with one boy upholding a thesis, another controverting it, and sometimes a third summing-up.[1] Whether for theme or declamation, composition was taught on the lines laid down by ancient rhetoric, and some of the ancient text-books were still in use, such as *Ad Herennium*, then believed to be the work of Cicero, Quintilian and Aphthonius, whose *Progymnasmata* in a Latin version was the main text-book for theme-writing.[2] Of modern aids to the writing of Latin the most popular was Erasmus's *De Copia*, a guide to the acquisition of a copious Latin style based partly on rhetorical precept, partly on the author's wide reading and long practice in writing Latin.

Latin prose-writing as taught in the grammar schools might be described as an exercise in variation, that is, in saying the same thing in a number of different ways. *Discant orationem infinitis modis variare* are the words used in the statutes of one school,[3] and anyone who has read Erasmus's *De Copia* will know that *infinitis modis* is hardly an exaggeration. Erasmus gives two examples of how a short Latin sentence can be varied, and in both cases he succeeds in doing it in well over a hundred different ways.[4] The *De Copia* deals with its subject under two heads, *Copia Verborum* and *Copia Rerum*, but the latter is not so very different from the former; *copia rerum* for Erasmus means what is in effect only another form of variation, by which a sentence is not merely paraphrased but expanded. And this was the method of school theme-writing. The aim was not to convey information or put forward original views, but to expand some moral commonplace by means of the various devices enumerated in the rhetorical handbooks.

The complete command of Latin at which the grammar-school education aimed involved the ability to express oneself in verse no less than in prose. Latin verse, as Brinsley puts it, was useful 'sometimes in occasions of triumph and rejoycing, more ordinarily at the funerals of some worthy personages, and sometimes for some other purposes'.[1] So we find versifying regularly mentioned as one of the school exercises. The rules of prosody would be learnt as part of the Latin grammar; there would probably be exercises in putting the words of a poet into their grammatical order and then turning them back into verse;[2] and in the upper forms one of the weekly tasks would be to produce a copy of elegiacs on a set subject. Composition in verse as in prose was largely an exercise in varying. 'The master', we read in the Westminster statutes, 'shall set a theme for varying, in verse to the sixth and seventh forms, in prose to the fifth.' In a book published by an English schoolmaster in 1597 could be found examples of no less than four hundred and fifty ways in which the same sentiment could be expressed in a single elegiac couplet.[3]

The increased knowledge of Greek among scholars, its importance as the language of the New Testament and of the best ancient authorities in philosophy, the prestige which Greek literature had had among the Romans and its place in their educational system, made it natural that Greek should be added to Latin in the grammar-school course. In the first half of the sixteenth century Greek scholars were few and the teaching of the language was, generally speaking, confined to the universities. But there was certainly some Greek taught in the schools in this period. Colet's statutes for St Paul's lay down that the Master is to be learned in Greek 'yf suyche may be gotten', and the first High Master was one of the few Englishmen of his day so qualified. He appears to have given some teaching in Greek from the early days of the school, if only to selected pupils, such as Thomas Lupset and John Clement, both of whom are said to have learned their Greek from him.[4] Greek was apparently being taught at Eton in the second and third decades of the century, for Sir Thomas Pope, who was born about 1507, records that when he was at the school 'the Greeke tongue was growing apace', and it has been plausibly suggested that the introduction of the language was due to Robert Aldrich, a friend of Erasmus, who was headmaster from 1515 to 1521.[1] Pope, writing in 1556, goes on to say that the study of Greek is 'now alate much decaied',[2] and there is no mention of it in the Eton curriculum of 1530, while in that of 1560 the two highest forms study Greek, but no more than the grammar. The earliest reference to Greek authors in a school curriculum appears to be in the statutes of East Retford school (1552); but a curriculum which, in a school of only four forms, includes Justinian's Institutes in the reading of the second form and both Greek and Hebrew in the work of the fourth form, gives the impression of being impracticable. By the 1560's, however, Greek was well established in the schools, and in the statutes of that period we find provision made for the reading of authors such as Isocrates, Homer and Euripides.[3]

Erasmus in his *De Ratione Studii* had suggested that Greek and Latin should be studied concurrently 'not only because these two languages contain almost all that deserves to be known, but also because each is so closely related to the other that both can be more quickly grasped together than either without the other, certainly than Latin without Greek'.[4] In fact it proved impracticable to begin Greek at the same time as Latin, if only because some knowledge of Latin was required in order to use the Greek grammar book. Latin, the international language of learning, was the medium of instruction in Greek; the Greek grammar was in Latin, as were the editions of Greek authors, and in class it seems to have been usual, though perhaps not universal, to construe from Greek into Latin.[5]

The Greek grammar book in common use during most of the sixteenth century was that of Clenardus, first published in 1530. A simpler book, better adapted to the needs of the young, was produced in 1575 by Edward Grant, headmaster of Westminster, but this was superseded by the grammar of Grant's successor, William Camden, published in 1597. This soon established itself as the standard grammar for the English schools, and though replaced at Westminster by Busby's in the mid-seventeenth century, retained its position elsewhere until the nineteenth century.

The usual first reading-book in Greek was the New Testament, but otherwise school reading was exclusively pagan and followed roughly the same lines as Latin reading. The *Tabula* of Cebes and Aesop in Greek provided some simple morality, and Lucian some lively dialogue.[1] Demosthenes and Isocrates corresponded to Cicero, and Homer and Hesiod to Virgil; historical writing was hardly represented, for when we find Xenophon specified, we may assume that the *Cyropaedia* is intended.[2] Menander, the Greek equivalent of Terence, was lost, and Erasmus's suggestion that Aristophanes should take his place was not carried into effect in schoolteaching. Euripides is mentioned in two curricula of the 1560's,[3] but is missing from those of the later part of the century, and it was not until considerably later that Greek plays formed a regular part of school work. Plutarch is found at Westminster; the Harrow statutes specify Heliodorus and Dionysius of Halicarnassus, and those of Durham Theognis or Phocylides.[4] The Blackburn statutes (1597) give an impressive list of Greek authors to be read, but there remains the suspicion that some of these, if read at all, were read only in the brief extracts appended to Clenardus's grammar.[5]

As Erasmus pointed out, there was a difference between Greek and Latin in that Greek was learnt more with a view to reading Greek authors than for use in conversation.[6] Less time therefore was spent on exercises in Greek than in Latin. None the less it was expected that a Greek scholar should be able to write the language if not to speak it,[7] and some school statutes refer to boys performing the usual exercises, epistles, themes, and verses, in Greek as well as Latin.[8] Those of St Bees (1583) provide the earliest example of the provision which appears in some statutes of the seventeenth century, that the master should be able to make Greek as well as Latin verses,[9] a provision which implies that Greek verse composition would be taught in the schools. In the early part of the seventeenth century the most important schools were noted for their Greek verse-composition,[1] and it seems likely that from the early days of Greek teaching the tendency was to ignore prose exercises in favour of verse. In a dialogue of Erasmus one of the characters asks 'Would you have ever believed it possible that in Britain or Holland boys would chatter in Greek (*Graece garrirent*) and amuse themselves not without success in little Greek epigrams?' The implication is that such accomplishments were not unknown among the schoolboys of this country. The ability to write a Greek epigram must have been very rare in the English schools in 1528, the date of Erasmus's dialogue, but by the end of the century it was probably not uncommon.[2]

CHAPTER II

THE UNIVERSITIES IN THE SIXTEENTH CENTURY

Erasmus distinguished two branches of knowledge, that of words and that of things. The mastery of language came first, but it led on to what was more important, the mastery of the knowledge expressed in language.[1] The distinction corresponds roughly to that between the grammar schools and the universities; the former taught the learned languages, the latter the 'arts', or, as we should now rather call them, the sciences. The traditional arts course of the universities comprised the old trivium and quadrivium, grammar, dialectic and rhetoric, arithmetic, geometry, music and astronomy, with the addition of moral and natural philosophy and metaphysics. So long as this scheme provided the basis of the university course there was little room in it for the study of language and literature, for grammar and rhetoric were of minor importance compared to the other arts, and were to a large extent covered by the grammar-school course. Though humanism in the sense of the study and imitation of the best classical authors found its way into the universities in the sixteenth century, its influence was limited, and it hardly affected the general scheme of university studies. Universities were a creation of the Middle Ages, and in them medievalism died slowly.

Humanism however meant more than the imitation of classical models. It meant also the rediscovery of ancient authors, the knowledge of whom contributed to learning in the traditional university subjects. The advance of scholarship brought to light new authorities in philosophy and science and thus involved a challenge to the traditional methods and text-books of the universities. In particular the spread of Greek scholarship had an importance which extended beyond the sphere of language and literature.

Almost all knowledge of things, said Erasmus, must be sought from the Greek writers.[1] Greek opened the way to the original Aristotle, the source of scholastic philosophy and the acknowledged authority in science, and, outside the arts faculty, to Hippocrates in medicine and in theology to the New Testament and the Greek Fathers.

Of the two English universities Oxford was the first to receive the new learning. The 'accurate scholars in both languages' whom Erasmus found in London in 1505, men like Linacre, Grocyn, More and Lily, were all Oxford men.[2] But their learning, in Greek at any rate, had, except in the case of More, been mainly acquired abroad. There was as yet no regular teaching of Greek in England. Grocyn had taught the language at Oxford for a few years, from 1491 to 1493, and it was probably from him that More acquired his Greek, but his lectures were not part of the regular academic course of studies and he had no immediate successors.

Humanist studies were first securely established at Oxford with the foundation of Corpus Christi College by Richard Fox in 1517. Fox's statutes made it clear that he was consciously introducing something new into the university. They established three public lecturers for the whole university, in Latin, Greek and Divinity. The lecturer, or professor, of Latin, or Humanity, was 'manfully to root up and cast out barbarity from our garden, should it sprout at any time'.[3] He was to lecture daily on the classics, choosing from among the following authors: in prose, Cicero's letters, speeches and *De Officiis*, Sallust, Valerius Maximus and Suetonius, and, for the more advanced, Pliny's *Natural History*, Livy, Cicero's rhetorical works and Quintilian; and in verse, Virgil, Ovid, Lucan, Juvenal, Terence and Plautus. The professor of Greek was to read the Greek grammar, with some of Isocrates, Lucian or Philostratus; Aristophanes, Theocritus, Euripides, Sophocles, Pindar, Hesiod or some other poet, together with parts of Demosthenes, Thucydides, Aristotle, Theophrastus or Plutarch.

Shortly after the foundation of Corpus Christi College Cardinal

Wolsey decided to found professorships of, among other subjects, Greek and Humanity. The history of these is obscure, but it appears that Wolsey's foundation merged with that of Fox, and that his professors were housed in Corpus Christi College.[1] Among the early professors or readers of Humanity were two pupils of Colet, John Clement and Thomas Lupset, and no less a person than Vives. Clement lectured with such success that, as More wrote to Erasmus, even those who had recently regarded good literature with dislike loved him, listened to him and gradually grew less stubborn.[2] Lupset, who succeeded Clement in 1519 or 1520, and lectured on both Greek and Latin, aroused admiration by his exposition of Cicero's *Philippics*. 'So plentifully', wrote the university authorities in 1521, 'does he bedew us with the figures of rhetoric and so eloquently does he daily strive to cultivate our taste, that, the dregs of barbarism having been removed, we trust that the very form of eloquence may soon live again.'[3] Vives, who came to Oxford in 1523 and lectured again there in the winter of 1524–5, was also well received.[4]

In spite of the welcome given to these lecturers the entry of humanism to Oxford had met with considerable opposition. A party was formed of men who called themselves Trojans, to oppose the introduction of Greek. Sermons were preached attacking not only Greek but all liberal studies. The matter reached the ears of Thomas More, who wrote from Abingdon, where he was in attendance on the king, a weighty letter to the university urging a more favourable reception of Greek. He pointed out that though Greek might not be necessary to salvation, students went to Oxford to study, and to study not only theology, but the poets, orators and historians, natural science and philosophy, while even for theology Greek was essential. It was not his purpose, he said, to defend Greek, whose utility was obvious, but rather to exhort the university not to let anyone be deterred from learning a language the teaching of which had been sanctioned by the universal church. He reminded them that among the Greek scholars of Oxford were some whose reputation had brought renown to the university abroad, held up the example of Cambridge, and ended by threatening them with the displeasure of the archbishops and of the king himself. There followed a royal letter in support of Greek which put an end to the opposition.[1]

In contrast to these excitements Greek came to Cambridge, as Erasmus remarked, quietly, thanks to the influence of the Chancellor, John Fisher.[2] Erasmus himself had introduced the language to the university in 1511, when he settled in Queens' College and taught the Greek grammar to a small class.[3] Three years later, in 1514, he left Cambridge. He left behind him a few pupils, such as Henry Bullock of Queens' and John Bryan of King's, the latter of whom as reader in logic lectured on Aristotle from the Greek text.[4] But the regular teaching of Greek in the university dates from 1518, when Richard Croke returned from abroad to be appointed reader in Greek. In his inaugural oration he spoke in eloquent terms of the greatness of the Greeks and the merits of their language. He dwelt on the utility of Greek in the fields of grammar, rhetoric, mathematics and music, and of its value to medicine and theology, and ended, no doubt with Fox's foundation in mind, by exhorting his audience not to let themselves be outstripped in the study of Greek by Oxford men and not to be deterred by the effort which it involved.[5]

Croke left Cambridge in 1529. In 1533 Thomas Smith succeeded to the readership of Greek, and for a few years lectured with success on Homer and Aristotle, Plato and Euripides.[6] In 1540 John Cheke, who had already taught Greek in his own college of St John's and in the University, became the first holder of the Regius Professorship founded by Henry VIII. His teaching aroused a widespread interest in Greek. Writing to a friend in 1542 or 1543 Roger Ascham described how Aristotle and Plato were now being read in the original:

Sophocles and Euripides are now more familiar than Plautus was when you were here. Herodotus, Thucydides and Xenophon are more widely quoted and read than Livy then was; Demosthenes is as familiar as Cicero once was; there are more copies of Isocrates in the students' hands than there were of Terence. Nor do we despise the Latin writers, but we eagerly welcome the best authors who flourished in the golden age. This zeal for literature has been kindled and sustained by the labours and example of Cheke. He has read in public lectures free of charge the whole of Homer and the whole of Sophocles twice, all Euripides and almost all Herodotus. He would have done the same in the case of all the Greek poets, historians, orators and philosophers, if an ill fate had not envied us our happy progress in literature.[1]

The fate which had such unhappy results was the intervention of the Chancellor, Stephen Gardiner, on the question of the pronunciation of Greek. When the language had first spread to the West it had been learned from Greeks, and they had naturally imparted their pronunciation along with the language. A method which reduced so many vowels and diphthongs to a single sound aroused the criticism of Erasmus in his work on the pronunciation of Greek and Latin published in 1528. A few years later Smith and Cheke took the matter up, and after some study of the question began cautiously to introduce a reformed pronunciation. Ascham, who was then lecturing on Isocrates, after some initial opposition came over to their side and became a strong supporter of reform.[2] In 1539 Smith went abroad and left the cause of Greek and of the new pronunciation to Cheke. In 1542 there came a decree from Gardiner ordering in severe terms a return to the old pronunciation. The effect was discouraging. Cheke no longer felt any pleasure in lecturing, nor his class in listening; according to Ascham, Gardiner's action 'completely extinguished almost all the ardour we had felt for learning Greek'. Now all sounds were the same, 'so subjected to the power of single letter iota, that you can hear nothing in Greek but a feeble chirping as of sparrows and an unpleasant hissing as of snakes'.[3] The scholars of the university obeyed their Chancellor, but proceeded to argue their case with him. Cheke engaged in a protracted correspondence with him, and Smith, who was now back in England, addressed to him a lengthy letter, more conciliatory in tone and perhaps more effective than Cheke's rhetorical appeals. Gardiner, as Ascham admitted, made a good case, but reason and learning were on the side of Cheke and Smith.[1] Neither side convinced the other. In spite of the initial compliance with the Chancellor's decree, the new pronunciation was not crushed; Gardiner continued to press his views on Cambridge until his death, after which the university was permitted to pronounce Greek as it chose.[2]

Cheke, as has already been said, gave public lectures on Homer, Sophocles, Euripides and Herodotus. In addition to these authors he read privately with pupils in his rooms Thucydides, Xenophon, Isocrates and Plato, and was intending to go on to Aristotle and Demosthenes when in 1544 he was summoned to court to be tutor to Edward VI.[3] These last two authors he continued to study after leaving Cambridge; he read Aristotle's *Ethics* with Edward VI, and in 1550 he was working on Demosthenes. Later on, when he left England under Mary, he had the opportunity to expound the Athenian orator, for whom he had the highest admiration, to a number of Englishmen at Padua. Sir Thomas Wilson, the first English translator of Demosthenes, who was one of his hearers, recalls 'his care that he had over all the Englishe men there, to go to their bokes: and how gladly he did reade to me and others certaine Orations of Demosthenes in Greeke'.[4]

Such records as we have of Cheke's lecturing suggest that he was a teacher of unusual gifts. Evidently he did not confine himself to verbal commentary, for it was his exposition of Herodotus that inspired Ascham with a love of travel.[5] Nor did he disdain the use of English. 'Better skill', says Sir Thomas Wilson, 'he had in our English speech. . . than any else had that I have knowne. And often he would Englyshe his matters out of the Latin or Greeke upon the sodeyne, by looking of the booke onely without reading or construing any thing at all.'[6] He was well aware of the educational and practical value of the ancient writings. He

held Demosthenes to be the orator best fitted to make an Englishman a good speaker in parliament or pulpit, and considered
Aristotle's *Ethics* superior to the *Cyropaedia* for training a young
prince.[1] As regards reading in general he was fond of saying that
a good student should study all authors Greek and Latin; 'but he
that will dwell in these few bookes onelie; first in Gods holie
Bible, and then joyne with it, Tullie in Latin, Plato, Aristotle:
Xenophon: Isocrates: and Demosthenes in Greke: must nedes
prove an excellent man'.[2]

With the departure of Cheke Cambridge lost her leading
Grecian. 'As oft as I remember', wrote Ascham, 'the departing
of that man from the University (which thing I do not seldom)
so oft do I well perceive our most help and furtherance to learning,
to have gone away with him.'[3] But there remained others to
carry on Cheke's work, among them Ascham, who lectured
daily on Greek at St John's, and Nicholas Carr, who succeeded
Cheke as Regius Professor and lectured mainly on Demosthenes
and Plato, but also on Homer, Sophocles, Euripides and Theocritus.[4] Carr was an eloquent speaker who drew large crowds to
his lectures; according to Francis Bacon, he and Ascham almost
deified Cicero and Demosthenes, and allured 'all young men that
were studious unto that delicate and polished kind of learning'.[5]

In 1550, when Ascham returned to Cambridge after tutoring
the princess Elizabeth, he reported to Sturm that the best authors
in Greek and Latin were being read, and that many inspired by
Cheke and Smith had entered upon such studies.[6] But it was not
long before humanism at Cambridge was checked. The effects of
Mary's accession in 1553 are described in vivid, if prejudiced,
terms by Ascham.

Judgement in doctrine was wholly altered: order in discipline very
sore changed: the love of good learning, began sodenly to wax cold, the
knowledge of the tonges (in spite of some that therein had flourished)
was manifestly contemned: and so, the way of right studie purposely
perverted: the choice of good authors of mallice confownded. Old

sophistrie (I say not well) not olde, but that new rotten sophistrie began to beard and sholder logicke in her owne tong: yea, I know, that heades were cast together, and counsell devised, that Duns, with all the rable of barbarous questionistes, should have dispossessed of their place and rowmes, Aristotle, Plato, Tullie and Demosthenes.[1]

So ended the first period of classical studies at Cambridge. Meanwhile in Oxford little had been done to follow up the work of the early lecturers on the foundations of Fox and Wolsey. Wolsey provided for a professor of the humanities in his Cardinal College, founded in 1525, and in the statutes directed that he should lecture on the Latin rhetorical authorities, and in Greek should either handle the more elementary authors, or, for the benefit of those more advanced, should lecture on one of the classical orators or poets, such as Homer, Aristophanes, Euripides, Sophocles, Pindar or Hesiod.[2] But Wolsey's college ended with the fall of its founder. It was succeeded by Christ Church, a foundation which included a Regius Professor of Greek. The first professor, Nicholas Harpsfield, soon vacated the post, and his place was taken by George Etherege, a man of varied accomplishments, physician, musician and poet in English, Latin, Greek and Hebrew.[3] But Oxford of this period had no Greek scholar of the calibre of Cheke, or if there was any such, he lacked an Ascham to hand down his virtues to posterity.

With the accession of Elizabeth I the atmosphere of the universities became more favourable to humanist studies than it had been during Mary's reign. Yet in the second half of the sixteenth century we find no progress in classical studies, and perhaps even decline. When John Bois was at St John's, Cambridge, in the 1570's, 'besides himselfe there was but one in the college could write Greek'.[4] A later writer interpreted this to mean that there were only two in the college who understood the language, and this has led to sweeping conclusions being drawn about the decay of Greek in Cambridge.[5] But at this time Greek lectures were given at St John's and were regularly attended; there must have been many undergraduates who knew something of the language, and it may be suggested that the two who could 'write Greek' were distinguished from the rest only by their skill in composition.[1] In any case it was not long before a revival took place, thanks largely to the work of Andrew Downes, who held the post of college lecturer in Greek for some years before his appointment to the professorship of Greek in 1586, and who, in addition to lecturing publicly five times a week, read privately with Bois 'twelve of the hardest, &, for dialect and phrase, both in verse and prose, most difficult Greek authors he could devise'.[2] Bois himself held the post of chief Greek lecturer in the college for ten years, and lectured every day, as well as holding classes at the daunting hour of four in the morning, which were attended by a number of fellows.[3]

At Oxford the humanist tradition was continued by John Rainolds, Greek Reader at Corpus Christi College from 1573 to 1578. He lectured on Aristotle 'whose three incomparable books of rhetoric he illustrated with so excellent a commentary so richly fraught with all polite literature, that as well in the commentary, as in the text, a man may find a golden river of things and words, which the prince of orators tells us of'.[4] But on the whole both in Oxford and in Cambridge the promise of the first half of the century was hardly fulfilled, and whatever other achievements may have made Elizabeth's reign glorious, it was not noted for Greek scholarship.[5]

One reason for this was that there was as yet no recognised place for classical scholarship in the universities. The arts course was supposed to lead on to the three other faculties, divinity, law and medicine. Ascham was one of the few to recognise that the universities needed men who could pursue the study of languages and philosophy for their own sake.

For law, physic and divinity, need so the help of tongues and sciences, as they can not want them; and yet they require so a man's whole study, as he may part with no time to other learning, except it be at certain times, to fetch it at other men's labour. I know universities be instituted only, that the realm may be served with preachers, lawyers, and physicians; and so I know likewise all woods be planted only either for building or burning; and yet good husbands in serving use not to cut down all for timber and fuel, but leave always standing some good big ones, to be the defence for the new spring. Therefore, if some were so planted in Cambridge, as they should neither be carried away to other places, nor decay there for lack of living, nor be bound to profess no one of the three, but bond themselves wholly to help forward all; I believe preachers, lawyers and physicians, should spring in number, and grow in bigness, more than commonly they do.[1]

It was rarely that a scholar of ability remained for long teaching the classics in the universities. Professional studies took many away. Some passed to divinity; law claimed Thomas Smith, and medicine claimed a number of scholars from Linacre onwards, among them John Clement, and two of the early Regius professors, Etherege of Oxford and Carr of Cambridge. Scholars were also in demand as tutors to princes—Cheke taught Edward VI and Ascham Elizabeth—or as diplomatists and men of affairs. A good command of Latin was necessary for the conduct of foreign affairs, and a bright boy who had begun by learning to write Latin letters in the grammar school might end, as Ascham did, by writing letters on behalf of his sovereign to foreign princes. Nor was it only skill in the writing of Latin that led to the employment of scholars in public life; they were also commended by the political wisdom which they imbibed from the study of the ancient orators, historians and philosophers. Henry Cuffe, professor of Greek at Oxford, became secretary to the Earl of Essex, as one who could 'suit the wise observations of ancient times to the transactions of modern times'.[2] His counsels, it may be added, brought both him and his master to the scaffold.

In the early part of the century the new learning had spread to the universities, partly through the work of individual teachers, but more by the encouragement of men like Fisher, Fox and Wolsey. Scholasticism was already weakened when in 1535

Thomas Cromwell sent his commissioners to the universities and the Royal Injunctions were issued which peremptorily ordered the abandonment of scholastic text-books and the establishment of Greek and Latin lectures in all colleges.[1] These injunctions gave the subjects of the arts course as logic, rhetoric, arithmetic, geography, music and philosophy. But it was not until 1549, under Edward VI, when the universities were provided with new statutes, that the course was precisely defined. Grammar, which had formed the initial stage of the old trivium, was now discarded, and arithmetic became the branch of study assigned to the first year, to be followed by dialectics and philosophy. The course for the Master's degree comprised philosophy, perspective, astronomy and Greek. The text-books prescribed were to a large extent classical; in philosophy Aristotle, with the addition of Pliny and Plato; in medicine Hippocrates and Galen; in dialectics and rhetoric Aristotle, Cicero, Quintilian and Hermogenes. The professor of Greek was to lecture on Homer, Demosthenes, Isocrates and Euripides, or some other classical author.[2]

While the Edwardian statutes were virtually the same for both Oxford and Cambridge, under Elizabeth I the two universities parted company. The Oxford statutes of 1564–5 returned to the arts course of the later Middle Ages, the trivium and quadrivium with the addition of the three branches of philosophy, omitting Greek altogether.[3] At Cambridge on the other hand the statutes of 1570 prescribed a course similar to that of the Edwardian statutes, except that rhetoric took the place of mathematics as a first-year subject.

But it was one thing to devise statutes and another to see that they were carried out effectively, just as to found a professorship did not necessarily mean that the professor would have an audience.[4] Already in the sixteenth century college teaching was encroaching on that of the university, and to get a true picture of the studies of Oxford and Cambridge we must look at college statutes as well as those of the university. For though college statutes might be, and eventually were disregarded, they at any rate reflect the educational ideas of the period when they were drafted.

We have already spoken of the statutes of Corpus Christi College, Oxford. Their full-blown humanism contrasts with the medievalism of Brasenose, whose statutes, dating from five years earlier (1512), speak only of the study of sophistry and logic for undergraduates and philosophy for Bachelors.[1] At Cambridge the original statutes of Christ's College (1506), founded under the influence of Fisher, make provision for lectures on poets and orators as well as on dialectics, logic and philosophy, but we have to wait until Fisher's revision of the statutes of St John's in 1530 for the introduction of Greek lectures into college teaching.[2] The Royal Injunctions of 1535 laid down that each college should maintain a daily lecture in both Latin and Greek, and at Oxford the commissioners of that date are said to have founded Greek lectures at Merton and Queen's and lectures in Greek and Latin at New College and All Souls.[3] In the two Oxford foundations of 1555, Trinity and St John's, provision is made for lectures in Greek and Latin. At the former college Latin poets, historians and orators were to be read, but there were to be only occasional Greek lectures; at St John's the Greek lecturer was to teach grammar or expound an author (those mentioned are Isocrates, Lucian, Philostratus, Herodian, Aristophanes, Theocritus, Homer, Euripides, Pindar, Hesiod, Demosthenes, Thucydides, Aristotle and Theophrastus), while the rhetoric lecturer was to handle not only the text-books of Aristotle, Cicero and Hermogenes, but also various ancient writers in prose and in verse.[4]

Full directions as to college teaching were given in the Elizabethan statutes (1560) of Trinity College, Cambridge. The foundation maintained nine lecturers, five in dialectic and four in other branches of learning. The five lectured mainly on Aristotelian texts. Of the four others the first taught Greek, the second Latin, the third mathematics and the fourth Greek grammar. The lecturer in Greek expounded Isocrates, Demosthenes, Plato, Homer, Hesiod or any other classical author, his lectures being attended by those who had already learned the Greek grammar, apart from Bachelors and those General Sophisters (third-year undergraduates) who were directed to attend the university lectures. The lecturer in Latin lectured particularly on Cicero; he also taught rhetoric, illustrating from the book on which he was lecturing, and instructed all those below the grade of Bachelor in verse composition. The lecturer in Greek grammar read with his class the work of either Clenardus or Ceporinus or Gaza.[1]

These statutes show how the colleges might supplement the teaching of the university. The Latin lecturer, though his duties included lecturing on rhetoric, also taught Latin verse composition. As regards Greek, whereas the university assigned the subject to the course for the Master's degree, the college expected all undergraduates to study it, and provided a class for beginners as well as for more advanced students. Similarly at St John's, Cambridge, in the 1570's there were three Greek classes; in the first the grammar was taught, in the second an easy author was explained, while the third involved more advanced work. It was common to attend the first class for one year and the second for two.[2]

Such a scheme of study was well suited to a period when there was little Greek teaching in the schools. By the end of the century it must have been somewhat out of date. By then Greek was well established in the schools, and a fair proportion of undergraduates must have come up with a respectable knowledge of the language. It is doubtful whether the universities had much to add to this. The pioneering days of Croke and Cheke were over and inevitably something of the old enthusiasm was lost.

CHAPTER III

THE SCHOOLS IN THE
SEVENTEENTH CENTURY

The seventeenth century was on the whole a period of steady progress on the lines already laid down in the previous century. The grammar-school system was well established, and it was no longer necessary to give detailed instructions as to curriculum in statutes and ordinances. Thus in the statutes of Monmouth school (1616) the choice of authors is left to the discretion of the master, 'providing for the attaining to the purity of the Latin tongue, those authors to have still chief place and use which the learned call classical, such as Tully, Caesar, &c, for prose,—Terence, Virgil &c for verse', and at Chigwell school in 1629 the directions to the master are 'for Phrase and Style that he infuse no other into them save Tully and Terence; for Poets that he read the ancient Greek and Latin Poets'.[1] The speaking of Latin in school was still required in new foundations, and still enforced in existing schools, as at Winchester, where about 1670 an observer remarked that 'they speake Latine everywhere', and at Westminster, where in 1682 Dryden's son was penalised for breaking the rule.[2] William Lilly, who was at school at Ashby-de-la-Zouch under Brinsley from 1613 to 1620, could then speak Latin as well as English, and at St Helen's about 1635 'all that were presumed by their standing able to discourse in Latine were under a penalty if they either spoke English or broke Priscian's head'.[3]

In a number of schools a third language was now added to Latin and Greek. Hebrew had entered the grammar schools in the sixteenth century; in the seventeenth it was taught at Westminster, St Paul's and Merchant Taylors', and in some schools in the provinces, though it does not appear to have taken much root in the important foundations of Winchester and Eton.[4] The addition of this language was no doubt the result of the Reformation and the interest it aroused in the language of the Old Testament, and it marked a departure from Quintilian and the grammar school of the ancient world. It did not, however, involve any significant change in the character of school education. Indeed the teaching of Hebrew was influenced by the spirit of humanism; it was conducted on much the same lines as the teaching of the classical languages, and Westminster boys in the seventeenth century were composing orations and verses in Hebrew, Arabic and other oriental languages as well as in Latin and Greek.[1]

In the classical languages the chief study was still the poetry of the ancients and the chief exercise its imitation. That useless but ornamental, and, to those who have any gifts for it, delightful accomplishment, the composition of Latin and Greek verse, was now, as it was long to remain, the characteristic feature of English education. Milton recalls how at St Paul's he studied not only orators and historians, but also 'the smooth Elegiack Poets... Whom both for the pleasing sound of their numerous writing, which in imitation I found most easie; and most agreeable to natures part in me, and for their matter which what it is, there be few who know not, I was so allur'd to read that no recreation came to me better welcome'.[2] Sir Simonds d'Ewes at Bury St Edmund's school in the early seventeenth century composed two thousand eight hundred and fifty verses, Latin and Greek, and William Lilly records that when at school at Ashby-de-la-Zouch he could 'make *Extempore* Verses upon any Theme; all kinds of Verses, Hexameter, Pentameter, Phaleuciacks, Iambicks, Sapphicks &c'.[3] At Westminster the two highest forms were practised in extempory verse, Greek and Latin, and at meal times the boys might receive a message from the prebendaries' table giving them a subject on which to improvise an epigram.[4] Evelyn, visiting the school in 1661, 'heard and saw such exercises at the election of scholars...to be sent to the university in Latin, Greek, Hebrew and Arabic, in themes and extempory verses, as wonderfully astonished me in such youths, with such readiness and wit, some of them not above twelve or thirteen years of age'.[1]

In the early part of the century Lancelot Andrewes, who was then Dean of Westminster, took an active interest in the work of the school. He encouraged the reading of the best classical authors, and would often take the place of the headmaster or the usher. 'He caused our Exercises', writes Hacket the biographer of Archbishop Williams, 'in Prose and Verse to be brought to him, to examine our Style and Proficiency.' He would summon the senior boys to his rooms in the evening, and keep them with him from eight to eleven 'unfolding to them the best Rudiments of the *Greek* Tongue, and the Elements of the *Hebrew* Grammar, and all this he did to Boys without any compulsion of Correction; nay, I never heard him utter so much as a word of Austerity among us'. Williams himself when Dean followed Andrewes's example. 'He was assiduous in the School, and miss'd not sometimes every week, if he were resident in the College, both to dictate Lectures to the several Classes, and to take account of them.'[2]

But the great period of Westminster was during the head-mastership of Richard Busby, who was appointed to his post in 1638, and held it until his death at the age of nearly ninety in 1695. Busby, as Samuel Johnson put it, 'advanced his scholars to a height of knowledge very rarely attained in grammar schools'.[3] He was famous for his Greek scholarship, and one of his pupils described him as far superior to all masters of his own age and preceding ages, perhaps also of future ages, both in the knowledge of Greek and in its teaching.[4] He 'strictly forbad the Use of Notes', and made his pupils use 'nothing but the plain Text in a correct and chaste Edition', which meant that in Greek the Westminster boy had to do without the Latin versions with which Greek texts were normally furnished.[5] Busby insisted on the observance of the Greek accents, and it was apparently he who was responsible for the practice which obtained for a time in Westminster and other

English schools of lengthening the accented syllables in pronunciation.[1] One curious detail of his teaching is preserved by Dryden; to end two consecutive lines of Latin verse with a verb was to earn a beating.[2] Dryden, it may be added, learned to write English as well as Latin verse under Busby; he records that while at Westminster among other exercises in English verse he translated the third satire of Persius.[3]

In the early part of the seventeenth century Westminster had a rival in the highly successful school conducted by Thomas Farnaby, who taught in the City until 1636 when he moved into Kent. Farnaby's was a private school and consequently little record of it has survived, but we are told that he had a great many boarders and day boys and sometimes as many as three ushers, an unusually large number for those days, and Anthony Wood describes him as 'the chief grammarian, rhetorician, poet, Latinist and Grecian of his time'.[4] The numerous school-books which he published give some indication of the authors he read and the methods he used; he wrote books on grammar and syntax, a Latin phrase-book and an *Index Rhetoricus*, and published editions of Juvenal and Persius, Seneca's tragedies, Martial, Lucan, Virgil and Ovid's *Metamorphoses*, as well as a collection of Greek epigrams.

A few years after Farnaby left London John Milton began to teach first his two nephews, then a few more pupils. His programme of reading was unusual and won the censure of Samuel Johnson. His nephew Edward Phillips gives a list of 'the many authors both of the Latin and Greek, which through his excellent judgment and way of teaching, far above the pedantry of common Public Schools (where such authors are scarce ever heard of) were run over in no greater compass of time than from ten to fifteen or sixteen years of age'. The Latin authors were the agricultural works of Cato, Varro, Columella and Palladius, a great part of Pliny's *Natural History*, Vitruvius, Frontinus's *Strategemata*, Lucretius and Manilius; the Greek authors Hesiod, Aratus, Dionysius *De Situ*

Orbis, Oppian, Quintus Smyrnaeus, Apollonius Rhodius, Plutarch *Placita Philosophorum* and *De Educatione*, Geminus on astronomy, Xenophon *Cyropaedia* and *Anabasis*, Aelian *Tactica* and Polyaenus *Strategemata*. The choice of authors shows that bias towards writers conveying useful information which we find in Milton's tract on education, but there is reason to believe that the curriculum was dictated not only by the interests of his pupils but also by the desire to fill in the gaps in his own reading. 'By teaching', writes Phillips, 'he in some measure increased his own knowledge, having the reading of all those authors as it were by proxy.'[1]

Returning to professional schoolmasters we may mention Charles Hoole, master of Rotherham school and subsequently of private grammar schools in London, and author of *A New Discovery of the Old Art of Teaching Schoole* (1660) based on his own experience. The subtitle of the book, 'Shewing how Children in their playing years may Grammatically attain to a firm groundedness in and exercise of the Latine, Greek and Hebrew Tongues', shows that Hoole's aims were the accepted ones of the contemporary grammar school. The scheme of work which he draws up, for a school of six forms, is remarkable for the wide range of authors included. Besides the regular authors, we find in Latin Juvenal and Persius, Lucan, Seneca's tragedies, Martial, Pliny's *Panegyricus* and the Quintilianic declamations; in Greek Hesiod, Pindar, Lycophron, Sophocles, Euripides and Aristophanes. Hoole's list of 'schoole authors' is moreover swollen by numerous 'subsidiary' works, which show the large number of aids to learning, commentaries, grammar books, handbooks to composition, etc., which had accumulated by the mid-seventeenth century. The long list of authors is to some extent deceptive, for Hoole preferred to read a small amount of a large number of authors rather than a large amount of a few. He regards two books of Homer as sufficient, and recommends only 'giving a taste of' Lucan, Seneca's tragedies and Martial. He explains that the young like variety, and that 'a Schoolmaster's aim being to teach them Languages, and Oratory, and Poetry, as well as Grammar, he must necessarily employ them in many books which tend thereunto'.[1]

His aim being to make his pupils orators and poets, Hoole gave careful attention to the writing of themes and verses, and his directions on this subject may be quoted in some detail as showing the methods of teaching composition in use in what was perhaps the most flourishing period of the English grammar school.

A theme is given out, for example, *Non aestas semper fuerit, componite nidos*. The boys begin by consulting what they have read in their authors concerning *tempus, aestas, occasio* or *opportunitas*, and note down anything appropriate in their commonplace-note-books. They read out what they have written, and each transcribes what the others have collected. Thus they have 'store of matter for invention ready at hand'. For vocabulary a number of dictionaries and phrase-books are available in the school library. In order to learn how to arrange their matter they study the model themes to be found not only in Aphthonius and humanist works, but also in more recent English books written for school use, such as the Merchant Taylors' Probation Book, the Winchester Latin Phrase-Book and Clarke's *Formulae Oratoriae*.[2] The boys learn

how to prosecute the severall parts of a Theme more at large by intermixing some of those *Formulae Oratoriae* which *Mr Clark* and *Mr Farnaby* have collected, which are proper to every part; so as to bring their matter into handsome and plain order; and to flourish and adorne it neatly with Rhetorical Tropes and Figures, always regarding the composure of words; as to make them run in a pure and even style, according to the best of their Authors, which they must always observe, as Presidents.[3]

For verse-composition Ovid's *Tristia* supplies lessons in scansion.

Let them scan every verse, and after they have told you what feet it hath in it, and of what syllables they consist, let them give the Rule of the quantity of each syllable, why it is long or short; the scanning and proving verses, being the main end of reading this Author, should more then any thing be insisted upon whilst they read it.

After scanning and proving, Hoole, contrary to the usual practice of his day, introduces English verse-composition. Returning to Latin, he takes some couplets, transposes the words into the prose order and makes his pupils turn them back into verse, while sometimes he requires them to vary a verse by transposing the words, or by keeping the same sense and altering the words.[1] For verse-composition his pupils 'comprise the sum of their Themes in a Distich, Tetrastich, Hexastich, or more verses, as they grow in strength' For poetical phrases numerous helps are available, ancestors of the modern Gradus, bearing such titles as *Phrases Poeticae, Index Poeticus, Aerarium Poeticum* and *Encheiridion Poeticum.* But, adds Hoole,

for gaining a smooth way of versifying, and to be able to expresse much matter in a few words, and very fully to the life, I conceive it very necessary for Scholars to be very frequent in perusing and rehearsing *Ovid* and *Virgil.*... And the Master indeed should cause his Scholars to recite a piece of *Ovid* or *Virgil,* in his hearing now and then, that the very tune of these pleasant verses may be imprinted in their mindes, so that when ever they are put to compose a verse, they make it glide as even as those in their Authours.[2]

Of teaching at Eton in the seventeenth century little is recorded,[3] but we have some interesting details of Winchester about 1670. This school was peculiar in that it did not provide the first stages of a grammar-school course, but took boys at twelve or thereabouts, when they had already begun Latin; 'none goe to Winchester schoole that are not fit to be in Aesop's fables, Ovid *de Tristibus* etc.' Winchester boys translated Virgil into English verse and Hesiod into Latin, while two features were already to be observed which were still characteristic of the school in the early nineteenth century, the dispensing with word for word construing and the practice of extensive learning by heart. 'One boy reads in Latine to such a stop and gives the English in grosse and not verbatim', and 'at Christmas and all such times they learne for Task abundance of Homer exactly'.[4]

Detailed accounts survive of the curriculum of two London schools in the seventeenth century, Merchant Taylors' in 1652 and St Paul's under Thomas Gale, High Master from 1672 to 1697.[1] At Merchant Taylors' Greek was begun in the fourth form and Hebrew in the sixth. In Latin reading began with *Sententiae Pueriles*, Cato and Aesop, and went on to the *Colloquies* of Corderius and Erasmus and Sturm's selection of Cicero's Letters. In the third form the *Andria* of Terence and Ovid's *Tristia* were begun. They were continued in the fourth, with the first book of the *Metamorphoses* as an alternative to the *Tristia* and with the addition of Cicero's *De Officiis, De Senectute, De Amicitia* or *Paradoxa*. The *Eclogues*, Horace's *Epistles* and select speeches of Cicero followed in the fifth, whilst the highest form read the *Aeneid* and Horace's *Ars Poetica*, or Juvenal or Persius (the *Odes*, we notice, are missing from the curriculum); Seneca's Tragedies; Sallust, Justin, Florus or Livy; and Pliny's Letters or *Panegyricus*. In Greek the fifth form read Isocrates *Ad Demonicum*, Pythagoras, Phocylides and Theognis, and the sixth more of Isocrates (*ad Nicoclem* and *Nicocles*), Plutarch *On the Education of Children*, select dialogues of Lucian and the *Cyropaedia*; the first two, or more, books of the *Iliad*; Hesiod, Theocritus and Greek epigrams; and a tragedy of Sophocles or Euripides. As regards exercises the second form translated sentences into Latin, the third practised varying an easy Latin sentence and imitating dialogues of Corderius and Letters of Cicero, and the fourth continued the exercises of the third form and began on themes and verses. In the fifth form the composition of Latin dialogues and epistles was added, and the writing of 'som *Parodiae* or imitations' of Latin and Greek verses. The sixth form, besides prose and verse themes, translated a passage of Cicero into English, then turned it 'into other Latine, one or more waies', and also into Greek and into Latin elegiacs and sapphics, and did the same, *mutatis mutandis*, with a passage of Greek.

At St Paul's, an eight-form school, Greek was begun in the

fifth form and Hebrew in the eighth. From the usual first reading-books the schoolboy proceeded to Erasmus, Ovid and Justin, while in the upper forms the authors were Martial, Sallust, Virgil, Cicero's speeches, Horace and finally, in the eighth form, Juvenal and Persius. Terence and Cicero's letters are missing, an omission which suggests a decline of interest in spoken and epistolary Latin.[1] In Greek the St Paul's boy passed from the New Testament to 'Minor Poets' (presumably Ralph Winterton's *Poetae Minores Graeci*, 1635) and Apollodorus, whose handbook on mythology was edited by Thomas Knipe in 1686 for use at Westminster, and had probably been read there before that date,[2] and thence to Homer, Aratus and 'Dionisius'. The last author could be either the literary critic of Halicarnassus or Dionysius Periegetes, whose geographical poem was edited by Winterton in 1633 and frequently reprinted after that date.[3]

For exercises the lowest forms had to translate verses out of the Psalms and Proverbs into Latin; this was varied in the fourth and fifth forms by the translation of passages from 'Heathen Gods', that is, the *Histoire Poétique* of Gautruche, or Galtruchius (1602–81), which was translated into English in 1671 under the title *Poetical Histories, a Collection of the Stories Necessary for Understanding the Greek and Latin Poets*.[4] Psalms were turned into Latin verse by the fifth form, and themes, verses and declamations constituted the exercises of the two highest forms. There is no mention of Greek verse-composition, but it is hard to believe that it was not taught, even though it may not have formed part of the regular school work. Milton had written Greek verses when at St Paul's.[5]

The use of the Psalms to provide material for Latin composition is a peculiar feature of the St Paul's curriculum. No doubt the intention was that religious sentiments should be imbibed at the same time as the Latin language. A similar intention inspired a Royal Recommendation of 1666, made as a result of a vote of Convocation, that Duport's translation of the Psalms into Greek hexameters should be used in schools 'for the better imbuing the boys' minds alike with piety and Greek learning', a recommendation which appears to have been duly ignored by the schools.[1]

The seventeenth century has been described at the beginning of this chapter as a period of steady progress in grammar-school education. Yet it was also the period in which we first hear serious criticisms of this education. One criticism was that of the religious extremists who condemned classical studies as tainted with heathenism, and either decried all learning or wished to base education on Christian authors. In 1650 William Dell, Master of Gonville and Caius College, Cambridge, advocated that 'in teaching youth the tongues, to wit, the Greek and Latin, such heathenish authors be most carefully avoided, be their language never so good, whose writings are full of the fables, vanities, filthiness, lasciviousness, idolatries and wickedness of the heathen'. He therefore advised that 'they learn the Greek and Latin tongues especially from Christians, and so without the lies, fables, follies, vanities, whoredoms, lust, pride, revenge, etc. of the heathens'.[2] George Fox, the Quaker, when he visited Durham in 1657, argued against the proposal to found a college there, pointing out that this

was not the way to make them Christ's ministers by Hebrew, Greek, and Latin and the Seven Arts, which all were but the teachings of the natural man. For the many languages began at Babel, and to the Greeks that spoke the natural Greek, the preaching of the cross of Christ was foolishness to them; and to the Jews that spoke natural Hebrew, Christ was a stumbling block to them, and as for the Romans that had Italian and Latin, they persecuted the Christians.[3]

Among the opponents of the classics must be counted Comenius, who deserves brief mention here as the leading educational theorist of the seventeenth century, and as one whose ideas had some vogue in England of the Commonwealth, though they exercised no immediate influence. Like the religious zealots already mentioned Comenius advocated banishing pagan authors from the schools, or at least admitting only a few unexceptionable moralists.[1] More important from the point of view of the future was his emphasis on the importance of learning things rather than words. That he devoted so much of his energies to devising a new method of teaching Latin does not mean that he shared the ideals of the contemporary grammar school. He had little interest in the elegances of style; Latin was for him the language of science and international communication, and his attitude towards it was practical rather than literary.

In the same way to Milton, when he wrote his tract on education, language was 'but the instrument conveying to us things useful to be known', and the primary purpose of learning Greek and Latin was to study 'the solid things in them'. Thus Milton had no use for the ornamental accomplishments of verse- and prose-writing which he himself had mastered in his youth. He pours scorn on the 'preposterous exaction' of 'forcing the empty wits of children to compose themes, verses and orations', and con-demns the prevailing school and university education as 'pure trifling in grammar and sophistry'.[2]

Some of Milton's criticisms of established methods reappear, expressed in a more urbane tone, in Locke's *Thoughts on Education*, published in 1693. Locke regards Latin as necessary for a gentle-man, Greek as necessary only for a scholar; for those destined for trade and unlikely to use the language in later life, Latin was a waste of time. He holds that Greek and Latin could be 'had at a great deal cheaper rate of pains and time, and be learn'd almost in playing', that grammar could be dispensed with and Latin learned by conversation. He prefers a private tutor to a school, but, he says, if a boy is to be sent to school, his parents should insist that he does not make Latin themes, declamations or verses. In theme-writing boys lack the knowledge and experience to handle the subjects set, and, as for verses, if a boy has no genius for poetry it is unreasonable to torment him and waste his time; if he has, it should be stifled and suppressed rather than encouraged.[3]

All these criticisms had virtually no effect on school teaching. Puritanism left the English grammar school unchanged; at Westminster school, so close to Parliament and so vulnerable to its influence, Busby continued to teach the classics throughout the civil wars and the Commonwealth.[1] Comenius's visit to England led to nothing; Milton and Locke could not drive themes and verses from the schools. Calm reigned in the educational world until the nineteenth century, when the demand for a more utilitarian education grew more pressing. But by then mankind had moved further away from the ancient world, and it was no longer necessary to acquire Latin and Greek in order to learn 'the things useful to be known'.

CHAPTER IV

THE UNREFORMED GRAMMAR SCHOOL

To all outward appearance grammar-school education remained throughout the eighteenth century much as it always had been. But during that century a slow and scarcely perceptible, but none the less real change took place which inevitably affected men's attitude to the classics. Latin gradually ceased to be a living language. As the language of everyday speech it had, of course, died long before; but at the beginning of the eighteenth century its literary uses were still considerable. By the end of the century they had shrunk to a narrow sphere. French had become the language of diplomacy; and even for the writing of books Latin was seldom used except for works on classical subjects.

The Reformation, though it made English the regular language of the church services, did not drive Latin altogether out of the church. In many grammar schools Latin prayers were prescribed, and in some they have continued to this day. Under Elizabeth I the Prayer Book was translated into Latin for use at the universities; the Act of Uniformity of 1662 permitted the use of the Latin version in College chapels, and in one foundation at least advantage was taken of this permission. At Christ Church, Oxford, the 'old thunderous Latin' recalled by Ruskin in *Praeterita* was regularly used for the daily services until 1861.[1] The Act of Uniformity permitted the clergy when gathered together in Convocation to use the Latin prayer book, and the Latin *Concio ad Clerum* has survived to our day; but though the English clergy were assumed, and indeed required by the canons of 1603, to know the old language of the Western church, the Reformation meant that, however learned they might be, they lost some of that familiarity with Latin which comes from its daily use in church, and in the nineteenth century a Catholic priest of relatively little learning might be more fluent in spoken Latin than an English divine of greater scholarship.[1]

The decline in Latin as a living language was reflected in school education. In the early eighteenth century the practice of making boys speak Latin in school seems to have been dying out. John Clarke, writing in 1720, refers to boys talking Latin barbarously among themselves in some schools and condemns the practice on the grounds that boys 'must not be put upon this Task of *Speaking Latin*, till they can write it pretty well...; that is to say, in almost all Schools never at all'.[2] The speaking of Latin in school probably came to an end in the course of the eighteenth century, leaving behind only a few words such as *cave, pax, pater*, and *mater*, which long formed part of schoolboy slang.[3] Samuel Johnson is an example of an eighteenth-century Englishman who spoke Latin as fluently as he wrote it, but since his time English scholars have in general been distinguished by an ability to write Latin combined with an inability to speak it.

The old conversation-books which had helped to teach colloquial Latin only gradually disappeared from the schools. When Dr Johnson drew up a scheme for a grammar school about 1736 he included the *Colloquies* of Corderius and Erasmus in John Clarke's edition, and these were still being used in some schools in the early nineteenth century.[4] But with the decline of spoken Latin they lost much of their point, and they are missing from the influential curriculum of eighteenth-century Eton. In the same way the composition of Latin letters, and with it the reading of Cicero's letters, seems to have dropped out; it was still a recognised part of school work in 1720,[5] but was apparently abandoned by the middle of the eighteenth century.

One schoolmaster, John Clarke of Hull, tried to adapt Locke's views on education to the requirements of school teaching and to revise the grammar-school system in the direction of common-sense utilitarianism by removing such useless tasks as learning by heart, composition in Greek and verse-making, the last of which

he regarded as at best 'a Diversion a Degree above Fidling'.[1]
Clarke advocated the reading of more of the historians and less of
the poets, and wished to ease the task of the schoolboy by the
provision of literal translations, a proposal which would have
horrified a nineteenth-century schoolmaster but had its advantages
in days when schools of six forms were normally staffed by two
masters and the boys were inevitably left to some extent to teach
themselves.[2] Clarke's views were not generally accepted. Indeed
the development, so far as there was any, was in the opposite
direction. As Latin became less a language for use, education
became less utilitarian and more purely literary. The study of
Greek advanced, while in Latin the prose-writers were neglected
in favour of the poets and verse-composition flourished more than
ever.

In the course of the eighteenth century Eton took the place of
Westminster as England's leading school. By about the middle of
the century its social pre-eminence was assured, and its scholarly
pre-eminence was attested by the success of Etonians in what was
then the hall-mark of classical culture, verse-composition. It is
significant that in 1750 was published the last edition of the
Westminster collection of verses, Lusus Westmonasterienses, and
that five years later there appeared the first volume of the Eton
collection Musae Etonenses.[3] The influence of Eton in the scholastic
world was considerable. Schoolmasters educated there brought
Etonian methods to other schools, such as Rugby, where Thomas
James taught with success in the later part of the century, and
Harrow, where a series of Etonian headmasters made the school
a close copy of Eton. In the early part of the nineteenth century,
as a perusal of Carlisle's Concise Description of the Endowed Grammar
Schools shows, many small local grammar schools professed to
follow the Eton system.

Winchester remained free from Etonian influence. Its best
known eighteenth-century headmaster was the minor poet Joseph
Warton, who can still be seen teaching his boys Greek in the

charming relief by Flaxman reproduced as frontispiece to this book. It was Warton's ambition, we are told, to inspire his pupils with his own love of literature, 'and under his auspices their ordinary classical lessons were often converted into an instructive lecture on the principles of good taste in composition'. As a pure scholar he was not strong, and some passages in the Greek authors were beyond him. When he came to a difficult passage in the chorus of a Greek play he would, so it is said, allow the boy construing to get through it as best he could, and hide his own ignorance by raising his voice and complaining of noises.[1]

While the well-established schools such as Eton, Winchester and Westminster could maintain a steady tradition of scholarship, at lesser schools much depended on the headmaster, and a school might rise to importance under an able master, but rapidly decline after his departure. In the early part of the eighteenth century Market Bosworth school enjoyed a reputation under Anthony Blackwall, author of an *Introduction to the Classics*, which it soon lost after his departure.[2] Taunton grammar school flourished under James Upton, an editor of classical texts, who held the headmastership from 1730 to 1749.[3] Wakefield grammar school, Bentley's old school, had from 1751 to 1760 a notable master in John Clarke, not to be confused with his namesake of Hull. Clarke read with his pupils a number of Greek authors not usually included in the school curriculum. His biographer recalls the 'happy flow of expression' with which he interpreted the comedies of Aristophanes.

When [he goes on] the divine Odes of Pindar were before him, he seemed to be full of the enthusiastic fervour which inflamed the Theban Bard. With Demosthenes he was all energy and vehemence. He sweetly moralised with Plato, as if walking along the flowery banks of the Ilissus. With Isocrates he conversed mild and gentle as the dew on the tender grass. With Longinus he assumed the dignity of an enlightened master of criticism, breathing the very spirit of sublimity.

His only fault was the excessive care he gave to correcting exercises; 'he scrutinised every word, and even weighed every syllable, with a diligence which was not, perhaps, always necessary'.[1]

The outstanding schoolmaster of the later eighteenth century was Samuel Parr, who, having failed to obtain the headmastership of Harrow in 1771, set up a school of his own at Stanmore near by, taking a number of pupils from Harrow with him. Parr was in some respects an unorthodox teacher. He taught Greek prose composition, which was then almost unknown in schools, and he read the Greek historians and philosophers, who were generally neglected elsewhere, including with the study of the philosophers a comparison of the systems of the different schools. Of the Greek poets he gave special attention to the dramatists, and, in the weeks at the end of the term when Greek plays were being read by the upper school, he would keep his boys at them for seven or eight hours together, sometimes until nearly eleven o'clock at night.[2] Parr was a stern taskmaster, but he was no mere grammarian; his pupils recalled with admiration his explanatory comment and literary illustration, whilst his recitations of parallel passages from English poets were so affecting that they moved some of his hearers to tears.[3] Parr was also the first English schoolmaster to make his pupils act a Greek tragedy; the *Oedipus Tyrannus* and the *Trachiniae*, without the choruses, were acted at Stanmore in 1775 and 1776. Parr intended to make these productions an annual feature, but falling numbers forced him to close the school and take the mastership of an endowed school, first at Colchester, then at Norwich, where he did not repeat the experiment.

It remains to describe in more detail the established routine of the ordinary eighteenth-century school. In doing this we shall draw to some extent on evidence from the early part of the following century, for in many schools changes came in slowly and old methods were only gradually abandoned. The picture that emerges is that of the unreformed grammar school, before the changes brought about by the great headmasters of the nineteenth century.[4]

The standard grammar book was still that of Lily, which survived with only small alterations as the Eton Latin grammar. With its confusing arrangement, its inclusion of much unnecessary matter and its use of doggerel hexameters for giving the rules for genders and principal parts of verbs, it must have made the path of learning a hard one for the schoolboy, but it only gradually gave way to more up-to-date compilations, and continued in use at Eton as late as the 1860's.[1] To learn this by heart was the first task of the young, though there were some masters who postponed the memorising of the syntax until some progress had been made in the language.[2]

The regular first reading-books of earlier days, Cato and Aesop, had lost favour. Cato seems to have disappeared in the eighteenth century,[3] and the Latin Aesop was perhaps mainly used in the obscurer schools,[4] its place being taken by Phaedrus's metrical fables, which seem to have come in as an easy book for beginners in the early eighteenth century.[5] At Eton the New Testament in Castalion's Ciceronian version was used in the lowest forms,[6] but most schools preferred the simpler classical historians, in particular Eutropius and Cornelius Nepos, two authors who first came into regular use in schools in the eighteenth century.[7] Caesar maintained his place in school reading, but Sallust seems to have lost favour somewhat.[8]

The striking feature of the Eton system was the small amount of prose read. Apart from some Caesar and Nepos in the middle forms the prose writers were known only from the book of selections, *Scriptores Romani*.[9] Even Cicero was neglected, and the only complete work of his with which the Etonian might be acquainted was *De Officiis*, which was recommended for private reading. In verse the Eton boy passed from Phaedrus to selections from Ovid and other elegiac poets, read some Terence in the middle forms and finally concentrated on Horace and Virgil.[10]

Latin was still the gateway to Greek, for the old grammar of Camden, written in Latin, was still in use. Editions of Greek authors were commonly, though not universally, furnished with

Latin translations;[1] at Eton in 1766 the sixth form construed Homer into Latin and as late as the 1820's boys at Winchester learned 'to translate Greek into Latin without a blunder'.[2] The system of learning Greek through Latin was an anachronism by the end of the eighteenth century and was already coming under criticism.[3] The nineteenth century saw the establishment of English as the medium for Greek teaching, a change which undoubtedly contributed to quicker learning and a better appreciation of Greek.

The pattern of reading in Greek was similar to that in Latin. At Eton, apart from Aesop in Greek, which was used in the early stages, the prose writers were known only through the book of selections *Scriptores Graeci*, a work which had replaced a selection of Lucian in the 1760's and in which Lucian was still well represented.[4] The beginner in Greek was plunged into 'Farnaby', a selection of epigrams and short lyric poems which continued to be known by the name of its original seventeenth-century compiler. From this the Eton boy passed on to another book of poetic selections, *Poetae Graeci*, and finally to Homer and Greek plays.

The addition of Greek plays to the programme of school reading was the most noteworthy development in the eighteenth century. Though they had occasionally been read before, it was now that they became a recognised part of the work of the highest forms in the more important schools. The *Persae* and the *Medea* are found at St Paul's in 1710, and in 1729 the *Choephori* and the two *Electras* were published for use at Westminster. In 1748 the *Hecuba*, *Orestes*, *Phoenissae* and *Alcestis* were published for Eton. Burton's 'Pentalogia', a collection used at Eton and elsewhere in the eighteenth century, consisted of the *Oedipus Tyrannus*, the *Oedipus Coloneus*, the *Antigone*, the *Phoenissae* and the *Septem*, while a later Eton collection, 'Pote's Pentalogia', comprised the *Hippolytus*, the *Medea*, the *Philoctetes*, the *Prometheus* and the *Plutus*. In addition to Burton's Pentalogia the *Supplices* of Euripides was read at Eton in 1766. We find occasional references to the reading of Aristophanes at school, but it is unlikely that any plays of his other than the *Plutus* and the *Clouds*, the two read at Eton, were at all generally used.[1]

The Eton curriculum, as has already been remarked, influenced a number of other schools, and at schools free from its influence the position was not very different. At Winchester Virgil, Horace and Homer formed the staple of the curriculum; at Westminster Henry Fynes Clinton, who went to the school at the age of fifteen and a half in 1796, found that of the Latin authors, apart from Sallust, only Virgil and Horace were studied, whilst in Greek, apart from six tragedies, reading was almost confined to Homer. Other schools had rather different programmes of reading; at Christ's Hospital at the end of the eighteenth century Cicero and Demosthenes were read in addition to Homer by the Deputy Grecians (the Grecians, the highest form, read Greek plays) and Horace was, surprisingly, neglected. But in general it is true to say that attention was concentrated on the poets and the aim was to read a few masterpieces rather than representative works of a wide selection of authors.

To read a work usually meant to read it through, sometimes twice over. John Clarke of Hull suggests that Terence should be read twice, as should the first six or seven books of the *Metamorphoses*; the *Eclogues*, the *Aeneid*, Horace and Juvenal should be read more than once entirely through, though of Homer he requires only ten or twelve books of the *Iliad*.[2] At Eton, if one stayed sufficiently long at the school, one might well read the *Aeneid* twice over, though not necessarily the *Eclogues* or the *Georgics*, all Horace except perhaps the *Epodes*, and the *Iliad* once and a half, though not the *Odyssey*.[3] At Winchester the whole of Virgil, Horace and Homer, with a few exceptions in the case of Horace, was read twice over.

The common practice was for boys to translate each word separately, sometimes also parsing, and then to follow with a translation into continuous English. Thus at Charterhouse in the early nineteenth century every single Latin and Greek word had to be

53

rendered by a single one in English, 'a process which sometimes resulted in ludicrous exhibitions of bald phraseology', after which the pupils attempted to 'exhibit the passage in English idiom'.[1] There were, however, some teachers who dispensed with this laborious process. At Winchester, as has already been said, the boys were encouraged to translate the whole of a passage into good English.[2] At Southwell Grammar school when Fynes Clinton was there from 1789 to 1796 the master's practice was to make the boys read over a sentence of the author, point out the principal verb, read the words in their grammatical order, and finally give the English of the whole sentence at once, a method which Clinton considers much superior to the usual practice of rendering each word separately.

Though the range of reading in the unreformed grammar school was narrow, it should be remembered that some schoolboys at any rate read the classics in their spare time. In those days before the multiplication of books for the young, when class work was unexacting and before the pressure of examinations had deepened the division between work and play, the schoolboy would turn to the classics for reading matter more naturally than he does today. Two extracts from schoolboys' letters of the early nineteenth century will serve to remind us that a narrow school curriculum did not necessarily mean narrow reading. In 1824 Charles Wordsworth writes from Harrow 'some of us do six or seven chapters of Thucydides, others of Herodotus, others Greek play—besides Juvenal, Livy, Tacitus &c—every day, extra! (that means beyond the ordinary school work)', and in 1835 J. D. Coleridge writes from Eton for Elmsley's Scholia to Sophocles and adds 'I also want you to send me my Lucan and Claudian for occasional reading.'[3]

Closely connected with the reading of authors was repetition. The traditional school practice seems to have been to learn by heart the books read in class, and the day commonly began with a saying lesson in which the passage construed the previous day was recited. At Eton all verse books read, with the exception of Greek plays, were, or were supposed to be, learnt in full, so that the Eton boy might in the course of his school career have learned nearly the whole of Virgil, Horace and the *Iliad* as well as numerous passages of lesser poets in the books of selections.[1] W. S. Walker while at Eton in the early part of the nineteenth century is said to have known every line of Homer, and if this could not be said of many, at any rate the Etonian would know his Horace pretty well by heart.[2]

Winchester had a peculiar institution known as 'standing up', at which boys in the middle or junior fifth, usually fourteen or fifteen years old, learned and repeated passages of Latin or Greek poetry chosen by themselves. Remarkable feats are recorded of youthful Wykehamists in the early part of the nineteenth century. One would offer to recite the whole of the *Aeneid*, another the whole of the *Iliad*; one, Lord Saye and Sele, learned several books of Homer in addition to the whole of the *Aeneid*.[3] Thomas Arnold once rose at three in the morning for six consecutive days to prepare for the recitation of some three thousand lines of Homer.[4] Similar feats are recorded from other schools. Among these we need only mention that of Charles Merivale, who, when at Harrow in 1824, repeated to his tutor the *Eclogues*, the *Georgics*, Catullus, Juvenal and all Lucan except for a few hundred lines.[5]

In addition to construing and repetition the schoolboy had to do his exercises. In Latin he began by translating stories from mythology or ancient history,[6] but in the higher forms virtually the only prose exercise was the theme. More important, however, than theme writing was the composition of verses. At Eton in the higher forms two copies of verses had to be produced each week to one theme, and in the lower part of the school the very names of the forms—Scan and Prove, Nonsense, Sense—recorded progress in the art of versifying. After learning the rules of scansion and prosody the boy proceeded to make nonsense verses out of words taken from a page of Terence, and then to turn into verse the words of some Latin poet given out of their metrical order (Sense).[1] After this he went on to original composition. The regular weekly task for the sixth form was to write twenty-six lines of elegiacs and six or seven stanzas of Horatian lyrics.[2] The editor of the 1755 volume of *Musae Etonenses* describes how there was keen competition for distinction in verse-composition, and paints a charming picture of the Eton boys strolling along the banks of the Thames, lying under a spreading elm, or sitting on a bench, meditating their verses, busily occupied when the ignorant traveller crossing the nearby bridge thinks they are least so.[3] Facility in Latin verse, particularly in elegiacs, or 'longs and shorts' as they were familiarly called, long remained the mark of the Etonian scholar. As an Eton master in the 1840's put it, 'If you do not take more pains, how can you ever expect to write good longs and shorts? If you do not write good longs and shorts, how can you ever be a man of taste? If you are not a man of taste, how can you ever be of use in the world?'[4]

Verse-making flourished at Harrow, where it was encouraged by a number of prizes, and at Winchester, where Sydney Smith made, if we can believe his own words, over ten thousand verses while at school.[5] Westminster required all boys in the upper school to write twenty lines of Latin hexameters on a sacred subject each week, while the two highest forms were given the strange task of turning an ode of Horace into Latin elegiacs.[6] Verse-making was indeed regarded as an essential part of education, and even in the smaller grammar schools the schoolboy would at least proceed through Sense and Nonsense to elegiacs and might at the same time escape prose-composition altogether.[7]

Greek exercises were few in comparison with Latin. At Eton there was a weekly Greek exercise for the sixth form consisting of translation from Latin, from either Latin prose or Phaedrus or Virgil. But original verse-composition in Greek was also practised, and the volume of *Musae Etonenses* published in 1795 shows that Etonians could write Greek elegiacs, hexameters, iambics and lyrics. Harrovians also learned to write Greek verse. Sir William Jones, when at Harrow in the 1750's, was noted for his Greek verse, and Byron recalled how he composed thirty or forty Greek hexameters when at the same school at the beginning of the nine-teenth century.[1]

The traditional curriculum which we have described had some merits, but it also had obvious defects. What was read was read thoroughly, but the narrow range of reading meant the neglect of much that is both interesting and educationally valuable; the *Edinburgh Review* had some ground for speaking of the 'obliquity of judgment' which (at Eton) preferred Lucian to Thucydides as a study for young men.[2] The neglect of the prose writers, particu-larly Greek, was a handicap to those who wished to pursue their studies further; Liddell, the lexicographer, who had read no Thucydides at Charterhouse, found considerable difficulty with this author when he first attempted him at Oxford—with the help of Hobbes's translation.[3] Moreover it is possible to have too much even of the best, and not a few boys left school with a distaste for the authors with whom they had been overdosed. Particularly was this the case with Horace, an author perhaps to whom schoolboys do not take naturally. Byron hated Horace as a result of his school experiences; Connop Thirlwall confessed that as a result of too much of him at Charterhouse it was many years before he could enjoy him, and Tennyson had much the same experience as a result of his father's teaching.[4] Nor was the restricted curriculum good for the teachers; as an Etonian, writing of his own school, put it, the clever or average boy did not suffer so much from the scantiness of classical diet as from 'the limited range of knowledge and the indifference growing out of monotony, which inevitably lowered the tone of ordinary teachers'.[5]

The practice of learning by heart gave the schoolboy a famili-arity with the masterpieces of ancient poetry rarely found today and supplied him with a store of classical quotations which would be useful in after life, at any rate in the company of those who had enjoyed a similar education. But in some schools at any rate it was possible to get away with only a few lines out of the prescribed task.[1] It was easy, too, to forget what one had learnt or to learn without understanding. Darwin at Shrewsbury used to learn forty or fifty lines of Virgil or Homer with ease during morning chapel and forget them entirely within forty-eight hours.[2] Leigh Hunt, who was at Christ's Hospital at the end of the eighteenth century, regarded Homer as 'a series of lessons which I had to learn by heart before I understood him', and Frederick Harrison, the Positivist, who was at King's College School under J. R. Major in the 1840's, records that he was nearly plucked in Little Go because although he knew Horace's *Odes* by heart he gave his own sense to the familiar sounds.[3]

The practice of requiring original composition from an early age made the schoolboy able to express himself in Latin far more readily than his counterpart today. There were indeed those who were more fluent in Latin than in their own language, such as W. S. Walker at Eton, who thought 'more vigorously and poetically' in Latin than in English, and Isaac Williams at Harrow, who was so used to think in Latin that on the rare occasions on which he had to write in English he had to translate his thoughts from Latin.[4] The prose theme was an exercise which on the whole aroused little interest, and as practised at Eton only fostered, according to the *Edinburgh Review*, a habit of 'vague pointless and vapid declamation';[5] but verse-making was enjoyed by those who had any gifts for it. To Isaac Williams Latin composition was the great charm of his life at Harrow, and another Harrovian, Cardinal Manning, confessed that he liked composition, though when in later life he turned up a quantity of school verses he burned them 'with a sense of shame at my idleness'.[6] Yet another Harrovian of later date, Henry Montagu Butler, describes how as a schoolboy it was his joy and pride to study the book in which prize compositions were written, and how he and his contemporaries could quote much of it by heart and would discuss it together. From Harrow too comes the story of C. S. Calverley (then Blayds) producing an elegant elegiac couplet in three minutes on a walk when challenged to give a version of two lines of English verse.[1] For those practised in verse-composition from early years, reading mainly Latin poetry and committing to memory what they read, there was no need to sit down with Gradus and dictionary. To Benjamin Kennedy at Shrewsbury 'the meditation of a solitary walk' was enough to produce a copy of verses, if he liked the subject set, and another Salopian, T. S. Evans, would employ his leisure 'in recording boyish adventures, happy thoughts, or any entertaining trifles in Latin or Greek lines'.[2]

On the other hand there were always some, perhaps the majority, who found the composition of verses too much for them. For such there was an easy way out. Everyone who knew anything of Eton, according to Archdeacon Denison, knew very well what came of the requirement of original Latin verse; 'it lies in two words: "Old Copies".'[3] When the boys of Eton were required to compose some verses on the death of George III the task was made easy by the discovery of some verses composed on the death of George II, sixty years earlier. When Goldwin Smith arrived at Eton in the 1830's a servant offered him a collection of old copies, indexed, so that he could be sure of finding something appropriate for any subject.[4] At other schools things were much the same. Darwin at Shrewsbury had a good collection of old verses which by patching together he could use for any occasion, and at Winchester, though the best boys wrote their own verses, others relied on 'small, but bulky quartos, the accretion of I know not how many generations of boys; in which almost every possible subject had been made the theme of a verse-task or vulgus' (Latin epigram).[5]

In 1830 the *Edinburgh Review* launched a vigorous attack on the Eton system of education which gave its readers the impression that England's leading school failed to teach effectively the only subject it professed to teach, the classics. A year later the *Quarterly Review* claimed that the great merit of Eton was that it aroused in its sons a love and enthusiasm for classical learning.[1] No doubt both were right. At Eton and other similar schools clever boys who took to Greek and Latin acquired an intimate knowledge of the ancient languages and literatures which remained with them through life; those who were less gifted or whose abilities lay in other directions learned little. For this antiquated methods and text-books and lazy conventional teaching were in part responsible. But it should be remembered that staffing was by modern standards quite inadequate, especially in the larger schools. Thomas Mozley recalls the crowding and 'insufficiency of teaching power' at Charterhouse under Russell, and at Eton in 1830 Keate had no fewer than one hundred and ninety-eight boys in his division.[2] In such circumstances it was easy to escape with the minimum of work and to learn next to nothing.

CHAPTER V

THE UNIVERSITIES IN THE SEVENTEENTH AND EIGHTEENTH CENTURIES

While Cambridge continued to be governed by her Elizabethan statutes until the nineteenth century, those of Oxford were given a thorough revision by Archbishop Laud in 1636. Under these statutes all undergraduates in their first year were to attend lectures on grammar and rhetoric. The grammar lecturer was to expound Priscian, Linacre or some other authority, or to explain passages from the ancient authors; the lecturer on rhetoric was to use the works of Aristotle, Cicero, Quintilian or Hermogenes. After the first year the undergraduate course was to consist of logic and moral philosophy, while natural philosophy and metaphysics belonged to the period after the Bachelor's degree. Greek lectures were to be attended by all students after their second year, including all Bachelors.[1] This scheme of study was conservative in character. Grammar, which at Cambridge had been abandoned nearly a century before, was still retained. Greek was now officially recognised, but its postponement to the third year had little reason now that the language was well established in the grammar schools.

It may, however, be doubted whether the seventeenth-century undergraduate was much affected by the Laudian statutes.[2] What mattered was college teaching, and this seems to have been conducted with little reference to the university requirements. In the two foundations of the early seventeenth century, Wadham and Pembroke, we find provision made for the teaching of the classics. The Wadham statutes (1612) established a prelector in Humanity, and laid down that lectures on Greek and Latin authors were to be given three times a week; also that all scholars must be able to write Latin verse.[1] At Pembroke, whose statutes date from 1624, lectures on rhetoric, which would no doubt include Latin composition, were to be attended by all undergraduates, while lectures on Greek were provided for those who had already learnt some Greek or were considered capable of profiting by them.[2]

Of classical teaching at Oxford in the seventeenth century not much is recorded. John Hales, later Provost of Eton, showed his 'exact knowledge of the Greek tongue' first as lecturer at Merton, later as Regius Professor.[3] John Harmar, professor from 1650 to the Restoration, 'was happy in rendring Greek into Latin, or Latin into English, or English into Greek or Latin whether in prose or verse'.[4] In the later part of the century Oxford's most distinguished Greek scholar was Humphrey Hody, author of the Prolegomena to the edition of Malelas which gave rise to Bentley's Letter to Mill. Hody was appointed to the chair of Greek in 1698, and delivered a series of lectures on the Greek scholars who revived the study of the language in the west, an unusual subject in an age when professorial prelections were normally devoted to the exposition of ancient texts.[5]

At Cambridge a decree of 1608 exempted Bachelors of Arts from the obligation to reside while qualifying for the Master's degree. If the studies of the University had been determined solely by the statutes this would have seriously affected the position of Greek, the study of which belonged by statute to Bachelors. But though the classes of the Greek professor may have been affected, college teaching, as we have seen, did not confine Greek to Bachelors, and the language continued to be taught and studied.[6] In the middle of the seventeenth century, if we can believe Isaac Barrow, Greek was flourishing.

Greek authors of every kind, poets, philosophers, historians, scholiasts, whom our ignorant forefathers not so long ago feared to touch, as if they were barbarians, even the younger sons of our Mother now go through fearlessly, reckoning such reading a light task; they approach the Lyceum or the Academy no less readily than if time had gone backward and they were conversing with Plato and Aristotle in Athens itself.[1]

Another speech of Barrow's gives us some information about the manner in which the Latin lecturer at Trinity carried out his duties. His functions were threefold; he read a Latin author with his class, he instructed them in theme-writing and he required them to compose Latin verses. For his author Barrow chose Ovid, and of Ovid's works the *Fasti*.

> From so many works of Ovid, all of equal genius though of different subject matter, I have chosen that which I thought it particularly worth while to explain; in which nothing relating to history, antiquity, philology, or even, I might almost say, philosophy and all the liberal arts, is missing; during the reading of which all our days will be holidays and none unfit to be numbered among the Fasti.[2]

On theme-writing his first requirement is that his students should keep their eyes on the subject set, his next that they should clothe their thoughts in correct and, if possible, elegant language. *Sententiae* should be neither too scattered nor too thick on the ground; the whole work should be suitably arranged, adorned with similes, illustrated by appropriate examples, seasoned with chaste wit, embellished by metaphors. After further advice he ends by insisting that each should show up only what is his own work. On verse-writing, after remarking that this form of composition should be particularly congenial to the young, he observes that it is epigrams that are to be written, and these must be witty and smoothly flowing. 'Far be it from me', he adds, 'to suspect that any of you will make a false quantity.'[3]

Cambridge did not lack able professors of Greek during the seventeenth century. Andrew Downes, who occupied the chair from 1585 for nearly forty years, was generally looked on as the leading Greek scholar of his day, and is said to have been so familiar with the language that he used it in everyday conversation, even in rebuking his servants.[1] He lectured on the Attic orators. In 1620 Sir Simonds d'Ewes attended his lectures on Demosthenes *De Corona*, and he also expounded Lysias *De Caede Eratosthenis* and Demosthenes *De Pace*, his notes on which were published in 1593 and 1621 respectively. A later editor of Lysias, John Taylor, while acknowledging Downes's services to the study of Greek, found his notes too laborious and prolix to merit reprinting.[2]

The next professor of note was James Duport, who occupied the chair from 1639 to 1654. Duport was chiefly noted for his translations of books of the Bible into Greek hexameter verse and for his *Homeri Gnomologia*, a collection of aphorisms from Homer, with parallels from the rest of Greek literature and from the Bible. He was also a diligent and successful teacher, by whom, in Barrow's words, 'grammatical austerity was seasoned with the variety of criticism, polished with oratorical charm and tempered with a pleasing urbanity'.[3] His lectures on Theophrastus's *Characters* survive, printed in Peter Needham's edition of 1712. They were delivered during the Civil War, and Duport explains in the opening paragraph that he had chosen the *Characters* as a work better suited to disturbed times than Demosthenes, on whom he had been lecturing,[4] in that it was broken up into short sections, so that it could be abandoned, if necessary, with less loss than a more continuous work. Duport's commentary on his author is elaborate and discursive; in a course which appears to have extended over about two years he covered only sixteen of Theophrastus's short chapters. The lectures, according to J. H. Monk, 'along with some schoolboy information adapted to the attainments of the junior part of his auditors, contain much sound scholarship and extensive learning of a higher character and are upon the whole calculated to give no unfavourable opinion of the state of Greek learning in the University at that memorable crisis'.[5]

In 1654 Duport was forced to resign, and Ralph Widdrington

was appointed by Cromwell in his place. He appears to have delivered only an inaugural oration. As his courtly successor Barrow put it, 'no one would have rendered a more distinguished service to this chair and to Greek learning if he had lectured as often as he lectured well, and if his health or at any rate his more important occupations had permitted this'.[1]

On his succession to the chair at the Restoration Barrow delivered an ornate oration in praise of his subject and of the more distinguished among his predecessors. A year later he delivered a second public speech, which he called an Oratio Sarcasmica, largely devoted to expatiating on the scanty audiences to which he had lectured on the plays of Sophocles during the preceding year. He elaborates his theme with all the wit and copiousness of which he had such a ready command.

> I have sat alone in this chair...like Prometheus on his rock;...not to mountains and woods, but to these walls and benches have I murmured my Greek sentences, figures, phrases and etymologies culled from every source; just like an Attic owl withdrawn from the company of all other birds. My Sophocles and I have acted on an empty stage; even his third actor was missing, no chorus was present, even one of boys; there was none to join in the music, applaud the dancing or interrupt the dialogue. If by chance some wandering Freshman, or an occasional shipwrecked Sophister, snatched by a random eddy, or carried away by the force of some unwelcome breeze, has now and then—though seldom do I recall this happening—landed on these shores, after scarcely making a hasty inspection or listening to a few words, no doubt with some tragic sound in them, in fear of being at once devoured, should he stay, by some barbarian Greek, he has hastily hurried away from my Cyclops cave.[2]

For the next year he decided to abandon Sophocles and choose another author, and his choice fell on Aristotle's *Rhetoric*.[3] What success attended this second course is not recorded. Not long after, in 1664, Barrow transferred to the Lucasian chair of Mathematics. As, he explained, there were many who would willingly and worthily undertake the duties of the Greek chair, he saw no reason why he should not follow his own inclination and retire from the 'grammatical mill'; though he had never disliked philology, he had a greater love of philosophy.[1]

In the seventeenth century the main studies of the undergraduate were logic and moral philosophy, and Greek and Latin were studied less for their own sake than as ancillary to the other branches of university learning. They had, however, another function in the life of the universities. Academic occasions were adorned with ornate Latin speeches which showed the wit and classical learning of the orator and his hearers. The art of verse-writing in the learned languages was highly valued, and the university scholar was expected to celebrate state occasions and academic functions with appropriate verses. Royal births, deaths and marriages were regularly celebrated by the universities in verses, mainly in Latin, but also in Greek, Hebrew and Arabic; between 1660 and 1700 Oxford issued as many as twelve volumes of such verses and Cambridge ten.[2] At Oxford there were also poems recited at the Encaenia, and at both universities verses treating the subjects set in the schools, known at Oxford as Lent verses and at Cambridge as Tripos verses. In spite of the small part played by the classics in their official studies the universities were pervaded by a classical atmosphere, an atmosphere which to a large extent faded in the course of the eighteenth century.

Though Oxford and Cambridge still retain their ancient language for academic ceremonies, it has for long been confined to this narrow sphere. The practice of speaking Latin at meals in Hall, enjoined in college statutes, died out as early as the seventeenth century. An attempt was made in the Commonwealth period to stop the already prevalent use of English,[3] but this seems to have had little effect. At Corpus Christi College, Oxford, in reply to a question of the visitor in 1664 it was stated that the students when sitting at table used Latin to a large extent; ten years later, when the same question was put, the answer was that they did not use Latin or Greek according to the exact sense of the statutes.[4] At

Trinity College, Cambridge, by the early eighteenth century it had long been the practice to speak nothing but English except in academic exercises, and no doubt the same was the case at other colleges.[1] By the end of the century English had become the regular medium for teaching and examining. At Cambridge the Senate House Examination was being conducted in English by 1773, while at Oxford the Examination Statute of 1800 allowed either English or Latin.[2] In the early part of the eighteenth century lectures seem to have been normally in Latin, but by the end of the century this was the exception.[3] Herbert Marsh, who was appointed Lady Margaret Professor of Divinity at Cambridge in 1807, remarked at the beginning of his lectures that his predecessors had used Latin for the few lectures they gave; since however that language had long been abandoned for other lectures, and to use it would mean to have no audience, he proposed to lecture in English.[4] An exception to the general rule was provided by the lectures of the Oxford professor of poetry; these continued to be given in Latin until the appointment of Matthew Arnold in 1857.

While the utilitarian Latin of everyday speech disappeared, the ornamental Latin of the formal oration and of verse-composition lost something of the honour in which it had been held. The practice of issuing volumes of verse on Royal occasions was abandoned. Verse-composition was still practised and still valued, but there was no longer quite the same appetite for, and interest in, such productions as in the seventeenth century. More important, however, than these changes was the abandonment, at Cambridge at any rate, of the old classical authorities in philosophy and science. By the eighteenth century the New Learning of the Renaissance was no longer new. Bacon had questioned the authority of the ancients. The seventeenth century had seen the growth of mathematics and experimental science and the new start in philosophy made by Descartes and Locke. Men were conscious of having outgrown their old masters. The two universities reacted differently to this situation. Oxford remained faithful to the ancients; Aristotle still reigned supreme and the moderns were kept out of the schools. Cambridge on the other hand abandoned the ancient authorities, and took Newton and Locke as her masters. The different course taken by the two universities in the eighteenth century was to have its effect on their attitude to the classics in the nineteenth. At Cambridge logic dropped out in favour of mathematics, and moral philosophy gradually shrank in importance. The old undergraduate course was transformed into one almost exclusively mathematical, and the result was that when the classics were officially recognised by the founding of the Classical Tripos they were regarded as a separate branch of learning divorced from other studies. Oxford on the other hand, because she had resisted modernisation in the eighteenth century, did not, when she came to devise her classical course, entirely forget the old idea that the main business of the university was to teach philosophy.

In the eighteenth century university teaching was in a state of decay. The professorships of Greek had become mere sinecures, and their holders apart from an inaugural oration gave no lectures. Teaching was monopolised by college tutors. At Oxford the degree exercises had sunk to a mere farce, so that tutors were at liberty to devise their own lecture courses, or leave their pupils to themselves. At Cambridge the century is marked by the development of the Tripos, or Senate House examination, mainly mathematical in content, in which classical learning counted for nothing.

While the classics had no place in the official studies of the undergraduate, they were encouraged by various prizes and scholarships, particularly at Cambridge, where, in addition to the Craven scholarships, founded at both universities in 1649, there were the Battie scholarships and Chancellor's Medals for classics, the Members' Prizes for Latin essays and the Browne Medals for Greek and Latin odes and epigrams, all of which date from the mid- or later-eighteenth century. These distinctions were the object of genuine competition, and, in the case of the scholarships and Chancellor's medals, were awarded as a result of an examination which was partly written. An account has survived of the examination for the Chancellor's Medal in 1762.[1] The candidates bring with them lexicon and dictionary. They are first given a passage of Greek to translate into English from a text without Latin translation, then a passage of English for translation into Latin. The next day the written part of the examination ends with Latin prose- and verse-composition, and after the written work has been looked over there follows oral construing from Greek and Latin. In 1781 when Porson sat for the Craven scholarship the examination included the translation of English into Greek iambics, and when Edward Maltby competed for the Chancellor's Medal in 1792 he was given a number of the *Spectator*, different parts of which were to be turned, at one sitting, into Latin prose, Greek prose, Latin verse and Greek verse; there was also a theme to be written, and a passage of Isocrates to be translated into English. For oral construing there were extracts from Simonides of Amorgos, Lysias, Livy and Manilius.[2] At the beginning of the nineteenth century the examination consisted of translation from Latin and Greek, prose and verse; translation of English prose into Latin, and sometimes Greek; original composition in Latin prose and verse, and sometimes Greek verse, and questions on history, geography and chronology.[3] Thus it was in the eighteenth century, well before the establishment of the Classical Tripos, that there developed the Cambridge type of classical examination, consisting largely of written translation from and into Latin and Greek.

In the college teaching of Cambridge there appear to have been two different methods in use, one involving the study of the classics together with other subjects throughout the undergraduate course, the other confining it to the first year. In the early years of the century Daniel Waterland of Magdalene drew up a scheme in which he divided the studies of the university student into three, philosophical (including mathematics and physics as well as logic and ethics), classical and religious, and recommended that all three should be pursued concurrently. He gives a long list of classical authors to be read in the course of the three undergraduate years, including many who would normally have been read at school, and recommends that the mornings and evenings should be devoted to philosophy and the afternoons to classics.[1] On the other hand another college tutor of the same period, Robert Greene of Clare, in his scheme of study confines the classics to the first year, and, in answer to the possible objection that this is not enough, points out that 'this is a course of University Studies, which always suppose Classicks already taught, and begins where the School ends'.[2] The same point of view is expressed by the school-master John Clarke, who observes that if boys are not taught the classics properly at school their Tutors are 'obliged to use them like School-Boys, by making them spend a great part of their Time, in the Reading of Latin and Greek Authors, which ought to be spent upon the Sciences. Thus their proper Business in the College is Jumbled together, with what properly belongs to a Grammar-School and should have been done there.'[3]

Turning to the later part of the century we find that in the 1770's St John's examined its students on classical books as well as on 'philosophy' throughout the undergraduate career. Thus in June 1774 the book prescribed for the first year was Demosthenes *On the Crown*, for the second year Cicero's Second Philippic and for the third three satires of Juvenal; in the following December, for the first year the *Ars Poetica*, for the second Livy XXI and for the third the *Antigone*.[4] But the practice in most colleges at this time was to confine classical lectures to the first year, a practice which was probably encouraged by the increasing importance of the Senate House examination and the consequent necessity of preparing for it in the last two years.[5]

King's was peculiar among the colleges in that its members could obtain degrees without performing any exercises or submitting to examination. The college was therefore exempt from the influences prevailing elsewhere in the university. It was purely classical, but mainly in the negative sense of being quite unmathematical. Eighteenth-century King's had little to add to what its undergraduates brought with them from Eton, though one King's tutor of the end of the century, Thomas Lloyd, made an effort to encourage what he called a 'manly way of reading the classics and suitable to the University'. His plan was to consider the classics under two heads, first, as serving to teach composition, secondly, as showing the need for Revelation. For the former purpose he lectured on Aristotle's *Rhetoric*, Longinus and Quintilian, for the latter on Plato, Aristotle's *Ethics* and Cicero's *De Natura Deorum*.[1]

At Oxford the normal practice of the mid-eighteenth century is probably reflected in the statutes of Hart Hall (1747), which lay down that every week the undergraduates are to write a theme or declamation or a translation, the translations being from Latin into English or English into Latin or, for advanced students, from English into Greek. The tutors are to instruct their classes for the first year in classics (composition and translation) and theology, and for the three following years in 'university learning [presumably logic and moral philosophy] not exclusive of other'.[2] Round about 1770 the practice became established in some colleges of submitting undergraduates to regular examination on classical books read during each term, a practice said to have been derived from Trinity College, Dublin.[3] Magdalen College at the end of the century had a regular scheme of classical reading distributed throughout the undergraduate years. In the first year the books read were Sallust and Virgil's *Aeneid*, Theophrastus's *Characters* and Xenophon's *Anabasis*; in the second year Caesar, Cicero *De Oratore* and *De Officiis*, *Iliad* I to XII and Dionysius Halicarnasseus *De Structura Orationis*; in the third Livy I to VI, Horace *Epistles* and *Ars Poetica*, Cicero *De Natura Deorum*, Xenophon *Cyropaedia* and *Memorabilia* and six satires of Juvenal; and in the fourth year Tacitus *Annals* I to VI, Cicero *Catilines*, *Pro Ligario* and *Pro Archia*, the *Georgics,* Sophocles *Electra,* Demosthenes in Mounteney's selection and Plato in Forster's. In addition a theme or declamation was required once a week.[1]

Corpus Christi College, the old centre of humanist studies, retained something of its repute in this field. Among its eighteenth-century tutors were John Burton, editor of the Pentalogia, and Thomas Burgess, a good Greek scholar, whose lectures are described as having been very able and instructive.[2] But in most of the colleges classical teaching was poor. Jeremy Bentham, who went to Queen's in 1760 at the age of thirteen, was forced to read Cicero's speeches which he already knew by heart or the Greek Testament which he had mastered years before. Gibbon was neglected by his tutors except for some readings of Terence. T. F. Dibdin, who was at St John's at the end of the century, wrote of his college lectures that they 'had only the air of schoolboy proceedings: nothing lofty, stirring, or instructive was propounded to us'.[3] Some tutors wisely dispensed their pupils from attendance at these elementary lectures. Thomas Burgess at Corpus was thus excused as he knew more of the classics than his tutor, and Robert Southey at Balliol was told that he would learn nothing from lectures and that he had better pursue his own studies.[4] Throughout this inglorious period in the history of Oxford there were always studious undergraduates who were encouraged by the unexacting routine of work to read widely on their own. To give one example, Sir William Jones, who was at University College from 1764 and was excused from attendance at lectures, 'perused with great assiduity all the Greek poets and historians of note and the entire works of Plato and Lucian, with a vast apparatus of commentaries on them'.[5]

Richard West, Gray's friend, who went to Oxford in 1735, described it as a 'country flowing with syllogisms and ale, where Horace and Virgil are alike unknown', and at the end of the century, according to Fynes Clinton the chronologist, 'Greek learning was perhaps at its lowest level of degradation'.[6] At Cambridge, though the University Calendar of 1802 might claim that the classics were in most colleges cultivated with great diligence and success, the importance attached to mathematics inevitably put classical studies in the background.[1] Yet while classical education languished in the universities, classical scholarship flourished. The great achievements of English scholarship in the eighteenth century were unrelated to university studies. Bentley, the founder of the English school, was neither college lecturer nor professor of Greek, and as Master of Trinity was mainly concerned to encourage studies other than classical. His successors, apart from Markland, who was for a time tutor of Peterhouse, lived and studied for the most part outside the universities; Porson, though Professor of Greek at Cambridge, gave no lectures. It is a curious fact, and one which should not be forgotten by those who put their trust in courses and examinations, that the date at which, according to A. E. Housman, the great age of scholarship in England came to an end, coincided almost exactly with the foundation of the Classical Tripos at Cambridge.

CHAPTER VI

THE SCHOOLS IN THE
NINETEENTH CENTURY. 1

England of the nineteenth century had inherited from earlier ages between seven and eight hundred grammar schools, unevenly distributed throughout the country, supported by endowments and governed by statutes dating in many cases from Tudor times.[1] At the beginning of the century the public school system which was to dominate education in the Victorian age was already beginning to develop. Certain schools such as Eton and Winchester had always been boarding-schools; others, owing to valuable endowments, good headmasters or other reasons, had developed into public schools, schools, that is, which drew their pupils from the country as a whole rather than from their immediate vicinity. But so far as curriculum and methods of teaching went there was little difference between one endowed school and another; from this point of view Eton was only the largest and most important of the grammar schools.

The grammar school had survived from the Roman Empire through the Middle Ages and the Humanist period. By the beginning of the nineteenth century the meaning of the term and the purpose of the institution were beginning to be questioned. But any doubts there might be were set at rest by the judgment of the Lord Chancellor in 1805 in the case of Leeds Grammar School, which laid down that the funds of the school could only be used for the teaching of the ancient languages.[2] Grammar had undoubtedly meant Latin and Greek at the time when most of these schools were founded, and, in spite of the change that had taken place in the position of Latin since then, the law still required them to carry out the intention of their founders.

Thus the classics owed their position in education, in part at any rate, to ancient endowment, and by the early nineteenth century there were many who were chafing at the dead hand of the past. Apart from the demand for a utilitarian education for those who had no intention of entering a learned profession, there were doubts about the value of an exclusive devotion to the study and imitation of the ancient poets. Grammar-school education of the eighteenth century had real merits, but its excessive conservatism laid it open to criticism. It might have been better for classical studies if they had been less securely established. In Germany, where the classics had fallen into sad decline by the early eighteenth century, the 'new humanism' of Gesner and Heyne, and later of von Humboldt, had all the appeal of novelty. For the Englishman a classical education was part of the established system, and its advocates in the nineteenth century had the disadvantage of being on the defensive; and because the education of the schools was exclusively classical, the classics bore much of the blame which should rather have been directed against defective organisation and natural human stupidity.

But if the classics had depended solely on endowment and ancient prescription, they would hardly have survived. That they did survive was due partly to the proved value of old educational methods, partly to the introduction of a new spirit into classical teaching. In spite of the limitations of the old grammar-school tradition there was enough life in it to enable it to recover and meet the challenge of the nineteenth century. It was from within the established system that reforms came; the great schoolmasters of the nineteenth century were classical teachers brought up in the old tradition. But they were also men who saw that the time had come for change. The old system was revivified. The changes introduced may at first sight appear to be slight, but they were none the less significant. Englishmen did not talk about a 'new humanism', but something which could with justice be so described gradually replaced the old humanism which had survived from the time of the Tudors.

Of these changes the most important was perhaps the increase in the amount of Greek done and the shift of interest from the Latin to the Greek authors. Latin literature was on the whole little regarded in nineteenth-century England, particularly in the first half of the century. The belief in the virtues of the original genius and the poetry of nature which grew up in the mid-eighteenth century gave the literature of Greece a greater prestige than that of Rome which was so largely derived from it. Coleridge records how James Bowyer at Christ's Hospital taught him to prefer Demosthenes to Cicero and Homer and Theocritus to Virgil,[1] and Bowyer's tastes were on the whole those of the nineteenth century. The trend of scholarship reinforced that of taste. The remarkable achievements of the English school in the field of Greek had their effect in schoolteaching; the great classical teachers of the nineteenth century, Butler, Kennedy and Arnold, were Greek rather than Latin scholars.

Ancient authors were no longer studied only as models of style, and more attention was paid to their subject matter and historical background. New authors were introduced to the curriculum, particularly prose writers such as Tacitus, Thucydides, Herodotus and Plato. Greek prose-composition came in and Greek verse-composition was more generally practised. Translation of English passages gradually replaced original composition in prose and in verse, and the written translation of Greek and Latin into English, which was little practised at the beginning of the century, slowly became a recognised part of school work.

The first important influence in nineteenth-century classical teaching was that of Samuel Butler, who found Shrewsbury school in a state of decay when he went there in 1798, and left it the leading classical school in the country. Butler, though his chief work of scholarship was his edition of Aeschylus, was more interested in the prose writers than most schoolmasters of his day. He included Tacitus and Cicero's speeches in the curriculum, and B. H. Kennedy recalled that Demosthenes was a favourite author

with him; some Thucydides was read, but not a great deal, and
Kennedy remembered no Plato.[1] Butler's pupils were also
taught ancient history and geography, subjects which had been
generally neglected before his time,[2] while once a week the two
upper forms had a lecture from their headmaster on Greek metres
or some subject connected with ancient literature.[3]

Butler retained the old exercises of the prose theme and original
Latin verse, but in addition to these he required translation into
Latin and Greek prose, while the prepostors did a Greek verse
exercise, usually a translation, in place of one or all of their Latin
exercises.[4] In this way Salopians acquired that proficiency in the
composition of Greek iambics for which they were noted at the
universities.

Butler's most important innovation was his use of regular
examinations to test the boys' acquirements and to determine their
place in school. But what was significant about his system was
not only the fact that he examined his boys but also the way in
which he did it. The examination was a written one, and 'the
Boys know not the subject of the Examination or the Nature of
the Questions until they are assembled in the room'.[5] It was in
fact an examination of the type in use at Cambridge for the University scholarships, consisting in the main of unseen translation
from Latin and Greek, translation into Latin and Greek and Latin
theme and original verse. It was small wonder that Salopians
excelled in the Cambridge examinations. They had been well
practised at school and the examination hall held no terrors for
them.

Butler's methods were widely admired and followed in the
scholastic world. But he owed his success to more than his system.
He had the power of bringing the classics to life and of interesting
his boys. One of his pupils, addressing his old headmaster on his
elevation to the episcopate, wrote: 'So beautifully solemn was
your Lordship's manner of unfolding the properties of the ancient
writers that those who heard could not but choose to learn; nor

is it strange if in me, among many of your pupils, there was kindled a flame which I hope will never be extinguished.'[1] The best of Butler's pupils did a remarkable amount of private reading. Kennedy, when he went to the university, had read by himself all Thucydides and Tacitus, all Sophocles and Aeschylus, much of Aristophanes, Pindar, Herodotus, Demosthenes and Plato, besides Cicero.[2] 'Dr Butler', said another of his pupils, 'certainly did succeed in making us believe that Latin and Greek were the one thing worth living for.'[3]

Butler was succeeded by Kennedy, who carried on the tradition of his old teacher. Between them the two headmasters produced a remarkable succession of able scholars who carried off with monotonous regularity the prizes and scholarships of Cambridge. There were those who said that Shrewsbury boys were crammed. When the Ireland Scholarship at Oxford was won in 1831 by a Salopian still at the school, Gladstone, an unsuccessful competitor, observed that 'this has contributed amazingly to strengthen a prevalent impression that the Shrewsbury system is radically a false one'.[4] But a Shrewsbury education produced not only scholarship winners, but men with a real love of learning and the ability to advance it. Among those who learned their classics from Butler and Kennedy were Shilleto, F. A. Paley, Robert Scott (of Liddell and Scott), E. M. Cope, James Riddell, H. A. J. Munro, Archer-Hind, J. E. B. Mayor and Heitland.[5]

But while Shrewsbury more than any other school left its mark on nineteenth-century English scholarship, from the point of view of education Rugby was more influential, thanks to the commanding personality of Thomas Arnold. We are not concerned here with the reforms which Arnold brought about in the general organisation and spirit of the English public school, but only with his work as a teacher of the classics. Even in this limited field his work was of considerable importance and did much to determine the character of nineteenth-century classical education.

As a young man Arnold reacted vigorously against much that was characteristic of the traditional classical education. As a schoolboy at Winchester he asked the headmaster to include Greek composition in the curriculum, admired the Greek orators and historians and professed himself 'quite tired of the pompous boasts of Cicero'.[1] At Oxford he preferred the philosophers to the poets and had little use for the niceties of language. His interest lay in 'things rather than words', and as a young man he would dismiss Latin verse-composition as 'one of the most contemptible prettinesses of the understanding'. In later life he modified his views, and as headmaster of Rugby became more favourably disposed to Latin verse, though he was never much of a versifier himself and set more store by prose-composition. Though he introduced other subjects, he had no desire to dethrone the classics. 'The study of language', he said, 'seems to me as if it was given for the very purpose of forming the human mind in youth; and the Greek and Latin languages...seem the very instruments by which this is to be effected.'[2] But with him the emphasis was not so much on the form as on the content of the ancient authors. His biographer claims that he was 'the first Englishman who drew attention in our public schools to the historical, political, and philosophical value of philology and of the ancient writers, as distinguished from the mere verbal criticism and elegant scholarship of the last [i.e. the eighteenth] century',[3] and the claim may be allowed, for Butler, in spite of his teaching of ancient history and geography, was primarily interested in accurate scholarship and not, as was Arnold, aiming to draw lessons from antiquity for the modern world.

The old type of theme—'virtus est bona res' was Arnold's scornful parody of the subjects commonly set—was replaced by subjects requiring solid knowledge and independent thought, while in selecting passages for translation into Greek and Latin Arnold chose extracts remarkable in themselves, taken from his favourite authors, so that composition in the classical languages became at the same time an education in modern literature.[1] His choice of books for school reading was largely determined by his own interests, and throughout his short life he was still learning. In 1835 he was reading Pindar and Aristophanes, the latter for the first time, and promptly introduced them into the school curriculum, though his strong moral sense made it hard for him to appreciate Aristophanes. Later he embarked with enthusiasm on the reading of Plato, and Plato was introduced to his sixth form.[2] Even Aristotle, for whom Arnold had a great admiration, was read at Rugby, in spite of his generally being regarded as essentially an author who belonged to the university.[3] In taking his classes through their books Arnold would insist on good English rather than word for word construes, though translation must at the same time be accurate and bring out every shade of meaning in the original. 'Every lesson', he held, 'in Greek or Latin may and ought to be made a lesson in English.'[4]

Of the London schools Westminster for long remained little affected by the spirit of reform, and in the early part of the century its place as the leading metropolitan school was taken by Charterhouse under Raine and Russell. Little is recorded of the teaching of Matthew Raine, but it may be surmised that, as a friend of Porson, he was a more genial character than his successor. Russell was a stern, unsympathetic teacher, and his regime left a lazy and sensitive boy like Thackeray with little knowledge or love of the classics,[5] but others of robuster temperament and more industrious habits gained from it a thorough grounding in the classical languages. But if thorough, it was also narrow. Liddell, the lexicographer, left the school in 1829 'a fair grammar scholar, but with very little classical reading'. Greek prose in particular was 'almost untrodden ground', and Herodotus and Thucydides were known only by name.[6] Yet though Russell and those who followed him at the old London Charterhouse before its removal to the Surrey hills have not gone down to history as great classical scholars, the school which produced Liddell, Henry Nettleship and Jebb certainly deserved well of classical scholarship. At St Paul's much of the new spirit in classical education had come in by the 1830's, when in the highest form far more time was spent on Greek than on Latin, and Pindar, Aristophanes, Demosthenes and Thucydides were read, as well as the tragic poets.[1] The teaching at that time is said to have been well adapted, if not to produce extreme accuracy of verbal scholarship, 'at least to imbue the minds of boys with a genuine love of literature'.[2]

Of the provincial schools other than the public schools already referred to perhaps the most distinguished in the first half of the nineteenth century was King Edward's, Birmingham, to which Prince Lee, who had been one of Arnold's ablest assistants, went as headmaster in 1838. At once the school began to challenge better-known foundations, and in the 1840's it provided Cambridge with four Senior Classics in as many years.[3] Lee was no pedant, and his pupil Bishop Westcott recalled 'the richness and force of the illustrations by which he brought home to us a battle piece of Thucydides, with a landscape of Virgil or a sketch of Tacitus'. Yet at the same time he insisted on accuracy.

In translating we were bound to see that every syllable gave its testimony. It might be possible or not to transfer directly into English the exact shade of meaning conveyed by the original text, but at least we were required to take account of the minutest differences in turns of expression, to seek some equivalent for their force and to weigh what was finally lost in our own renderings.

It was this belief of Lee's in verbal accuracy that impressed itself on his pupils. 'If I am to select one endowment', said Westcott, 'which I have found precious for the whole work of life beyond all others, it would be the belief in words which I gained through the severest discipline of verbal criticism.'[4]

There are no doubt many other schools which might be mentioned here, schools which maintained a respectable though not remarkable standard in classics, or which under a good headmaster attained for a time a level from which they afterwards declined.

Among the latter was Sedbergh during the headmastership of
J. H. Evans (1838–61), before the school's sad decline in the 1860's
under Day.[1] As befitted a school closely connected with St John's
College, Cambridge, Sedbergh taught more mathematics than
was usual at that time, but the classics were also studied thoroughly
and there was much private reading. According to J. M. Wilson
it was part of the tradition of the place that everyone should have
read Homer, Thucydides and Sophocles before he went up to the
university, and a good many other books such as Virgil, Horace,
Catullus, Euripides and even Lucan were regarded as necessities.
'We read the classics', says Wilson, 'literally with our feet on the
fender.'[2] Wilson's reminiscences remind us of the educational
advantages of an isolation from the world which is unattainable
in the modern school. There was only one tolerably readable
book, he says, in the school library, Schömann's *De Comitiis
Atheniensibus*, and so this was read.[3] It is not surprising that those
who turned for recreation to a book in Latin on the Athenian
constitution should leave school with the taste and ability for
hard work.

While the endowed public schools and grammar schools were
the main strongholds of the classics, there were in the early part
of the nineteenth century a number of private schools which
prepared for the university and gave a classical education on
grammar-school lines. Later on, as the public schools became less
barbarous, such establishments tended to die out and by the middle
of the century a private school was generally a non-classical or
semi-classical school. In addition to the regular private schools
there were clergymen who took pupils in country rectories, some
of whom prepared boys for the universities, such as Mr Preston,
who taught Macaulay and who sent his pupils to Cambridge well
able to hold their own with the products of the best public schools.
For those who were themselves sons of scholarly clergy the home
could provide at least the early stages and sometimes the later
stages too of a classical education. Tennyson, apart from a brief

period at the local grammar school, received his education from his father, and went from Somersby rectory to Cambridge thoroughly grounded in the classics.

Whether he received his early education in the rectory study or with a private tutor or at a private school the nineteenth-century boy would begin his classics at an early age and might reach a high level of proficiency before his regular schooling began. Not many, it is true, could like Connop Thirlwall read Latin at the age of three and Greek at four,[1] but it is not uncommon in the memoirs of the period to read of boys starting Latin at home at the age of five or earlier and Greek not much later.[2] Conington at the age of eight would amuse himself by comparing different editions of Virgil, and even before then could repeat one thousand lines of Virgil to his father.[3] Roundell Palmer, afterwards Lord Selborne, was fairly well grounded in Horace and Virgil by the age of nine, and before he went to school had read some Homer and the *Prometheus* of Aeschylus; George Osborne Morgan at the age of eleven was reading the eleventh book of the *Aeneid* and Xenophon's *Anabasis* and was making Latin verses.[4] The hero of *The Way of All Flesh* had read 'the greater part of Virgil, Horace and Livy and I do not know how many Greek plays' before he went to school at the age of twelve. There is doubtless some exaggeration here as regards Livy and Greek plays, but the examples already quoted show that the clergy did not let their sons off lightly. In private schools or with private tutors boys advanced no less rapidly. Macaulay was reading Xenophon and Homer and doing Latin verses at the age of twelve and J. A. Froude had read the *Iliad* and the *Odyssey* twice under the rector of Buckfastleigh before he went to Westminster at the age of eleven.[5] Frederick Harrison under Joseph King, a schoolmaster who used unorthodox methods, could read Homer and Virgil, Herodotus and Livy accurately by the age of eleven.[6]

The nineteenth century also saw the development of a new type of private school whose purpose was to prepare boys for the public schools. These preparatory schools in many cases brought their youthful pupils to a remarkable degree of proficiency. For example, at the school at Mitcham opened at the end of the eighteenth century the boys were made to tear out the Latin translations of Greek authors and use a plain text only; they composed Latin themes and verses and, towards the end of their time, Greek verses. Pusey, who attended this school before going to Eton, once remarked that half the boys there could have passed Oxford Moderations, except for the logic paper, before they were eleven.[1] Then there was Eagle House, Hammersmith, under Edward Wickham, father of the editor of Horace. Here was given what by the standards of earlier times was a complete grammar-school course. Henry Montagu Butler when he left at the age of twelve had read two Greek plays with choruses, a fair amount of the *Iliad*, of Xenophon's *Hellenica* and of the Greek Testament, Cicero's *De Amicitia*, much of Virgil, a book of Horace's *Odes* and a little Livy. In addition to this he had composed themes and, every week, sixteen lines of original hexameters.[2] It is doubtful whether so high a level of scholarship, in Greek at any rate, was reached at so early an age before the nineteenth century, and certain that it is not reached today. For those who went from a good private to a good public school, the nineteenth century was the golden age, if not of classical scholarship, at least of classical education.

CHAPTER VII

THE SCHOOLS IN THE NINETEENTH CENTURY. 2

In the 1860's the government, for the first time, began to take a serious interest in secondary education in England and Wales. In 1861 a Royal Commission under Lord Clarendon was appointed to inquire into the state of the nine schools somewhat arbitrarily classified as public schools, and this was followed in 1864 by a second commission under Lord Taunton which inquired into the endowed grammar schools and secondary education in general. The reports of these two commissions, published in 1864 and 1868 respectively, give us a valuable picture of the state of classical education in the mid-Victorian period.

The most striking feature in the picture is the decline of the old grammar schools. With some notable exceptions these schools had ceased to play any important part in the life of the country. The words 'grammar school' called up the picture of an antiquated schoolroom and listless, conventional teaching from out-of-date grammar books to a few boys who would be unlikely to stay at school long enough to get anything out of the classical education which was all that was offered them. Not a few of the schools had given up teaching the classics altogether, in spite of the requirements of their statutes. In some cases the amount of classics done was small, even farcical; at one school in London the highest class read aloud the beginning of the Latin grammar for one hour a week, without explanation or knowledge of the meaning, in order to satisfy founder's intention.[1] According to the Schools Inquiry Commission, of the endowed grammar schools only 27 per cent were conducted as full classical schools; 23 per cent were semi-classical, that is, taught Latin but little or no Greek, and 43 per cent taught no Latin or Greek.[2]

The decline had begun in the early part of the century. Already in 1818, when Carlisle compiled his *Concise Description of the Endowed Grammar Schools*, there were schools which had ceased to teach the classics because there was no demand for them,[1] and the reports of the Charity Commissioners on educational endowments in the 1820's and 1830's give further evidence of this development. By the 1860's things had become worse. The state of affairs reported by the commissioner who visited the Yorkshire schools for the Schools Inquiry Commission was typical. 'It not infrequently happened', he wrote, 'that on visiting foundation schools, which are now sunk to a far lower level than an ordinary national school, I have been met by trustees who are now magistrates and country gentlemen, and informed that in their youth they received a good drilling in Latin and Greek within the same walls.'[2]

The grammar schools which did teach the classics did not on the whole teach them well. The Commissioners may have had severe standards and may in some cases have been hasty in their judgments, but their reports certainly suggest that much of the classical teaching was wasted effort. One of them reported that in eight schools which he examined where Latin was taught, no boy could give correctly the Latin for 'He was a good boy' or the English for 'epistulam quam misi vidit'.[3] Another found that in his area there were no boys who with any amount of time and unlimited use of the dictionary could translate with decent correctness an ordinary passage of Cicero or Virgil.[4] In Northumberland, outside Newcastle Grammar School, there was only one boy who could even attempt to translate an English sentence into Latin, and in Yorkshire a boy who could read Latin 'with ordinary fluency' was hardly to be met with.[5]

The demand for a classical education varied in different parts of the country. In Devon the farmers and tradesmen were opposed to Greek for their sons, but in favour of Latin, because, they said, it was so often quoted in the newspapers.[6] In Westmorland 'a love and respect for the ancient classics' was still to be found; in Cumberland the farmers wished their sons to have a chance of learning the classics, and there was said to be a remarkable demand for Greek and Latin in the neighbourhood of Kendal.[1] Westmorland and Cumberland were somewhat peculiar; they were abnormally well supplied with grammar schools, and in the early part of the century there had been a widely diffused knowledge of the classics in those counties. In Westmorland at the time of the Schools Inquiry Commission men were still to be met with in the humbler walks of life who spoke with pride of their recollections of Virgil and Homer.[2] But even in this unusually civilised part of the country the demand for a classical education had fallen off, and few of the old schools were conducted as full classical schools.

Elsewhere in England the 'mercantile and trading classes', to use the language of the day, and in general those whose sons were unlikely to go into a learned profession or continue their education after the age of about sixteen, had no use for Greek and perhaps tolerated Latin, but in any case objected to the exclusively classical education provided by the grammar schools. In Yorkshire, for example, the masters of grammar schools put the blame for their unpopularity on the apathy and ignorance of parents bent on money-making, and in Lancashire, apart from a few schools, Greek had virtually disappeared as a result of the general demand for a short and practical education.[3]

To meet the demands of parents who considered classics useless innumerable private schools had sprung up. In these the classics had only an insecure place. The laws of supply and demand operated, and masters of private schools, dependent as they were on fees, had to take into account the views of the parents. 'If I dared', said one private schoolmaster, 'I would teach more Latin in my school, but the parents won't let me.'[4] The spirit of the age was utilitarian; the vast populations of the new industrial towns judged education solely by its usefulness, and they had their spokesmen in men like Cobden, who declared that one copy of

The Times contained more useful information than the whole of Thucydides.[1]

The grammar schools lost ground not only to the private schools but also to the public schools, for by now there was a clear distinction between these and the grammar schools. 'The classical education', as the Schools Inquiry Commission put it, 'of the highest order is every day to a greater degree quitting the small grammar schools for the great public schools.'[2] With the coming of the railways boarding schools were more in demand, and men who had themselves been educated at a local grammar school sent their sons to Rugby or Shrewsbury, or to a new foundation like Marlborough. The grammar schools suffered accordingly. In Norfolk, it was stated, the reduced number of classical scholars in local schools was 'mainly owing to the increased facilities for travelling, which enable gentlemen of independent means, although themselves educated in Norfolk schools, to send their sons to Eton, Harrow and Rugby'.[3] Much the same was reported from other parts of the country, and indeed it is unnecessary to quote evidence for what is a well-known fact of English social history.

The public schools recruited to their staffs some of the best classics of the universities, and fellows of colleges who, in the eighteenth century, might have gone to be headmasters of country grammar schools, in the later nineteenth century went as assistants to Rugby or Harrow. The standard in the public schools was high, and the smaller local schools could not compete. Classical scholarship tended to be concentrated in a comparatively small number of schools, and this tendency was encouraged by the establishment of open entrance scholarships at Oxford and Cambridge. To win these one had to be well trained.[4]

Of the public schools Eton was the most conservative. In the 1860's it taught the classics very much as it had taught them in the eighteenth century. A few new authors had come into the curriculum; the upper forms read a little Thucydides, Demosthenes and Tacitus. But the staple of the curriculum remained

Virgil, Horace and Homer, and the old extract books were still in use, though they were abandoned, along with the Eton Latin Grammar, shortly after the Public Schools Commission. Eton boys were still required to learn by heart most of the verse writers construed in class; there was still a large amount of original Latin verse and little translated. The weekly Latin theme continued until 1868, when it was replaced by translation into Latin prose, which had only occasionally been required before then.[1] There was very little Greek prose composition and much less Greek than Latin verse. But there were Eton boys whose facility in iambics matched the traditional Etonian facility in Latin elegiacs. Oscar Browning, who was at Eton in the 1860's, wrote his first Greek iambics without difficulty and without previous practice; 'we all', he says, 'knew how to write Greek Iambics as if we had learnt the art in our cradles.'[2]

Winchester, like Eton, remained faithful to old traditions. The practice of 'standing up' and the writing of vulguses still continued. There was a large amount of original composition, and little or no Greek prose was written.[3] New methods had however begun to come in with the appointment of E. C. Wickham in 1857 to tutor the senior boys in composition. He is said to have brought new life into the school. 'Many of us', writes a Wykehamist of the period, 'would turn out thirty or forty lines of passable Latin, either in prose or verse, per hour', but it was 'slipshod stuff'. Wickham introduced translations from English into Latin and Greek with fair copies and careful correction, and gave the boys their first exercise in minute accuracy of thought and expression.[4] A feature of Winchester, though it was not peculiar to the school, was the reading of Pindar by the highest form. The tradition went back at least to the 1820's, and continued under the Victorian headmasters, Moberly and Ridding.[5] Moberly's favourite authors were Pindar and Thucydides; Greek plays he 'did not care about a bit'.[6] Tacitus, Plato and Aristophanes, authors who were by that time read in not a few schools, were unrepresented at Winchester in 1861; of these Plato had come in by the 1870's, but not the other two.[1]

At Harrow the old eighteenth-century tradition of elegant scholarship had been modified by Rugbeian influences introduced by Vaughan. Authors such as Plato, Lucretius, Tacitus and Aristophanes, who had been unknown to Harrow in the early nineteenth century, were now read by the sixth form, though the range of reading is said to have been narrow compared to that of some schools.[2] Henry Montagu Butler, who succeeded Vaughan as headmaster in 1859 and remained until 1885, was a teacher who combined scholarly thoroughness with enthusiasm, and who inspired 'a feeling for the fine diction, the deep thoughts, the music and humanity of an ancient author'.[3] Butler's chief interest was in composition. He was himself an accomplished versifier and succeeded in inspiring his boys with something of his own enthusiasm for the art; competition was keen for the school prize compositions, the subjects set were difficult and the standard was very high.[4]

At Shrewsbury Kennedy's long reign came to an end in 1866. He was the foremost classical teacher of his age, known throughout the scholastic world for his Latin grammar and other educational works, an accomplished writer of verses and sufficiently distinguished as a pure scholar to end his days as professor of Greek at Cambridge. But above all he excelled in the classroom, impressing himself on his sixth form by his vigorous personality and his power of making the ancient world come alive. 'He was never tedious', wrote his pupil Heitland; 'a lesson—and we had long lessons in short hours—was got through at a terrific pace.... His tall and striking figure, never—or hardly ever—at rest, his bright piercing eye, his mighty voice echoing among the rafters, all combined to fix attention.' His translations of the authors read in class were dramatic and impressive. 'He is not merely', to quote Heitland again, 'translating Demosthenes: he *is* Demosthenes speaking extempore in English.'[5]

Classical reading was wide at Shrewsbury compared with most other schools.[1] In the sixth form Greek reading exceeded Latin, and included such advanced authors as Pindar and Aristotle. Since Butler's day Attic Greek had been the speciality of Shrewsbury, and Homer was comparatively neglected. Non-Salopians alleged that this neglect was due to a fear that the boys' compositions might be contaminated by non-Attic Greek,[2] but no doubt the simple fact was that if many other authors had to be included there was not room for the large amount of Homer that characterised school education in earlier days. The situation was much the same in other schools, and Sir Charles Oman even states, though this is hard to believe, that no Homer at all was read at Winchester when he was there in the 1870's.[3]

At the time of the Public Schools Commission Shrewsbury still had a large amount of original Latin composition in prose and verse. There was very little Greek prose-composition— Kennedy believed that if you read Thucydides you could write Greek prose well enough for a schoolboy[4]—and less Greek verse than might be expected in view of the well-known excellence of Salopian iambics. A Rugby sixth-form boy did more Greek verse than a Salopian. Kennedy did not worry his pupils with verse-composition if they showed no gift for it. 'Those who are unable', as he put it, 'may be allowed to "hang up the pipe to Pan".'[5]

At Rugby the tradition of wide and varied reading and a choice of books interesting in themselves established by Arnold was continued by his successors. Frederick Temple, headmaster from 1857 to 1869, introduced Lucretius to the sixth form, and even read with them so advanced a work as the *Philebus*.[6] He was particularly remembered for his analyses of the subject-matter of the authors read and his power of making their character and meaning clear. 'Whether it was Lucretius or Thucydides, Guizot or de Tocqueville, Plato or St Paul, it was marvellous how it all fell into shape in our minds.'[7]

The amount of original composition required at Rugby, though considerable, was noticeably less than the amount of translation into Greek and Latin. The sixth-form boy did twice as much translated Latin prose as original, and fifteen copies of translated Latin verse a year to ten of original verse. His Greek compositions, all translated, were fewer in number than his Latin, but numerous compared to those at Eton, Winchester and Shrewsbury. In all— I give these figures so that my readers may be able to compare them with their own experience as teachers or taught—he did in the course of a year fifteen Latin essays and about three hundred lines of original Latin verse; about six hundred lines of translated Latin prose and four hundred and fifty of translated Latin verse, while his Greek compositions consisted of about four hundred lines of prose and the same amount of verse.[1] Careful correction and the giving of fair copies, features absent from Shrewsbury under Kennedy, were characteristic of the Rugby method.

The reports of the Public Schools Commission and the Schools Inquiry Commission show that in the 1860's traditional methods of teaching still survived to a considerable extent. They must have lost ground rather rapidly after that date. Learning by heart did not entirely disappear, but the amount exacted diminished, and at Shrewsbury in the 1890's there was hardly any.[2] Original composition was already under fire in the 1860's. Distinguished Rugbeians interviewed by the Public Schools Commission spoke of the 'utter miseries of original composition'; the Salopian C. E. Graves recalled how he had grumbled at too much of it when at school, and declared that he saw no advantage whatever in original Latin verse.[3] The eighteenth century might survive at Eton, where, as W. R. Inge tells us, the Collegers of his day (1870's) wrote in Ovidian couplets more easily than in English,[4] but elsewhere what had been in earlier days the delight of the more gifted boys had now become a burden. The influence of the universities must have helped to kill original composition, for though there were medals and prizes for such composition, and though it was still required in University Scholarships, it had no place in the Tripos or the Oxford Honour Schools. Added to this was the very real educational value of translation into dead languages. There are few better ways of grasping the essence of an author than by attempting to express his words in an alien language, and there are probably many who have learned more about English literature from their classical compositions than from their English lessons.

This, however, would mean little to the less gifted boys who simply could not do verses. The wise example of Kennedy was not generally followed. Latin verse-composition was still almost universally regarded as an essential part of education. There was, it is true, one headmaster of a good classical school in the mid-nineteenth century, T. H. Key of University College School, who dispensed with verses entirely.[1] But Key was an exception among schoolmasters; in the Public Schools verse-making was compulsory, and for the majority it was a painful and unprofitable drudgery. Junior masters whose task it was to teach the art to the duller boys lost faith in its value. In 1867 F. W. Farrar, the author of *Eric, or Little by Little*, then an assistant master at Harrow, published a paper in which he urged the abandonment of Greek and Latin verse as a necessary element in a liberal education and a diminution of the value hitherto set on this accomplishment.[2] His headmaster, H. M. Butler, in spite of his own love of verse-composition, apparently shared to some extent his assistant's views. In the same year in which Farrar's essay appeared he exempted some of the lower forms from verses, observing that experience had convinced him that to a very large proportion of boys this kind of instruction was useless.[3] So verse-composition began to lose its old position as an essential part of English education.

Another change which marked the classical education of the later nineteenth century was the spread of annotated editions. In the earlier part of the century plain texts were commonly used or editions which hardly gave the sort of help a modern schoolboy needs. The best scholars flourished under the discipline of tackling a plain text of Plato or Thucydides with the help only of dictionary and grammar, and could hardly reconcile themselves to commentaries. When Charles Gore at Harrow in the 1850's asked B. F. Westcott, then an assistant master, for an order for Poppo's Thucydides, Westcott almost shivered at the idea of using a commentary at so early an age; he himself had had nothing but Bekker's plain text till he was twenty-three.[1] But there must have been many who resorted to the forbidden crib.

From about the middle of the century dates the extensive production of the familiar school editions which are now characteristic of English education. The middle years of the century saw the production of the *Grammar School Classics* and the editions of the industrious T. K. Arnold; Rivington's *Catena Classicorum* dates from 1867, and from about the same period those series of texts published by Macmillan and the two university presses which are still familiar to schoolboys. One reason for the increased output of such works was no doubt the growth of external examinations. The London matriculation examination, which began in 1838, and the Oxford and Cambridge Local examinations, first held in 1857, did much to influence curriculum and teaching at what were then known as 'middle-class schools', schools where classical teaching did not reach a high level and which did not normally send boys to the universities. In 1874 came the Higher Certificate examination of the Oxford and Cambridge Board, designed for the sixth forms of schools which prepared for the two universities, and this was followed in 1884 by the Lower School examination. These examinations had their 'set books', and annotated editions gave the boys the necessary help in the way of explanatory notes.

The two Royal Commissions of the 1860's differed somewhat in their attitude to classical education. The Public Schools Commission, though it approved of the introduction of other subjects, was strongly in favour of maintaining the classical tradition. It was important, the commissioners held, that there should be 'some one principal branch of study, invested with a recognised, and, if possible, a traditional importance, to which the principal weight should be assigned'. The classics at present occupied that position and had the advantage of long possession, 'an advantage so great that we should certainly hesitate to advise the dethronement of it'. But long possession was not the only ground for the retention of the classics. The ancient languages, the Commissioners believed, provided the finest and most serviceable models there were for the study of language. Greece and Rome gave us 'the most graceful and some of the noblest poetry, the finest eloquence, the deepest philosophy, the wisest historical writing'; their languages supplied the key to modern languages, their poetry, history, philosophy and law the key to the poetry, history, philosophy and jurisprudence of modern times, and this key would seldom be acquired except in youth.[1]

This enthusiasm for the classics is not to be found in the report of the Schools Inquiry Commission. Surveying the whole chaotic field of secondary education, the commissioners were impressed by the failure of the traditional classical education to meet the needs of the country as a whole, and at the same time by the general belief of the schoolmasters of the day in the virtues of Latin, particularly of Latin grammar. Latin was the only subject taught thoroughly, and, as the Commissioners put it, 'it would plainly be in the highest degree inexpedient to dislodge it from its place till we are sure of getting something better'.[2] Thus they regarded Greek as unnecessary except for first-grade schools (schools, that is, which kept their boys until eighteen and prepared for the universities), they recommended that Latin should retain its place as an important subject in second-grade schools, with a leaving age of sixteen, while in third-grade schools, with a leaving age of fourteen, it was suggested that the elements of Latin should be taught, though the language should not be allowed to take up too much time.[3] These proposals were not put into effect, but the attitude to Greek and Latin shown by the Commissioners has been to some extent reflected in educational practice since their day, in the divergence between the school with a classical sixth form, where Greek is on a level with Latin, and the school where of the two languages only Latin is effectively taught. In the latter case Latin becomes not what it was in the major classical schools of the nineteenth century, one of the constituents, perhaps the less important one, in the study of the ancient world, but something valued mainly as a linguistic discipline, teaching accuracy of thought and expression and contributing to the understanding of modern languages, but doing little to enlarge and stimulate the mind.

In the last quarter of the nineteenth century there were few changes in the general pattern of classical education throughout the country. At the public schools the standard of classical teaching was generally maintained, and in some of them it was advanced, as at St Paul's, where F. W. Walker was High Master in the last quarter of the century, and at Westminster, where the learned W. G. Rutherford, who had been an assistant master under Walker, went as headmaster in 1883. At Charterhouse the late-Victorian headmaster Haig-Brown, himself a sound classical scholar, had an outstanding assistant in T. E. Page, an old Salopian, who taught the classical sixth for many years from 1873. Among the large town schools Manchester Grammar School came to the fore in the later part of the century. At the time of the Schools Inquiry Commission it was not one of the leading classical schools; by the 1890's its classical teaching was as good as anywhere. In London the older schools found a new rival in the City of London School, a nineteenth-century foundation which became known as a classical school under Mortimer, headmaster from 1840 to 1865, and even more under his successor Abbott. In the days of Mortimer boys began Latin and Greek later than was usual else-where,[1] but they did no less well in open scholarships, and in the 1850's and 1860's three Chancellor's Medallists and Senior Classics at Cambridge were Old Citizens. Abbott brought with him from Cambridge an enthusiasm for comparative philology, and gave better teaching on the subject than was available at Oxford for many years afterwards.[1] Under him the classics, and other subjects as well, were excellently taught; J. S. Reid, L. R. Farnell and R. S. Conway, not to mention H. H. Asquith, learnt their classics in the gas-lit fog of the City.

As a result of the reorganisation of educational endowments carried out by the Endowed Schools Commission set up in 1869 and by the Charity Commission which took over its functions five years later, many of the old grammar schools revived, and by the end of the century were far better than they had been at the time of the Schools Inquiry Commission. But a grammar school was no longer what it had been in earlier days. As the old school-room in the shadow of the parish church was replaced by a commodious red-brick building on the outskirts of the town, so the curriculum was brought up to date. Where the classical tra-dition had been lost it was not easy to recover, especially as the classics had now to contend not only with the ordinary parent anxious for a useful education for his son, but with a government uneasily conscious of Britain's weakness in scientific and technical education and willing to provide financial aid for this purpose, but with no desire to subsidise or even encourage the classics. The century ends with the Royal Commission on Secondary Education of 1895, which confined itself entirely to questions of adminis-tration and was content to leave matters of curriculum to the local authorities, who were now to be charged with the new and important task of directing a state system of secondary education.

CHAPTER VIII

THE UNIVERSITIES, 1800–1850

The most important feature of nineteenth-century university education was the development of examinations. Cambridge had pointed the way in the eighteenth century with the mainly mathematical Senate House examination or Tripos, but until the nineteenth century neither university had any degree examination in classics. The Oxford examination statute of 1800 and the establishment of the Classical Tripos in 1824 gave a new direction to classical studies. Throughout the century the work of undergraduates and their teachers was to be increasingly dominated by examinations.

The Oxford statute of 1800 established a single examination for the Bachelor's degree. The subjects were Grammar, Rhetoric, Logic, Moral Philosophy and the elements of Mathematics and Physics. Candidates could be examined in either all or some of these subjects; 'but always and for every degree, an examination in Humane Literature is to be set on foot, and especially one in the Greek and Roman writers, three of whom at fewest, of the best age and stamp, are to be used'. The examiners were also to test the candidates' command of Latin by making them translate at sight from English.[1]

These regulations clearly derive from the system embodied in the Laudian statutes, but a new concept has been introduced, that of Literae Humaniores. The examination was to be in the main a classical one, and already we find the characteristic feature of the Oxford system, the examination on a number of books chosen by the candidate. The examination was at first entirely oral, and must have been a casual affair compared with the ordeals of later years.[2] It was soon superseded by the statute of 1807, which established the separate Honours Schools *in Literis Humanioribus* and in Mathematics and Physics.

Literae Humaniores were now defined as the Greek and Latin languages, rhetoric and moral philosophy 'in so far as they are derivable from the ancient authors', and logic.[1] In 1830 a new definition was promulgated. The authorities now decided that humane letters included the histories of Greece and Rome, rhetoric and poetry and moral and political science 'in so far as they may be drawn from writers of antiquity, still allowing them occasionally as may seem expedient to be illustrated by the writings of the moderns'.[2] The statute of 1807 had allowed the examiners to require written as well as oral work, and as time went on the proportion of the former to the latter increased. In 1819 a candidate had two days of written and one of oral examination; in 1842, when Frederick Temple was examined, there were five days of written work, followed by the viva voce examination.[3] Though the statutes made no mention of any composition other than Latin prose, Greek prose was included by the 1840's, and the ability to write good Attic prose was regarded as essential.[4] Verse-composition, though not specifically mentioned in the statutes before 1850, was introduced in 1830, and in the 1840's the written work ended with a 'taste paper', containing, among other matter, passages for Greek and Latin verse. It was, however, said to be possible to obtain a first class without a single verse.[5]

Although there was no official definition of what was meant by a 'book' and no regulation as to what books should be chosen, it was generally known what was expected of the 'class man'. In the early days of Literae Humaniores one who aimed at the highest honours might offer Homer, Pindar, one or more of the Greek dramatists and Thucydides, while of the Latin authors, besides the Augustan poets, Livy, Tacitus, Cicero and Lucretius were the authors most usually 'taken up'. In addition to these 'books', Aristotle's treatises were used for ethics and rhetoric, with Cicero's *De Officiis* and Quintilian as an easier and often chosen alternative, while the *Politics* could be added at the option of the student.[6] In the 1840's the books regarded as necessary for

Honours were divided into three categories. First came 'science'. Here the *Ethics* and *Rhetoric* were essential, with the *Politics* and *Poetics* occasionally thrown in. Plato was sometimes added; though it was possible to obtain a first class without him, it was advisable to offer at least one dialogue, which was usually the *Phaedo*.[1] Under the heading 'History' the books were Herodotus, Thucydides (with Xenophon's *Hellenica* sometimes added), the first decade of Livy, or, rarely, the second, and Tacitus *Annals* I to VI or *Histories*.[2] Finally there was poetry; in this category, of the Greek poets it was enough to offer Aeschylus, Sophocles and Aristophanes or Euripides, with four plays of each (or six of Euripides) as the minimum. Pindar, the Bucolic poets and Homer (not less than twelve books) might be added, but were not necessary. In Latin the usual list comprised Horace, Juvenal and Virgil; Plautus, Terence and Lucretius might be added, but their omission did not prejudice one's chances of a first class. In the second quarter of the century the list of books had become stereotyped; it was observed that authors regularly studied in the first quarter, such as Homer, Demosthenes, Cicero, Lucretius, Terence, Plutarch, Longinus and Quintilian, had almost entirely disappeared from the university course.[3] As an Oxford man put it, 'four years are spent in preparing about fourteen books only for examination. . . . These are made text-books, read, re-read, digested, worked, got up, until they become part and parcel of the mind.'[4] Authors outside the customary list might be neglected, and it was noted with surprise by a Cambridge man that at Oxford it was possible to obtain a first class without having read any Plato or Demosthenes.[5]

In the second quarter of the century critical scholarship of the Porsonian type was little cultivated at Oxford.[6] Nor was the skill in Latin verse-composition which characterised the older generation of scholars much valued. In 1846 William Linwood, himself an accomplished composer, lamented that verse-composition was no longer regarded as it should be in his university.[7] Latin literature was neglected by comparison with Greek. In the 1830's it was being said that but for the Hertford scholarship (founded in 1834) all knowledge of Latin would have been extinct in Oxford, and in the middle of the century it was observed that an intimate acquaintance with the Latin poets such as characterised the Oxford men of the early years of the century was now rare.[1] The substance rather than the form of the ancient authors was what Oxford studied.

Moreover from its inception the school of Literae Humaniores was to some extent a school of philosophy, including as it did logic and moral philosophy. At the beginning of the century the only ancient authority known to Oxford was Aristotle, and in the college lecture rooms, as Sir William Hamilton put it, it was 'Aristotle today, ditto tomorrow'.[2] It was the pride of Oxford that her students did not learn their philosophy from men who might mislead the young with ideas of their own, but rather by 'the regular and docile study of a fixed theory', that is to say, of Aristotle's *Ethics*.[3] But although the text-book remained the same, the treatment changed. The dons who had to teach Aristotle began to study him and Aristotelian scholarship developed. Mark Pattison distinguished four periods of Aristotelian study in the first half of the century. The first was the 'scholars' period', when only the *Ethics*, the *Politics* and the *Rhetoric* were known, and were studied as a part of Greek literature; then came attempts to interpret Aristotle by the light of common sense, when the *Ethics* was discovered to be a practical treatise about the affairs of everyday life. Next there came the 'critical school', which compared the *Ethics* with other works of Aristotle, and finally the 'scientific', when Aristotle's system was studied in relation to the general course of knowledge.[4]

In the 1830's there was a new development in Oxford philosophy, when William Sewell, professor of Moral Philosophy, began to lecture on Plato, particularly on the *Republic*, which he regarded as a kind of prophecy of the Catholic church.[5] His lectures were discursive and unsystematic—it was said that his class did not know whether he was lecturing on St Paul's Epistles or Plato's dialogues[1]—but they were an exciting change from the common run of lectures, and the undergraduates who flocked to the hall of Exeter went back to read their Plato.[2] The seed that Sewell sowed was watered by Jowett, who began lecturing on Plato in 1847 as tutor of Balliol, and according to his biographers was responsible for the introduction of the *Republic* as a book to be taken up in the schools.[3]

The study of ancient history, which was later to become so important a part of Literae Humaniores, had hardly developed beyond the reading of texts in the first half of the century. Thucydides, Herodotus and Livy were read in college lectures, but the lecturers had no contribution of their own to make towards interpretation, and in some cases were not even aware of the work that others had done. A. P. Stanley going to Balliol from Arnold's Rugby in 1834 was surprised to find that his Livy lecturer had apparently not heard of Niebuhr and recommended to his class the work of Nathaniel Hooke, by then nearly a century old.[4] By the 1840's, however, the standard modern authorities were being recommended for reading in connection with the ancient historians, and, as Sellar put it, Herodotus and Thucydides read and re-read by the light of Thirlwall and Arnold, and Livy by the light of Niebuhr, provided a 'good historical propaedeutic'.[5]

Gaisford, who held the professorship of Greek until 1855, followed the eighteenth-century tradition of giving no lectures, and, apart from philosophy lectures such as those of Sewell or his predecessor Hampden, classical teaching was in the hands of the college tutors and lecturers. Each college made itself responsible for teaching all subjects; undergraduates clever and stupid were taught together and the general standard was low. College lectures were mere schoolboy construing lessons. The undergraduate who came from the sixth form of a good school, said Mark Pattison in 1855, 'finds that in exchanging lesson for lecture he has gone back a couple of years in the standard of requirement'.[1] This was no new thing. Thomas Arnold had this experience when he went to Corpus from Winchester in 1811, although he was only sixteen years old, and Hogg, Shelley's friend, says that lectures at University College were decidedly less difficult and less instructive than the lessons received in the higher forms of a Public School.[2] Robert Lowe, who went to Oxford in 1829, recalled the distaste with which he began construing Livy chapter by chapter.[3] Even Balliol had little to teach Rugbeians like Stanley and Clough;[4] and at the lesser colleges things were worse. A Pembroke man of the 1830's spoke of the 'hundred of hours utterly and on my part unavoidably wasted by being compelled to hear portions of books construed with which everyone was familiar at school'.[5]

A new era in college teaching opens with the appointment of Jowett as tutor of Balliol in 1842. Jowett was not a great scholar, or even a very accurate one. He had no interest in minute scholarly investigations; for him the function of the scholar was to bring Greek ideas into contact with the modern world, and the purpose of university education was to produce not scholars or researchers but statesmen and men of the world. This is not to say that he neglected teaching for the Schools; Balliol men must win the honours of the University no less than those of the world outside. An undergraduate in his first year might have to show up compositions to him three times a week, and his lecture class might be called upon to translate *Rasselas* into Latin, or construe Demosthenes, at sight.[6] But his teaching had a lively and stimulating quality which was new. He gave lectures, not immediately related to the university examinations, on the history of philosophy, and above all he had that mysterious thing personality, which made it a liberal education to sit in his rooms while he kept silent for long periods and occasionally uttered some remark of devastating rudeness. But Jowett belongs more to the second than to the first half of the century, and we must now turn to the sister university.

Whereas at Oxford the classics were the main subject of under-graduate study from the beginning of the nineteenth century, at Cambridge there was no Classical Tripos until 1824, and from that date until the 1850's the examination did not of itself qualify for a degree, but was open only to those who had already obtained mathematical honours. Yet though the classics were apparently so little regarded, the standard of classical scholarship and teaching was higher than in contemporary Oxford.

The study of the classics was encouraged at Cambridge before the days of the Tripos partly by the University Scholarships and Chancellor's Medals and partly by the fact that the largest and most influential college in the university made a practice of ap-pointing fellows on the grounds of their classical attainments.[1] Classical scholarship at Cambridge in the early nineteenth century was very much centred in Trinity. Other colleges gave little encouragement to anything but mathematics. St John's, the other large society, although it was the college of Butler and Kennedy, whose scholarship, through their pupils, had so great an influence on Cambridge, for long remained relatively indifferent to the classics.[2]

In 1822, thanks largely to the efforts of Christopher Words-worth, Master of Trinity, the establishment of a Classical Tripos was approved, and two years later the first examination was held. The regulations were simple. There were no prescribed books; translation, it was stated, 'shall be required of passages selected from the *best* Greek and Latin Authors'.[3] In addition there was composition (translated, not original) in Greek and Latin, both prose and verse. Candidates were required to answer questions arising out of the passages set for translation, but these were regarded as of little importance, and the examination in effect consisted entirely of translation into and from Greek and Latin. Unlike the Oxford examination in Literae Humaniores it included no logic or moral philosophy and was entirely written. At first it lasted four days and comprised eight papers, four of composition and four of translation; in 1836 two more translation papers were added. In translation the greatest accuracy was required. Verse-composition was important, though it was possible to get a first class without high marks in verse; but of the four types of composition it was believed that most weight was given to Greek prose.[1]

The Tripos thus differed from the usual type of university examination, based on a recognised course of study and designed to test the candidate's knowledge of certain prescribed texts and subjects. Its peculiar features are due in part to the fact that it was a voluntary additional examination for those who had already obtained mathematical honours. It was thus not very different in purpose from the University Scholarships and Chancellor's Medals, and indeed it was clearly modelled on the existing examination for those awards. The only important difference was that in the Tripos no original composition was required, in order that the examination 'should not be of such a searching character as to militate against the zealous pursuit of mathematics'.[2] More-over the Cambridge tradition of examining was formed under the influence of mathematics. In the Mathematical Tripos it was customary to arrange the candidates in order of merit as well as in classes, and the same practice was transferred to classics. In order to carry this out effectively it was necessary to examine only on what could be accurately measured. It is easier to put candidates in order of merit on translation papers than on essay questions.[3]

In the early part of the nineteenth century college teaching followed the pattern of the eighteenth century. Classical texts were read in college lectures at the beginning of the undergraduate course, but as the Tripos drew near the classics were usually dropped. Annual examinations on the books read had been estab-lished at Trinity and St John's in the eighteenth century, and in the early nineteenth other colleges followed suit.[4] At Trinity the practice was to lecture on three books in the first year, a Greek play, a Greek prose book and a Latin book; a further book might be read in the second year, but there was no classical teaching after that.[1] Examination papers were long and exacting, with many detailed questions on the subject-matter, language and text of the books read.[2]

College teaching continued on these lines after the establishment of the Classical Tripos, though it bore little relation to that examination. The detailed study of a few books was not likely to be particularly useful for an examination which demanded wide reading and gave little scope for the display of that general information known in undergraduate slang of the day as 'the cram'. Nor did colleges make it their business to coach their students in composition. It was probably assumed, and in many cases rightly, that they had been sufficiently well trained at school for further teaching to be unnecessary. Macaulay, who was a good enough composer to be able to turn some lines of Plautus into Greek comic iambics while walking in the Isle of Wight, went through at least two years of Cambridge life without practising composition at all, and B. H. Kennedy wrote no verses while an undergraduate except for prizes and in examinations.[3] Macaulay's undergraduate days belong to the period before the Classical Tripos, Kennedy's to its early days. Later on, though J. E. B. Mayor claimed that undergraduates of his day (the 1840's) were not engrossed by the Tripos, this is not the impression we get from other sources.[4] The highly competitive Cambridge system and the prestige attaching to a high place in the Tripos led to careful training for examination purposes, and since the colleges gave so little help, it was regarded as almost essential to resort to a private tutor.

The latter might be a young fellow of a college putting in time until a suitable job turned up, or a professional coach such as Richard Shilleto, who, having disqualified himself for a fellowship by marriage, set up as a coach in the 1830's and for some thirty years was the great trainer of Cambridge classics, the man to whom everyone went who aspired to high honours. Heitland's description of Shilleto, though it depicts him in his later years, may be quoted here.

For many years he had lived a most exhausting life, coaching single pupils from 9.0 a.m. to 8.0 or 9.0 p.m., with short intervals for meals. His habits had told upon an originally tough constitution and he looked older than his real age. He did not smoke, but took snuff freely.... He generally drew his pinch from a large tinfoil packet that stood in the middle of the table. On each such occasion he needed a handkerchief and that speedily. It was somewhere on the floor among the books with which the whole room was littered. In his search for it he was apt to catch his foot in a book and sneeze prematurely. I have known him get an awkward fall in the attempt. Found and used the handkerchief was dropped on the floor again.... It was understood that during the day he drank a quantity of tea: at night, when I saw him, a pint pot of beer stood handy on a pedestal. When it was low ebb in this vessel, he placed it in a pigeon hole close to the door and rang the bell. Soon a stealthy hand withdrew it and put it back refilled. So much liquid refreshment entailed other embarrassing phenomena. Among these various doings the work went on. Criticism of an exercise consisted chiefly in telling you what you had done wrong and what you had better have written.... He spoke with authority, and the outpouring of references (by chapter, section and line) without opening a book, simply took your breath away.... In his own kind he was unrivalled.... But whether it would have been well to enjoy a great deal of this instruction may be doubted.[1]

At the beginning of the century classical scholarship at Cambridge was dominated by Porson and by his followers, Dobree, Blomfield and Monk. Of these Monk was the most important influence in the university, since he had charge of the classical teaching at Trinity in the years of his tutorship from 1807 to 1822, and was one of those who played an active part in the establishment of the Tripos. Lecturing on a Greek play he would begin with brief introductory remarks on Greek tragedy in general, after which he would put his class on to construe in turn, now and again putting questions on history or geography or asking them to quote parallel passages. His manner was stiff and formal, his language was pompous and he was averse from anything in the nature of a joke.[1]

In 1825 Dobree died, and by that year Cambridge had already lost Blomfield and Monk to the Church. The Porsonian school died out. Scholefield, who succeeded Dobree as Greek professor, was a mediocre scholar, but he was the first holder of the chair for many years to give lectures, and his lectures, though dry and without popular appeal, were found useful by the undergraduates. He lectured on the major Greek authors in turn, and his lectures differed from those given in college teaching in that he did not put the class on to construe, but himself translated, confining himself to the more difficult passages and adding critical and grammatical comment.[2]

While Scholefield lectured slowly and methodically year after year, other more stimulating teachers came and went. The later 1820's and early 1830's were the period of Julius Hare and Connop Thirlwall, who brought to the Trinity lecture room a knowledge of German scholarship and an interest in history, philosophy and philology that were new in Cambridge. Their aim in lecturing on an author was 'the discovery of his thoughts, not the dry elucidation of his words'.[3] There was no change from the old methods; the class still construed, still 'hammered at the words and the sense', but F. D. Maurice, after attending Hare's lectures on the *Antigone*, felt that he had never learned so much about that particular play, about Greek dramatic poetry and about all poetry as in that term.[4] Hare followed the *Antigone* with the *Gorgias*. Here too he stuck close to the text, and included no general remarks on Plato's philosophy, no comparison of him with Aristotle or with the moderns,[5] but he evidently aroused an interest in Plato, and we hear of a 'Platonist club' being founded at Cambridge at this period.[6]

Cambridge had none of Oxford's devotion to Aristotle. When Thomas Arnold was hesitating whether to send one of his sons to Cambridge, 'Aristotle turned the scale' in favour of Oxford.[7]

Aristotle was not, however, unknown in Cambridge. Thirlwall lectured on the *Ethics* and the *Politics* at Trinity, and his lecture room was crowded with the rising young classics of the time.[1] Hare and Thirlwall aroused a new interest in ancient philosophy at Cambridge, and their successors on the whole followed their methods. Whereas Oxford aimed at teaching philosophy by means of the ancient authorities, Cambridge approached Plato and Aristotle through classical scholarship, eschewing tendentious interpretations and letting each author explain himself.

Though the nature of the Tripos might seem to make any form of cramming impossible, it is not surprising to learn that undergraduates and their tutors had discovered certain short cuts to success in the examination hall. Apart from the intensive practice in composition that was desirable for those at any rate who had not been well trained at school,[2] it was not uncommon to make a special study of hard passages likely to be set for unseen translation.[3] But on the whole the system encouraged wide reading, and the aim of the best students was to have as few gaps as possible in their reading list. A typical first-class Cambridge classic of this period would be intimately acquainted with the recognised classical authors, though less well-read outside this field. He would probably have little claim to be a philosopher and his interest in and knowledge of history might be slight, for though tutors recommended Niebuhr, it was well known that Niebuhr was of no use for the Tripos.[4] He would be a skilled composer with a good sense of language and a love of literature. His training had given him a taste for hard work, and when his examinations were over he would be ready to master new fields of knowledge.[5]

As we have seen in this chapter, there was a marked difference between the classical schools of the two universities, a difference which, though greatly lessened by the changes of the second half of the century, is still perceptible. In 1843, when the Tripos and Literae Humaniores still stood in marked contrast to one another, the characteristics of the two universities were summed up by a

Rugby schoolboy who was destined to have a distinguished career at Oxford.

Cambridge [he wrote, with that precocious maturity which characterised Arnold's pupils], from its verbal criticism and philological research, as well as its mathematical studies, imparts a system of education valuable not so much for itself, as for the excellent discipline which prepares the mind to pass from the investigation of abstract intellectual truth to the contemplation of moral subjects. Oxford, on the contrary, seeks without any such medium to arrive at the higher ground at once, without passing through the lower, leading the mind before it has been sufficiently disciplined, to investigate the highest and most sacred subjects at once. Cambridge men too often view the intellectual exercise as sufficient in itself, instead of as a preparation for higher things. Oxford men, without any such preparation, which they affect to despise, proceed to speculate on great moral questions before they have practised themselves with lower and less dangerous studies.... Cambridge appears to have seen that the province of a university is not to give a complete education, but to furnish the mind with rules drawn from lower subjects to be applied in after life to higher; Oxford wishes to give a complete education and by attempting too much, does the whole very imperfectly.[1]

CHAPTER IX

THE UNIVERSITIES, 1850-1900

The previous chapter has shown that the universities had, on the whole, little reason to be proud of their classical teaching in the first half of the nineteenth century. When we consider that school-teaching was almost entirely classical and that at Oxford at any rate the classics formed the main business of the university, we cannot avoid the conclusion that the general level at the universities was considerably lower than it might have been. The main reason for this no doubt lay in the numerous restrictions which surrounded college fellowships. The exclusion of Nonconformists was of less importance than might have been expected from our point of view, since good classical teaching was at that time rarely to be found outside Anglican schools. More important was the restriction of the great majority of fellowships to celibate clergy; not many scholars, it is true, disqualified themselves for fellow-ships by declining to take Orders or by early marriage, but many held their fellowships for only a brief period and then sought careers in the Church or schoolmastering, where they would be free to marry, and would also earn more than the modest stipends offered by their colleges. The universities were unable to retain the services of their best men; those who were left to make a career there would include a large proportion of the unambitious, the lazy and the disappointed.

Moreover the clergy, if they took their sacred calling seriously, might find that their main interests lay outside the classics it was their business to teach. This must have been the case with many at Oxford in the 1830's and 1840's, the period of the Tractarian movement, when religion and theology were the absorbing interest. When Tractarianism as an Oxford movement came to an end with Newman's conversion to Rome in 1845, 'our thoughts', in Mark Pattison's words, 'reverted to their proper channel, that of the work we had to do'.[1] Cambridge remained by comparison unaffected by religious uncertainties. Cambridge scholars took orders as a matter of course, and stuck to their classics. Paley, it is true, moved via ecclesiology into the Roman church, but he remained none the less the Salopian scholar; the author of the *Manual of Gothic Mouldings* was also the editor of Aeschylus, and, though outside the academic establishment, spent a good part of his later life in his old university.

But more harmful to learning than the requirement of celibacy and Holy Orders were the local restrictions on fellowships. At Oxford the vast majority and at Cambridge a considerably smaller proportion of the college fellowships were closed, confined, that is, to natives of certain parts of the country or those educated at certain schools. In most of the colleges, at Oxford at any rate, the dons might be men of very mediocre ability, and as professorial teaching had fallen into decay and almost all effective instruction was in the hands of college tutors, the university as a whole suffered. Frederick Temple in his evidence before the Royal Commission of 1850 put the matter simply and bluntly. 'The interests of learning are intrusted to those who have neither talents nor inclination for the subject.... The undergraduates suffer a double loss; in first being deprived of the legitimate stimulus to study, and, secondly, in having their instruction intrusted to an inferior body of men.'[2] The fact that those colleges where all or most of the fellowships were open, Trinity at Cambridge and Oriel and Balliol at Oxford, easily outstripped the others, clearly indicates the harmful nature of these local restrictions.

Thus though the ancient universities still had almost a monopoly of the learning of the country and still trained most of its best scholars, they were, thanks to their obsolete organisation, unable to make proper use of the talent at their disposal, and the reforms in university organisation which followed the Royal Commissions of 1850 had an important effect in bringing about an improvement in scholarship and teaching.

The second half of the century opens at Oxford with the examination statute of 1850, which divided the work of the old classical honours school between two examinations, Moderations and Literae Humaniores. Philosophy and history now formed the substance of the final examination, while Honour Moderations consisted of composition in prose and verse, papers on a number of books, a philological and critical paper and one on logic, an incongruous survival from the old single examination. 'We wish', said the statute, 'the preference to be given to the poets and orators.'[1] The authors to be offered were to include Homer (twelve books), Virgil, Demosthenes (*De Corona* with Aeschines *In Ctesiphontem*, or other speeches of comparable length) and Cicero (*Verrines* or eight speeches of comparable length).[2] A fairly long list was given of other books from which choice might be made, but by the 1860's custom had narrowed the field. It was usual to offer either Aeschylus or Sophocles (five plays) and Horace, and to fill up the list with historians—five books of Herodotus or Thucydides and Livy (six books) or Tacitus (*Annals* I to VI or *Histories*)—as these would be useful for Greats.[3]

In the final examination 'scholarship' was represented by composition, in prose only, and translation from books, but the main part of the examination was in philosophy and ancient history. The candidate for honours was expected to take up eight 'books', and though in theory he had some choice, in practice there was little or no variation. In philosophy the *Ethics* remained the primary authority, and of all books was the one most thoroughly studied. Of other works of Aristotle the *Politics* was the one most commonly chosen; the *Rhetoric*, which had been often taken up in the days of the single honours examination, soon dropped out of the new Greats. Plato was now represented by the *Republic*; though other dialogues might be offered, in the 1860's there was 'practically no choice'.[4] In history things remained much as they had been;

Herodotus, Thucydides, Livy and Tacitus were the essential books.[1] But the new examination *in Literis Humanioribus* differed from the old in that it was more a matter of subjects and less of books. There were papers on Logic, Moral Philosophy, Political Philosophy, the History of Philosophy, Greek History and Antiquities and Roman History and Antiquities.[2]

The purpose of the new arrangements was partly by the institution of Honour Moderations to promote accurate scholarship and partly by dividing the work of the old final examination to ensure greater proficiency and ease the burden on the student.[3] The last object, according to Mark Pattison, was hardly achieved. 'We congratulated ourselves on having notably alleviated the burden of preparation. Little did we foresee that we were only giving another turn to the examination screw, which has been turned several times since, till it became an instrument of torture which has made education impossible and crushed the very desire of learning.'[4] As for the first object, it may be doubted if Moderations quite fulfilled the expectations of those who hoped to see pure scholarship flourishing at Oxford. It is true that the study of the poets, or at least of those regularly 'taken up', revived. Virgilian studies flourished under the leadership of Conington and Nettleship, and Homer, who had been neglected by pre-1850 Oxford, returned to favour, and found an able exponent in D. B. Monro. But a greater prestige attached to the final school than to Moderations, and most of the talent of Oxford went into Greats teaching. Classics being the main business of the university, the colleges could afford some degree of specialisation in teaching. It was usual for one tutor to take philosophy, another history and a third 'Mods work'; the last was not usually the most gifted of the three.[5]

For some years after the middle of the century the general level of college teaching remained low. Construing was still the rule. 'Pass and Class men', to use the language of the day, were taken together, and the blundering and perfunctory performances of the former were painful to the better scholars.[1] As a writer of the 1860's put it, 'college lectures are, as a rule, perfunctory, repressive, irritating', and 'almost universally quoted by undergraduates with contempt and dislike'.[2] Though Oxford had no coach of the fame of Shilleto, private tutors flourished, and it was almost universal to resort to one in the last three terms of the undergraduate course.[3] Gradually, however, the coaching system declined as college tutors gave their pupils more individual attention. One of the first to do this was E. C. Wickham, tutor of New College from 1859 to 1873, who was remembered for his careful criticism and correction of compositions.[4] The later part of the century also saw the development of inter-college lecturing. This spread slowly. The old idea of the college as the self-sufficient unit was not easily broken down, and in the 1870's the scheme was still in an embryonic stage and most undergraduates depended entirely on the teaching of their own college.[5]

When Gaisford died in 1855 he was succeeded as professor of Greek by Jowett, who occupied the post till his death in 1893. Liddell had refused the chair on the ground that a head of a house should not be a professor. But Jowett's appointment did not mean that the Greek professorship would now claim the whole time and energies of its occupant. He combined it with his Balliol tutorship and later with the Mastership. His teaching as professor was on the same lines as his tutorial teaching and his attitude to scholarship remained unchanged. He read and re-read the classics of Greek literature, ignored 'pamphlets, periodicals and programmes',[6] translated Plato and encouraged men to read Thucydides sitting in an arm chair. He remained a stimulating influence, but those who valued the refinements of scholarship had to go elsewhere than to the Greek professor.[7]

In 1854 John Conington was appointed to the newly founded professorship of Latin. Gifted with a marvellous memory and a fine literary sense, he had made his name as a Greek scholar in the old tradition of verbal scholarship. But his undertaking of the editorship of Virgil, followed by his appointment to the Oxford chair, turned his interests towards Latin. As professor he took classes in verse-composition, the most interesting feature of which was his analysis of the piece set for translation and his comparison of modern with ancient poetic style; gave courses on Persius, Plautus, Virgil and other authors, and occasionally delivered as public lectures literary essays on Latin authors or translations of Virgil.[1] To those who thought that a professor should be in touch with the latest research Conington, who was not widely read and knew little German, was a disappointment. Liberals like Jowett disapproved of him as one who had deserted the cause.[2] Mark Pattison, who was both a liberal and a believer in research, devoted to him some of the severest pages of his autobiography.[3] Conington, with his purely literary outlook and his lack of interest in philosophy and history, would perhaps have been more at home at Shrewsbury and Cambridge than Rugby and Oxford. One can imagine him as fellow of Trinity unconcerned with religious and social problems, continuing the tradition of Porsonian scholarship. As it was, he was somewhat out of place in Oxford; but even Pattison allowed that his was 'a remarkable mind', and to many undergraduates Conington's conversation on Oxford walks or vacation reading parties was as much part of their education as the formidable silences of Jowett's breakfast parties.[4]

In 1869, when Conington died, John Wordsworth, who had done pioneering work at Oxford in lecturing on early Latin literature and was shortly to publish his *Fragments and Specimens of Early Latin*, stood for the chair. He was a believer in research and a critic of verse-composition, the typical activity of traditional classical scholarship, and his candidature was regarded as a challenge to the older type of learning.[5] The challenge failed; the chair went to Edwin Palmer, an accomplished versifier and scholar of the old school, who left little mark on Oxford classical studies before he exchanged the professorship for the archdeaconry of Oxford.

Mark Pattison, though his researches lay outside the classics, had an important influence on classical scholarship at Oxford through his followers, that 'small band of academic reformers who thought that a university should be organised with a view to learning and research as well as with a view to education'.[1] Chief among these were Bywater and Henry Nettleship.

Bywater was a thorough representative of the new school. He did not write verses, and seldom spoke of such exercises without a shudder.[2] His aim was to make himself a thorough master of the limited field he had chosen for himself; in editing a text he hoped to make further labour in the same field unnecessary.[3] His lectures as tutor of Exeter and later as Reader (1883) and professor (1893) of Greek were impressive. His hearers felt that they were in the presence of a master. It was a new thing to listen to a scholar who could meet the Germans on their own ground. '"Vahlen *thinks* that I agree with him, but I DON'T" was the antithesis of Jowett's "Do not dispute about texts: buy a good text".'[4]

Nettleship, though he concerned himself more with literary history and lexicography than with textual criticism, filled much the same place in Latin studies as Bywater in Greek. As fellow of Lincoln he had come under the influence of Mark Pattison, and encouraged by him studied for a while at Berlin. He came back an admirer of German methods, critical of the traditional English education and anxious to promote a more thorough and scientific study of the classics. As he himself wrote, the lectures of Haupt in Berlin introduced him to a method of teaching unknown in Oxford at the time. 'We learned in Oxford to read the classics, to translate them on paper, to think and talk about them, to write essays on them; but of the higher philology, of the principles and methods of textual criticism, in other words, of the way to find out what the classical writers really said, we were taught next to nothing.'[5] After a brief period of schoolteaching Nettleship returned to Oxford in 1873 as fellow of Corpus, and five years later succeeded Palmer in the chair of Latin, which he held to his death in 1893. As a college tutor he was remembered for his sympathetic tuition of individuals and his ability to interest his pupils, as well as for his lectures on Virgil, in which he combined minute criticism of the text with a more general exposition of the character of the poet's work.[1] As professor he found to his disappointment that he no longer commanded the large audiences which listened to a college tutor lecturing with a view to the schools.[2] Research students were as yet unknown, and the average undergraduate could hardly be expected to take much interest in such figures as Verrius Flaccus and Nonius Marcellus.

Though Jowett might say 'Aristotle is dead, but Plato is alive',[3] Aristotle remained very much alive at Oxford, and many of the ablest men in the university devoted themselves to his interpretation. The brief Oxford career of Richard Congreve, editor of the *Politics*, belongs to the middle of the century. Vigorous and ambitious, a man of the world, travelled and well read, rather than a scholar in the technical sense, he taught by Socratic questioning and aimed at making his pupils good citizens. His teaching at Wadham was highly successful, but in 1854 he left Oxford to study medicine and propagate the gospel of Comte, and was lost to the world of scholarship and teaching.[4] Congreve's *Politics* was closely followed by the editions of the *Ethics* by W. E. Jelf and Alexander Grant. Oxford men now had adequate commentaries on their staple text-book, but much of the Aristotelian lore of the university remained in lecture note-books, and in 1876 it could still be said that no considerable work had appeared in Oxford on the philosophy of Aristotle as a whole.[5] In the last two decades of the century Aristotelian study flourished as much as at any time. In the 1880's an Oxford Aristotelian Society was founded, and in it the pure scholarship of Bywater joined with the more philosophic approach of the Greats men. Ernest Barker, looking back on Oxford of the 1890's, remarks on the fascination Aristotle then had for many of the best minds in the university, and recalls that J. A. Smith used to read *De Anima* in bed and leave it under his pillow, a practice that was paralleled at Cambridge some years later, where R. D. Hicks, who was blind, would read Aristotle in bed with the braille under the bedclothes.[1]

Perhaps the most striking development in Oxford classics in the later nineteenth century was in the field of ancient history. Though the separation of Moderations and Greats gave an increasing importance to this branch of study, it was some time before teaching of the subject reached a level equal to that reached in philosophy.[2] According to Warde Fowler, who was an undergraduate from 1866 to 1870, at that period 'lecturer and student alike were ignorant of history'.[3] There was, however, at least one good ancient historian, W. L. Newman of Balliol, who was appointed college lecturer in 1858 and left behind him the memory of a brilliant teacher when he retired in 1870 from ill-health—to live another fifty-three years. He was described by T. H. Green as the best lecturer he had ever heard, and his treatment of ancient history showed a new independence and imagination. Characteristic of his teaching was his use of illustrations from modern history and law and the close connection he maintained between history and philosophy.[4] Among his pupils was Evelyn Abbott, author of a lengthy history of Greece, who taught ancient history at Balliol in the later part of the century. But whether because, so long as Greek history was centred in Athens, there seemed little to be added to Grote, or because of the stimulating quality of Mommsen's work, it was in Roman history that the most distinguished work of the Oxford school was done. At Balliol there was Strachan-Davidson. 'An enthusiast for constitutional theory', wrote a pupil of his, 'with a keen sense of politics and political capacity, he conveyed to us with individuality and a fine interpretation of his own the traditions of the Oxford school of ancient history, which he had received from W. L. Newman.'[5] But the leading figure in the field of ancient history in the later nineteenth century was H. F. Pelham. As fellow of Exeter he was a colleague of Bywater, and he shared his older contemporary's belief in the importance of research. As tutor of Exeter he attracted listeners from other colleges besides his own, and, by 1882, was filling the college hall week by week. His popularity as a lecturer increased with his appointment to the Camden professorship in 1889. As professor he confined himself to Roman history, giving courses on the constitutional history of the Republic and Empire designed for undergraduates taking their Schools, while he reserved one term for lectures on a variety of topics less closely related to examinations. Lucid and authoritative, slow and somewhat formal in his style of lecturing, he was considered one of the best teachers of his day.[1]

One further development marks the last two decades of the century, the growth of an interest in classical archaeology. In 1855 an attempt had been made to give this type of learning a footing in the university by bringing back C. T. Newton from the British Museum to fill the professorship of Greek.[2] But Newton had refused the offer. In the mid-nineteenth century literature, history and philosophy absorbed the interests of the Oxford classics and archaeology was ignored and neglected. In 1879 Walter Pater gave a course of lectures on archaic Greek art distinguished more for literary charm than scientific expertness.[3] Then in 1885 the Lincoln professorship of Classical Archaeology was founded, and two years later Percy Gardner began his long tenure of the chair. In the same year, when Farnell, fresh from his studies in Germany, was lecturing and Jane Harrison, over from Cambridge, supplemented his archaeological learning with her feminine enthusiasm, it could be said that there was a remarkable interest in archaeology in the university.[4] But this new branch of learning had to contend with the hostility of Jowett and others, and Gardner and his allies strove for many years in vain to obtain some place for it in Literae Humaniores, though in 1890 the history of Greek sculpture was made one of the optional subjects in Moderations.[5]

At Cambridge the second half of the century opened with two changes in the examination system. The mathematical requirements were relaxed, and a paper in ancient history was added to the Classical Tripos.[1] Though Whewell still advocated compulsory mathematics on the ground that the university should add something to school teaching, he was fighting a losing battle; in 1857 the mathematical requirement was completely abolished and the Classical Tripos by itself qualified for a degree. By 1863 the average number of those who took this Tripos was more than twice that in the years 1824 to 1850, and it could be said that 'classical studies are now equally esteemed and not much less practised than mathematical'.[2] The introduction of Ancient History did little to encourage the study of the subject, and the paper was at first ill done. In the years 1853 to 1855 the average percentage mark in this paper obtained by first-class men was 35; that obtained by second-class men was 21, by third-class men 10.[3]

The general character of the Tripos was unchanged, and the reformers were not satisfied. The report of the Royal Commission of 1850 shows that many of the Cambridge classics considered that the Tripos left something to be desired. The commissioners themselves suggested one criticism when they asked whether it was desirable to specify books, so as to exclude 'those undesirable on moral or other grounds'. Opinion on this point was divided and no action was taken. Nor did the suggestion that verse-composition be omitted lead to anything.[4] A more important criticism was that more attention should be directed towards the subject-matter of the authors read. It was alleged that the Tripos demanded merely linguistic skill and that it was possible to obtain high honours without acquiring any real knowledge of antiquity.[5] In particular there was a good deal of support for the proposal to add a paper on Ancient Philosophy, a project which had been put forward in 1849, but defeated.[6] As one of the supporters of the proposal put it, 'attention could be directed to such studies as tend to cultivate the robuster mental faculties and supply an antidote to the enervating effects of Latin elegiac verses'.[7]

It was in this direction that the next reform of the Tripos took place. In 1872 (the scheme had been approved two years earlier) three papers were added, two consisting of translation from and questions on set books, mainly philosophical, and one on classical philology.[1] This alteration, we are told, proceeded from the feeling that the Classical Tripos prolonged unduly a piecemeal method of study more suited to schoolboys, and that in the past there had been too much attention to form and not enough to matter. But students were warned against spending too much time on the prescribed authors; the bulk of the examination, they were reminded, still consisted of unseen translation.[2]

The final development took place in 1882, when the Tripos was divided into two parts. Part One now consisted of composition and translation, with a paper on history, literature and antiquities and one on grammar and criticism, while in Part Two the candidate chose one of a number of subjects for special study, Ancient Philosophy, Ancient History, Archaeology or Language, Literature and Criticism being added to the list in 1895.[3] The new regulations brought the Tripos nearer to the Oxford Classical Schools, but the similarity was less close than it might seem to be, for, whereas Greats was an integral part, and the more important part, of the Oxford course, at Cambridge it was not at first necessary to take Part Two in order to obtain a degree; it was a voluntary examination taken by only a small proportion of those who took Part One.

As the Classical Tripos gradually freed itself from its position of inferiority to the mathematical, so more attention was given to the provision of classical teaching. By the middle of the century it had become the common practice to provide classical lectures throughout the three undergraduate years, those in the second and third years being designed to prepare for the Previous Examination and for the Ordinary B.A. respectively. Many of the books lectures were depressing experiences for the good scholar. College lectures, according to a writer of 1850, were 'rarely above, and generally far below, the level of the lessons of the head class in a well-conducted Public School...owing to the mixed classes of ignoramuses and proficients lectured together under the College system'.[1] D'Arcy Thompson, who migrated to Pembroke from Trinity about the middle of the century, wrote of his experiences in his new college: 'I felt as though the dial of my days had run back ten years when...I heard a bearded man called upon to parse "*tuleram*", and heard the wretch go without a smile through the mystic, but nearly forgotten formula of—"*Fero, tuli, latum, ferre*".'[2] At this period a few colleges provided special lectures and composition classes for Honours men, but there was as yet no individual tuition, and the division of Honours from Pass men did not take place until after the first year. The Master of Trinity justified this on the grounds that 'the less advanced learn, not only by what the lecturer delivers but by the performances of their abler fellow students', but the latter were not so appreciative of the benefits of the system.[3] G. O. Trevelyan records how at his first lecture one of his fellow freshmen construed from the prologue of the *Helen* 'μορφώματα having taken, ὄρνιθος the form, λαβὼν of a swan'. 'That', adds Trevelyan, 'was my earliest experience of Greek in the college of Porson.'[4] In the 1860's things began to change; the old composition class, in which the lecturer confined himself to pointing out grammatical blunders and giving a fair copy, began to be replaced by individual tuition.[5] As usual Trinity led the way. Henry Jackson, appointed lecturer and assistant tutor in 1866, extended to all classical students the individual tuition in translation and composition previously given only to those about to take the Tripos. 'We superseded classical coaching', said Jackson.[6] At the same time the system of inter-collegiate lectures began; the scheme, which was initiated in Trinity, was in operation in the late 1860's.[7]

In 1853 Scholefield died, and was succeeded as professor of Greek by W. H. Thompson. Thompson was a fine lecturer, who always commanded a large audience. He was particularly remembered for his translations of the books read. He 'stood at his desk and read his author into English with neither manuscript nor even notes before him...in a style which reflected the original with exact fidelity....The happiest renderings were passed from mouth to mouth and so made the round of the university.'[1] When Thompson succeeded to the mastership of his college in 1867, the Greek professorship went not to any of the resident classics of Cambridge, but to the elderly schoolmaster B. H. Kennedy. The professorship was now attached to a canonry at Ely, and the electors no doubt had to consider the interests of the cathedral chapter as well as of the university; Shilleto, who was generally considered to be Cambridge's best Greek scholar, was, although in Orders, hardly fitted to be a canon.[2] By 1889, when the next election was made, this awkward arrangement was abandoned. It was possible once more for a layman to hold the professorship, and there was a Cambridge scholar of outstanding gifts in the person of R. C. Jebb ready to fill the chair. As professor he gave carefully prepared lectures on the history of Greek literature; the matter was excellent, but the manner was found by his hearers to be 'deficient in life and vigour'.[3]

Cambridge had to wait until 1869 for a professorship of Latin. There was, it may be supposed, no doubt about who should be its first holder. H. A. J. Munro was duly appointed, but he resigned after three years in favour of J. E. B. Mayor, who held the professorship for thirty-eight years from 1872. Mayor's lectures were on Juvenal, Martial, Seneca, the younger Pliny, Tertullian, Minucius Felix, and occasionally Plautus, Terence, Quintilian, Ausonius and Lactantius.[4] With his encyclopaedic knowledge and simple-minded enthusiasm for learning combined with a complete absence of any sense of proportion or of what his listeners wanted, he was not a successful lecturer. His method was to dictate long lists of references, unaccompanied by translation or commentary, in the hope that his listeners would look them up after the lecture. His class would dwindle to one hearer

who remained faithful out of kindness, and who might be re-
warded after the lecture with a copy of the *Vegetarian Magazine*
or the reading of Mayor's correspondence with one of the Old
Catholic bishops.[1]

The outstanding figure among the Cambridge classical dons in
the later nineteenth century was Henry Jackson. His lectures were
an exhilarating experience and he was as stimulating outside the
lecture room as within; to some he seemed a reincarnation of
Socrates, to others a second Dr Johnson.[2] The alterations in the
Tripos in 1872 created a demand for specialised teaching in Ancient
Philosophy, and Jackson more than anyone else met this demand.
From 1872 onward he lectured regularly on philosophical texts
and on the history of Greek philosophy. His 'primary aim was to
develop the meaning of the author as he meant it, not as it could
be interpreted or applied under modern conditions'.[3] The high
Cambridge standards of verbal scholarship were maintained, and
Jackson and his pupils would amuse themselves by noting where
Jowett fell short of these standards.[4]

Ancient History had, as we have seen, been introduced to the
Tripos in the middle of the century, but it was not until the division
of the examination into two parts that any real encouragement
was given to this branch of study. The chair of Ancient History
was not founded until 1899, and in the later part of the century
specialised historical study did not develop to the extent that it
did in contemporary Oxford. Cambridge had no ancient historians comparable to Pelham, Strachan-Davidson and Greenidge.
Philology was represented by John Peile, of Christ's, who was
teaching Sanskrit and lecturing on Greek and Latin etymology in
the 1860's and was the first holder of the readership in comparative
philology established in 1884. Sidney Colvin introduced Cambridge to classical archaeology when as Slade professor in the 1870's
he lectured, among other subjects, on the Olympia sculptures.
He was conscious of the weakness of Cambridge classical education
on the aesthetic side and wished to see the art of Greece studied

no less than her literature.[1] It was not long before Archaeology had a place in the Tripos, and in Charles Waldstein, who was brought in to teach the subject in 1880, Cambridge had a teacher able to do justice to the aesthetic as well as the historical side of it.

While these newer disciplines found their way into the university, the study of the Greek drama, the traditional activity of Cambridge scholarship, continued to thrive. Jebb, whose editions of Sophocles began to appear in the 1860's, added a new interest in literary interpretation to the old verbal scholarship of the Cambridge school. His English translations, so little to the taste of the present day, were a welcome change from the literal crib-like versions which had been bred by the Cambridge insistence on accuracy.[2] In the 1870's Verrall began to lecture and his novel interpretations made men look anew at the familiar plays. He had a gift for lecturing, and the exciting matter was matched by the dramatic delivery.[3] The lively interest in Greek drama prevalent in Cambridge in the later nineteenth century is shown by the performance of the *Ajax* in 1882, the first of a series of productions which has continued to the present day.

The classical world of Cambridge in the later nineteenth century lacks the striking contrasts of personalities and ideals that we find in contemporary Oxford, and presents no parallel to the opposition of Pattison, the champion of research, and Jowett, the believer in training for public life. In Cambridge the classical dons, who formed a smaller proportion of the total establishment than at Oxford, were more uniform in character. In them the newer scientific approach joined happily with the older elegant scholarship, nor was there the same specialisation as at Oxford. Munro, Cambridge's leading Latinist, and Jebb, her leading Greek scholar, were both composers of verses as well as editors of learned editions; Archer-Hind published both editions of Plato's works and a book of translations into Greek; J. S. Reid was both the leading Ciceronian scholar of his day and Cambridge's first professor of Ancient History.

By the end of the nineteenth century Mathematics had lost its old primacy at Cambridge, but the new study of the Natural Sciences had taken its place. In 1900 Natural Sciences was the most popular of the triposes, being closely followed by Classics; the others, apart from Mathematics, were still small and unimportant. At Oxford the situation was different. The Final Honour School of Literae Humaniores was the largest in the University, while Mathematics and Physics and Natural Science were relatively small schools. The classics dominated the university as they did not, and had never done, at Cambridge.[1] Moreover, so long as school education remained predominantly classical, new honours schools could be established at the universities without seriously disturbing that unity of outlook which was given to the men of learning by their common classical background. The time was still to come when the classics would have shrunk to being one of a number of specialisms, and when a classical quotation at the High Table would be met by a blank stare.

CHAPTER X

NEW UNIVERSITIES

This chapter will inevitably be a short one. Throughout the nineteenth century the ancient universities so dominated the scene so far as classical studies are concerned that there is little to say about the new foundations.

Among these Durham, founded in 1832, stands by itself. A small residential university, closely connected with the cathedral chapter and designed mainly for the training of clergy, it followed closely the model of the older universities, particularly Oxford. Its classical honours course, like that of Oxford, included logic and Aristotle's *Ethics* and a number of prescribed books, and in the latter part of the century there was an arrangement somewhat similar to that at Oxford, by which poets predominated in the first examination (taken at Durham at the end of the first year) and historians and philosophers in the Finals.[1]

Durham's first professor of Greek, Henry Jenkins, soon transferred to the chair of Divinity, while T. W. Peile, the editor of Aeschylus, who was a classical tutor in the early years of the university, left in 1841 to become headmaster of Repton. Little is recorded of John Edwards, professor from 1840 to 1862, but his successor, T. S. Evans, is remembered as one of the most accomplished writers of Greek and Latin verse of the nineteenth century. 'It was', we are told, 'a matter of conscience with him to impart his very best to his pupils; to some this painstaking seemed superfluous, whereas in fact it gave his lectures that perennial freshness and finish which distinguished them.'[2] Evans was succeeded by Herbert Kynaston, the editor of Theocritus, who is described as 'an able teacher of those who were willing to learn'.[3] But able though some of its professors were, Durham University remained small and undistinguished throughout the nineteenth century.

A greater interest attaches to the two London institutions, University College and King's College, which were less directly influenced by the older universities.

In the early days of University College a course was designed, derived from those of the contemporary Scottish universities, in which Latin and Greek were confined to the first year and were to be followed by various branches of philosophy and science.[1] But in practice few students followed this course, for, since it led to no degree, there was no incentive to do so. Each enrolled for whatever courses he wished, and the different departments of knowledge were pursued independently. In 1836 the University of London was founded as a degree-giving institution. At first a condition of obtaining a degree was the pursuit of a course of instruction in one of the London colleges, or some other approved institution, but in 1858 this restriction was removed, and the degree became open to any who could pass the examination. The London degree in its early days, before the separation of science from arts, was a general one, requiring a competent knowledge of four branches of learning: Mathematics and Natural Philosophy; Chemistry, Animal Physiology, Vegetable Physiology and Structural Botany; Classics; and Logic and Moral Philosophy. Provision was also made for Honours examinations, in Classics among other subjects; these, however, did not constitute an alternative means to a degree, but followed the pass examination. For Honours in Classics the candidate was examined on a large number of books, in addition to which there was composition in Greek and Latin prose and an English essay. Later in the century the number of prescribed books was reduced and a paper of unseen Latin translation added.[2] A peculiar feature of the examination was the inclusion of passages for retranslation into Latin and Greek.

The London degree, useful as it was in setting standards for those working on their own or in newly founded colleges, too often meant merely getting up set books to satisfy a remote and impersonal examining board, and apart from Sir William Smith, the editor of classical and other dictionaries, London graduates of the nineteenth century contributed little to classical study apart from those annotated editions and text books which are inevitably bred by examination syllabuses.

Of the London colleges, King's remained, until the reorganisation of London university in 1899, little influenced by the university. It had its own courses, and few of its students took the London degree.[1] In classics its best students would proceed to Oxford or Cambridge; it provided a useful intermediate stage for those who had not been at a first-class school, like F. W. Farrar, who left King William's School, Isle of Man, at the age of sixteen, and put in a few years in the Strand before proceeding to Cambridge. At University College the London degree was more in favour, and for most of the students the road to Oxford and Cambridge was at first barred by the religious tests in force there. But when these were removed, the older universities exercised their attractive force here too, and in the 1880's it was usual for the best classics from Gower Street to go on to Oxford or Cambridge with scholarships after two or three years.[2]

Though the London degree schemes owed little to Oxford and Cambridge, the classical staffs of the two London colleges, and of the later foundations in the provinces, were drawn almost exclusively from the old universities. The early classical professors at University College, George Long, T. H. Key and Henry Malden, were all of Trinity College, Cambridge. Of these Long, who held the Greek professorship from 1827 to 1832 and that of Latin from 1842 to 1846, was the most prolific writer, Key, professor of Latin from 1828 to 1842, was perhaps the most original scholar,[3] but the most influential, if only from his long tenure of the chair, was Henry Malden, professor of Greek from 1832 to 1876. Malden, Macaulay's schoolfellow, brought to Gower Street the accurate and refined scholarship of the Cambridge school. Conscientious, precise and painstaking he 'preferred to examine exhaustively a corner of a great subject, to attempting anything like that rapid and general survey of it which would have given his students a larger familiarity with the language'.[1] Very different from Malden was F. W. Newman, professor of Latin from 1846 to 1863. A man of eccentric habits and strange enthusiasms, far removed in his views from his brother the cardinal, he was one of the minor 'characters' of the nineteenth century. As a professor he was something of a disappointment; at first his lectures were brilliant, but soon he neglected them for other interests.[2] Another eccentric who held the Latin chair later in the century was Robinson Ellis. 'In the class room', an old pupil records, 'he was the strangest mixture of hyper-efficiency and lamentable incompetence.... He was always fully prepared, and easily master of his subject. But he was deplorably, pathetically, unfit to manage and control the high-spirited, mischievous boys who formed the bulk of his junior class.'[3] After six years of Gower Street he returned in 1876 to the more congenial atmosphere of his old university.

In the 1880's the classics at Gower Street were in low water, and for a time the professorships of Latin and Greek were held concurrently by one man. In 1892, however, they were once more separated, and the appointment of A. E. Housman to the Latin chair and W. Wyse to that of Greek, in which he was shortly to be succeeded by J. A. Platt, ensured that the classics were taught by men of fine scholarship, even if, to use Housman's words, they seldom had pupils who possessed a native aptitude for classical studies or intended to pursue them far.[4]

At King's College, the first professor of classics was Joseph Anstice, a young man of brilliant promise who died at the age of twenty-eight after holding the chair for only four years. His successor, R. W. Browne, author of histories of Greece and Rome and of Greek and Latin literature, is described as an elegant and tasteful scholar, particularly strong in Greek iambics.[5] He was succeeded in turn by J. G. Lonsdale, J. B. Mayor, brother of

J. E. B. Mayor and editor of Cicero's *De Natura Deorum*, and G. C. W. Warr. But in the second half of the century the 'Department of General Literature and Science', in which the classics was included, declined; there was no longer the same demand as there had been in the 1830's for the type of education it provided, and revival had to await the incorporation of the college in the new London University.

By the end of the century, the Victoria University, comprising colleges at Manchester, Liverpool and Leeds, and the University of Wales, with the three constituent colleges of Aberystwyth, Bangor and Cardiff, were in existence, and there were colleges at Birmingham, Sheffield and Bristol which were soon to develop into independent universities. These institutions had different origins. Some of them had developed from colleges of science and acquired arts departments as they advanced towards university status. Others aimed at teaching all the usual university subjects from the beginning. In the case of the oldest of them, Owens College, Manchester (1851), the committee appointed to draw up a scheme of study decided that the classics should be one of the basic subjects of the education provided there, observing that

in a locality where men's minds and exertions are mainly devoted to commercial pursuits, it seems particularly desirable to select as an instrument of mental training a subject which, being general in its nature, and remote from the particular and daily occupations of the individual, may counteract their tendency to limit the applications and, eventually, the power of applying the mental faculties.[1]

But it is probable that theoretical considerations, at Manchester and elsewhere, counted less in the development of the courses than the requirements of the London degree. In none of the new colleges did the classics enjoy the same prestige as in the old universities, nor was the level of attainment likely to be so high, as long as a scholarship at Oxford or Cambridge remained the goal of the sixth-form boy in a classical school.

CHAPTER XI

SCOTLAND FROM THE SIXTEENTH
TO THE EIGHTEENTH CENTURY

Whereas in England before the nineteenth century the development of education was a haphazard affair determined largely by the endowments of private individuals and subject to little public direction or control, in Scotland there was what may justly be called a national system of education. Though the ambitious plans for educational reorganisation advanced in the *First Book of Discipline* were never put into effect, it remained the object of the Scottish Reformers to establish a school in every parish, and by the end of the seventeenth century this had been effected. The universities were more numerous and more popular in character than those of England, and took their pupils not only from the grammar schools of the Burghs but also direct from the parish schools. They took them at an earlier age than was usual in England. The average age of entry to the Scottish universities remained about fourteen until the nineteenth century, with the result that the grammar-school course was much shorter than in England and the amount of classics done was consequently less. Moreover, whereas in the English universities the medieval system slowly decayed and died, in those of Scotland it was adapted to new circumstances and remained alive and vigorous. Only towards the end of the nineteenth century did the Scottish universities develop specialised honours courses of the type that characterised Oxford and Cambridge. For the greater part of the period with which we are concerned they provided a general arts course in which the classics had only a small place. The Scottish system was thus not very favourable to advanced classical study. In particular until the nineteenth century little Greek was learned at school and not a great deal at the university.

Scotland of the sixteenth and seventeenth centuries produced a notable line of humanist scholars. George Buchanan was famous throughout Europe for his learning and his Latin verse, and the collection *Delitiae Poetarum Scotorum* (1637) attested the continued life of the Scottish school of Latin poets. But eminent though the Scottish humanists were, their influence on their own country was limited. The poverty of Scotland and the relative weakness of its seats of learning sent them abroad to study and in some cases to live. In spite of the great name of Buchanan humanism never took root in Scotland to the extent that it did in England.

About the middle of the sixteenth century we first hear of teaching of a humanist character in Scottish schools. The statutes of Aberdeen Grammar School (1553) lay down that the headmaster is to prelect on Terence, Virgil or Cicero,[1] and in the 1560's James Melville read Cicero's letters, some of the *Eclogues* of Virgil and the *Epistles* of Horace at Logie, Montrose.[2] At about the same time we find a five-year scheme of study at Glasgow High School which includes the usual grammar-school authors, Cicero, Sallust and Caesar in prose and in verse Terence, Ovid, Virgil and Horace.

While there was naturally much in common between the Latin course in the English schools and that in the Scottish, there were certain differences which deserve mention. Scotland had her own grammar books, and Scottish teachers showed more enterprise than those of England in producing new Latin grammars. At first the book in use was that of Despauterius. This was superseded to some degree by the grammar book of Andrew Simpson of Dunbar (1587), commonly known as the Dunbar Rudiments. An attempt at imposing an official grammar on all the schools of the country was made in 1612, when Alexander Hume's grammar was prescribed by the Scottish Parliament, but this work did not succeed in ousting the Dunbar book and that of Despauterius, the latter of which continued in use in some schools and was revised by James Kirkwood in 1674. All previous books were, however, superseded by Thomas Ruddiman's *Rudiments of the Latin Tongue*, first published in 1714, which became the standard grammar book of the Scottish schools of the eighteenth century.[1]

So far as classical authors are concerned reading was on much the same lines as in England, except that Suetonius, an author who does not to my knowledge appear in any English grammar-school curriculum, is found at Edinburgh in 1614 and Aberdeen in 1700, and the Aberdeen curriculum of 1700 includes the rather surprising item 'Virgil's Epigrams and Moretum'.[2] Though the Distichs of Cato were regularly read until well into the eighteenth century,[3] there seems to be no evidence of the Latin Aesop being used in the schools of Scotland. The *Colloquies* of Corderius, Erasmus and Castalio were as well known in Scotland as in England.[4] Sulpitius's poem *De Moribus in Mensa* was still being used in Scotland when it was probably forgotten south of the border;[5] peculiar to Scotland was the almost universal reading of Buchanan's Psalms, which conveyed religious instruction in classical Latin and classical metres to many generations of Scottish schoolboys.[6]

As regards school exercises it appears that the version, or translation of English into Latin, which was the characteristic feature of Scottish teaching in the nineteenth century, was from early times more practised than in England. Thus at Glasgow in the sixteenth century the highest class every other day 'translates into Latin a theme written in the vernacular'. Original composition was, however, also practised, and we find references to themes in most of the early curricula.[7] Verse-composition was prescribed at Glasgow in about 1570 and 1685, and at Edinburgh in 1614 and 1640, while at Aberdeen in 1659 it was ordained that a prize should be given at the annual visitation to the boy who made the best verse. But at Glasgow verse-making was only for those who had the faculty for it, and the scheme of study for Edinburgh High School in 1614 contains the phrases 'that thair exercises be in... making of versis as thair spirits servis thame' and 'that thai be exercised...in verse quhois gift serves thaim'. It appears that advantage was taken of the latitude permitted, for in 1645 the General Assembly noted the decay of verse-making and ordained that no schoolmaster should teach in a grammar school unless skilled in Latin verse.[1]

The earliest certain case of the teaching of Greek in Scotland is at Montrose in the 1550's where Andrew Melville learned the language from the Frenchman Petrus de Marsiliers.[2] There is evidence that in the later sixteenth century schoolmasters were expected to be able to teach Greek as well as Latin. In 1562 there were complaints that the headmaster of Edinburgh High School had 'nane or litill eruditioun in gramer greik or latene';[3] at Banff in 1585 the headmaster was required by the charter to be well versed in both Greek and Latin, and in 1591 the master of the school at Haddington undertook to instruct 'whole bairns sufficiently in their Greek and Latin grammars'.[4] In 1602 John Davidson founded a school at Prestonpans for the teaching of Latin, Greek and Hebrew, and Greek was either learnt or could be learnt at Stirling and Dumfries in the seventeenth century.[5] But the language had an insecure place in the Scottish schools and the amount done was small. At Glasgow about 1570 only the grammar was taught, and no Greek is included in the Edinburgh curriculum of 1598. At Edinburgh a fifth class was added for the teaching of Greek in 1614, and the scheme of study for that year includes the rather mysterious words 'and to teitche the greik gramer *Lyesiod* and *Theogius*', where the corrupt words no doubt stand for Hesiod and Theognis.[6] Greek had, however, dropped out of the Edinburgh curriculum by 1640 and from that of Glasgow by 1685.

The reason for this was no doubt that the language was regarded as belonging to the universities, and since those who studied it at school might be tempted to omit it at college, the university authorities discouraged its teaching elsewhere. In 1645 the General Assembly forbade the teaching of Greek except as preparation for entry to the university; it was not to be studied with a view to exemption from the Greek class.[1] Much the same was said in a document of about 1690 attributed to the Regents of St Andrews, which insisted that whatever progress had been made in Greek, logic and philosophy before entry to the university, the student should start in the lowest class.[2] Further evidence of the monopolistic attitude of the universities is provided by the Act of the Privy Council of 1672 prohibiting persons not publicly authorised from teaching philosophy or Greek, and by the request of St Leonard's College, St Andrews, to the Parliamentary Commission of 1695 that 'all teaching of Greek in Grammar Scholes be strictly prohibite, because there are a number of silly men, who, haveing hardly a smatter of Greek themselves, do take upon them to teach others, to the great disadvantage of many good spirits'.[3]

Such development as there was in the schoolteaching of Scotland in the eighteenth century was in the opposite direction from that in contemporary England. Whereas in England Greek advanced, in Scotland it remained at best stationary, and while in the English schools reading was mainly confined to poetry and verse-composition was held in high honour, in those of Scotland more attention was paid to prose writers and versifying died out almost completely.

At Edinburgh High School no Greek was taught during the eighteenth century until 1772, and when a Greek class was started there were protests from the university.[4] At Glasgow High School some Greek was taught in 1786, but at Aberdeen Grammar School there is no record of anything but Latin being taught throughout the century. It was probably in the smaller towns, away from the influence of the universities, that Greek flourished most. There are records of its having been taught at Banff, Wigtown, Huntly, Monquitter and Peterhead, and at Elgin in 1795 the highest class had got as far as reading Homer.[5] At Dumfries under George Chapman, headmaster from 1751 to 1774, Greek was begun in the fourth year of school, and in the fifth year the New Testament,

Aesop in Greek and the *Tabula* of Cebes were read, with a book or two of the *Iliad*; if another year was spent at school, more Homer was read, with the *Memorabilia* and sometimes the *Cyropaedia*. This was probably about as much as any eighteenth-century school in Scotland attempted in Greek, and indeed when the normal leaving age was about fourteen not a great deal more could be expected.

In Latin Chapman's programme of reading began with Corderius's *Colloquies* and went on through Phaedrus and Cornelius Nepos and other easy historical writers to Caesar and Sallust, Ovid's *Metamorphoses* and Virgil; the fifth year was occupied by Virgil and Horace, two or three books of Livy, a play of Terence and Cicero's *De Amicitia* and *De Senectute*; after which, if the schoolboy stayed another year, he passed to Pliny's Letters and Cicero *De Officiis* and sometimes Tacitus *Agricola* and *Germania*. At Aberdeen in 1796 the authors in the two highest classes were Virgil, Terence, Livy, Cicero, Sallust, Caesar and Horace, and the greater part of the time was taken in reading prose authors.

After the early part of the eighteenth century verse-composition became almost extinct. Ruddiman compiled a prosody, but did not print it, because 'the age has so little taste, the sale would not pay the expense', and according to a writer of 1813 prosody and poetry had been completely exiled from most Scottish schools for almost a hundred years.[1] At Dumfries in the eighteenth century it was the custom for the boys to compose a Latin poem each August addressed to the Magistrates and Town Council, requesting an autumn holiday. The headmaster, however, admits that he was obliged to help them in composing the poem, and describes the practice in somewhat apologetic terms: 'Though the poetical spirit cannot be expected, unless in those whom nature has endued with a particular genius for poetry, yet an exercise of this kind, once in the year, is neither impracticable nor improper for those in the highest class.'[2]

Andrew Dalzel, professor of Greek at Edinburgh at the end of the century, is said to have attributed Scotland's inferiority to England in Latin verse to Presbyterianism. Sydney Smith claimed to have heard him muttering to himself in the street one dark night: 'If it had not been for that confounded Solemn League and Covenant, we would have made as good longs and shorts as they.'[1] There is, however, no evidence that the Scottish church was hostile to Latin verse, and the General Assembly at least showed its loyalty to one of Scotland's own Latin poets when in 1740 it recommended to schools the reading of Arthur Johnston's paraphrase of the Song of Solomon.[2] Probably verse-composition had never flourished much in the Scottish schools. We have already seen that in an earlier period two of the chief schools did not force it on those who had no gift, and in the prosaic age which followed the Act of Union the same principle was pushed further. George Chapman, the eighteenth-century master of Dumfries school, warns students 'not to do violence to nature, by indulging a turn for versification, if they be not endued with an original genius for poetry'.[3] If this was the attitude of the schoolmasters, it is not surprising that verse-composition dropped out.

From the mid-sixteenth to the mid-nineteenth century there was little fundamental change in the arts curriculum of the Scottish universities. Throughout this period the degree course involved a regular progression from one subject to another, and though there were alterations in the course of time, and variations between one university and another, the basis remained the late medieval system under which the student passed through an abbreviated form of the trivium and quadrivium, involving mainly logic, rhetoric and arithmetic, to moral and natural philosophy. The humanist movement brought the introduction of Greek, which was firmly established in the sixteenth century and remained for three centuries or so the regular first-year subject, which by the nineteenth century extended into the second year. In the early period the teaching was in the hands of regents, each of whom taught his students all the subjects throughout their university career; this system survived a number of attempts to change it, and only gradually gave place to the professorial system by which a separate teacher was attached to each subject. Regenting was abolished at Edinburgh in 1708, at Glasgow in 1727, at St Andrews in 1747, at Marischal College in 1753 and at King's College, Aberdeen, not until 1798.

The introduction of humanism to the Scottish universities is due more than to anyone to Andrew Melville. Melville had left St Andrews with the reputation of being the best philosopher, poet and Grecian of any young master in the land; he had studied in Paris, and in 1574 he returned to Scotland and was appointed principal regent of Glasgow university. Here among other subjects he taught Greek, and lectured on a wide variety of ancient authors in connection with the traditional university subjects; he illustrated rhetoric from Homer, Hesiod, Phocylides, Theognis, Pythagoras, Isocrates, Pindar, Virgil, Horace and Theocritus, while for ethics he used Aristotle, Cicero and some of Plato's dialogues.[1] In 1575 his nephew James as regent at Glasgow read Isocrates *Ad Demonicum*, a book of the *Iliad*, Phocylides and Hesiod's *Works and Days*, and illustrated rhetoric from Cicero's *Catilines* and *Paradoxa*; in his second year of regenting he read for logic and ethics Aristotle in Greek, Cicero's *De Officiis* and Plato's *Phaedo* and *Axiochus*.[2] Melville's ideas were incorporated in the scheme of studies drawn up after the new foundation of the university in 1577. In this the first year was occupied by Greek grammar, with the reading of Isocrates, Lysias and Libanius, and rhetoric, with the reading of Cicero, Demosthenes, Homer, Aristophanes and the Greek epigrammatists. Rhetoric was continued in the second year, with Aristotle and Cicero's *De Oratore* as text books and various classical authors to provide illustration. In the third year, along with mathematics, there was the reading of Aristotle's *Logic*, *Ethics* and *Politics*, Cicero *De Officiis* and selections from Plato, while the final year was occupied by

Aristotle's *Physics*, the doctrine of the spheres, cosmography, universal history and Hebrew.[1]

Meanwhile the other universities were moving with the times. When James Melville was a student at St Andrews from 1571 to 1574 the curriculum was thoroughly medieval. 'I wald', writes Melville, 'haiff gladlie been at the Greik and Hebrew toungs, because I red in our Byble that it was translated out of Hebrew and Greik; bot the languages war nocht to be gottine in the land.'[2] But in 1579, a few years after James Melville left the university, it was reorganised, and a new scheme of study was introduced in which Greek and Latin were to occupy the first year, and in the second year the study of rhetoric was to be accompanied by the reading of authors, Greek and Latin, and composition in both languages, while Aristotle in Greek and Cicero in Latin were to be used for logic, ethics and politics in the third year.[3] In 1580 Andrew Melville himself came to St Andrews, and his nephew has left a vivid account of the reactions to his attacks on the medieval Aristotle. The regents 'cryed "Grait Diana of the Ephesians", thair bread-winner, thair honour, thair estimation, all was gean, giff Aristotle sould be sa owirharled in the heiring of thair schollars'.[4] In the meantime at Aberdeen Alexander Arbuthnot, a friend of Melville, appointed principal of King's College in 1569, had introduced Greek, and the scheme of study drawn up for that university in 1580, like that of St Andrews of the previous year, included the reading of authors Greek and Latin and practice in composition.[5] When Marischal College was founded in 1593, it was laid down that one of the regents should teach Greek, explain the easiest authors in both Greek and Latin and make the students compose first in Latin then in Greek.[6]

At Edinburgh University, founded in 1582, the first year was occupied by the study of the classical languages and in Greek the student proceeded in one year from Clenardus's grammar to the New Testament, Isocrates, Homer, Hesiod and Phocylides.[7] The same list of authors appears in the Glasgow curriculum of 1648,[8] while at the Aberdeen colleges of the same period Demosthenes was added and Hesiod omitted.[1]

Latin was the medium of instruction in the sixteenth and seventeenth centuries, and no doubt it was assumed that all those who entered the university would have been sufficiently well grounded in the language at school. Consequently it had not the same place in the universities as Greek, and Latin authors were read primarily to illustrate the traditional university subjects such as rhetoric and moral philosophy. But experience must have shown that the grammar-school training was not always enough. In 1597 Edinburgh University found it necessary to appoint a 'private professor' of Humanity to teach a class below the university level, and at the beginning of the eighteenth century Humanity became a recognised part of the university course, occupying the first year.[2] At Glasgow an additional class for Humanity, to precede the Greek class, was established in 1648, but was abolished about forty years later.[3] Professors of Humanity were appointed intermittently in the seventeenth century, and in 1706 the subject gained a permanent professor and a permanent place in the curriculum. At St Andrews a professorship of Humanity was founded in 1620 at St Leonard's College by Sir John Scot of Scotstarvet. The new professorship met with opposition both from the existing members of the college and from the Burgh schoolmaster, who feared that he would lose his pupils, and it was not until 1644 that it was finally established.[4] At King's College, Aberdeen, there had been from the early days of the college a 'humanist', whose duties included the teaching of the elements of Latin, but in 1753 it was decided that in view of the existence of grammar schools this elementary class was now entirely useless and should be abandoned.[5] At Marischal College, though some provision was made for the teaching of Latin, there was no regular professor of Humanity until 1841.[6]

The establishment in the early eighteenth century of Latin classes with their own professors at Glasgow and Edinburgh is an indication of the change which was taking place in the position of the language. It could no longer be assumed that all students would be familiar with it. At the beginning of the century it was found that the Glasgow students were regularly ignoring the rule that only Latin should be used in conversation,[1] and at the same time the practice of lecturing in Latin was dying out. James Wodrow, professor of Divinity at Glasgow from 1672 to 1705, used English as well as Latin, and Andrew Ross, professor of Humanity from 1706 to 1735, taught Latin through the medium of the vernacular; later in the century Francis Hutcheson the philosopher and Adam Smith the economist lectured in English.[2] At Edinburgh in 1741 the professor of 'Universal Civil History and Roman Antiquities' used Latin for his lectures, as did the professor of Logic, while the lecturer on Church History followed each Latin lecture with a recapitulation in English; but soon after that date Latin died out as the general medium of teaching.[3] It seems to have lingered on longest in the medical faculty; examinations in medicine were still being conducted in Latin in 1826.[4]

At Glasgow and Edinburgh the eighteenth-century professors of Humanity, in addition to their ordinary class, held a 'private class' for more advanced work. In this Andrew Ross of Glasgow dealt with criticism and Roman customs, and lectured on authors, and William Richardson, a man of some note in his day as a poet and miscellaneous writer, lectured on 'the peculiarities and beauties of the Roman language, on the principles of classical composition and on Roman antiquities'.[5] John Kerr of Edinburgh in 1741 read with his private class Terence, Cicero, Horace, Tacitus, Suetonius and the younger Pliny.[6] In Greek the attempt to complete the Greek course in a single session had apparently been given up by the mid-eighteenth century; at Edinburgh in 1741 there were two classes, in the more advanced of which the professor read some Homer and Demosthenes and two plays of Euripides, and by the end of the century a third Greek class had been established at both Edinburgh and Glasgow.[7]

The Greek professors of this period were of necessity confined in the main to elementary work, and one of them, Robert Hunter of Edinburgh (1741–72), is described as having used a method which 'did not differ materially from that of most country school-masters'.[1] By the end of the century, however, we find them giving lectures of a more popular character. This was the great age of the lecturing professor. Graduation, except at Aberdeen, had fallen into disuse, and students often ignored the curriculum and attended what classes they chose. In these circumstances professors who wished to be successful had to be effective lecturers who impressed their personality on their hearers. Such a one was John Young of Glasgow, professor from 1774 to 1821, of whom it is recorded that 'nothing could be more captivating than the eloquence with which he treated of the liberty, the literature and the glory of ancient Greece, while tears of enthusiasm rolled down his cheek'.[2] Grecian liberty was also one of the themes of Young's friend, Andrew Dalzel of Edinburgh. Dalzel was a man of attractive character and an enthusiastic teacher, who did much to promote an interest in Greek in his university and who, according to his biographer, 'identified his happiness with the success of his class and his students and with restoring the study of Greek in Scotland'.[3]

Young and Dalzel had large classes, but it may be doubted whether their pupils learnt much Greek from them. The defects of the Scottish system, as well as its merits in the hands of an able lecturer, are clearly indicated in Lord Cockburn's reminiscences of Dalzel.

At the mere teaching of a language to boys he was ineffective. How is it possible for the elements, including the very letters, of a language to be taught to one hundred boys at once, by a single lecturing professor? To the lads who, like me, to whom the very alphabet was new, required positive *teaching*, the class was utterly useless. Nevertheless, though not a good schoolmaster, it is a duty, and delightful, to record Dalzel's value as a general exciter of boys' minds.... Mild, affectionate, simple, an absolute enthusiast about learning—particularly classical and especially Greek...he was a great favourite with all boys and with all good men.... He could never make us actively laborious. But when we sat passive, and listened to him, he inspired us with a vague but sincere ambition of literature, and with delicious dreams of virtue and poetry. He must have been a hard boy whom those discourses, spoken by Dalzel's low, soft, artless voice, did not melt.[1]

CHAPTER XII

SCOTLAND:
THE NINETEENTH CENTURY

In the early nineteenth century there was a feeling abroad that classical studies in Scotland were in an unsatisfactory state. As the Royal Commission appointed to inquire into the Scottish universities in 1826 put it,

> Those very high attainments in Classical Literature which distinguished some individuals in Scotland at the close of the sixteenth century are no longer to be found. Men's minds are now turned to more important and useful pursuits than consummate elegance in classical composition; but it is a matter of regret that an intimate acquaintance with the classics, particularly the Greek authors, is not more general among the best educated classes of society in Scotland.[1]

Sir William Hamilton was more emphatic. 'In Scotland', he wrote in 1836, 'our higher and lower seminaries are, perhaps, worse calculated for the promotion of ancient learning than those of any other European country.'[2] Though the schools provided a sound grounding in Latin, the nature of the educational system made it difficult to acquire more than a superficial knowledge of Greek, for, as Hamilton put it, 'professorial prelections are no substitute for scholastic discipline'.[3] Improvement in the position of the classics could only come with a lengthening of the grammar-school course and the consequent provision of more time for Latin and Greek before the university. This in fact took place in the nineteenth century. In the 1820's the average age of entry to the universities was fourteen, and in the case of Marischal College as low as twelve. By the end of the century it had risen to eighteen.

It was in Edinburgh High School that the first advances were made in classical teaching. From 1768 to 1809 the school was presided over by Alexander Adam, of whom Lord Cockburn wrote that he was born to teach Latin, some Greek and all virtue.[1] In Latin he confined himself to a few authors, Virgil, Sallust and a little Horace, but he made a point of teaching ancient history and geography as well.[2] His successor James Pillans, appointed in 1810, introduced new Latin authors and extended the Greek teaching. The opposition of the university was now a thing of the past, and in 1814 the Town Council recognised the teaching of Greek at the school by presenting a gold medal for the subject. Pillans also developed the teaching of classical geography; but his chief innovation was the introduction of Latin verse-composition. He had been a private tutor at Eton, and had returned to Scotland with a belief in the value of some features of English education. Two years after his appointment to the High School he actually published a collection of Latin poems by his pupils, most of them under fifteen years of age.[3] During the rectorship of Carson (1820–45) the High School was said to be distinguished for a 'union of strict classical studies with a proper amount of useful collateral knowledge', and under his successor, the German-born Leonard Schmitz, we find a wide range of Greek reading in the highest form and some Latin and Greek verse-composition.[4]

Meanwhile the old High School had acquired a new rival in Edinburgh Academy, which opened in 1824. Unlike a number of 'academies' which had been founded in the eighteenth century primarily to teach modern subjects, that at Edinburgh was designedly a classical school. Lord Cockburn records that he and Leonard Horner had often discussed the causes and remedies for the decline of classical education in Scotland, and finally decided that there could be no improvement so long as there was only one classical school in the capital. 'So one day on the top of the Pentlands—emblematic of the solidity of our foundations and of the extent of our prospects—we two resolved to set about the establishment of a new school.'[5] The first headmaster of the Academy was the Welshman John Williams, a friend of Sir Walter Scott, who considered him 'the best schoolmaster in Europe'[6] and had sent his son to Wales to be educated by him. Williams is described as a man of 'varied scholarship and kindly manners, with an aptitude for imparting knowledge in an attractive and easy, though somewhat desultory way',[1] and when he left Edinburgh to become the first Warden of Llandovery College he had given the Academy a good start. He and his two successors were Oxford men and Anglican clergy, and the school thus grew up under the influence of English educational methods. Verse-composition was encouraged, and Greek was begun earlier than at other Scottish schools; W. Y. Sellar, who was at the Academy from 1832 to 1840, was writing Greek iambics at the age of fourteen.[2] It was at Edinburgh Academy that D'Arcy Thompson taught for eleven years before going to Galway as professor of Greek, and, as his *Daydreams of a Schoolmaster* show, he was a teacher of unusual qualities.

Outside Edinburgh the most important classical school was Aberdeen Grammar School, where James Melvin was Rector from 1826 to 1853. In the first year of his rectorship it was decided that Greek should be taught in the two highest forms, but the amount done remained small, and the school under Melvin was almost exclusively a Latin one.[3] The authors read were few —Caesar and Livy, Virgil, Horace and Buchanan's Psalms—and the quantity got through was not large. Every sentence was gone over at least five times; it was read aloud, translated first word for word, then as a whole, and analysed first etymologically, then syntactically. There was little verse-composition, but constant practice in versions, to which two entire days were given up in every week. Closeness to the original and grammatical accuracy were the qualities on which Melvin insisted.[4]

This efficient but narrow system owed its character to the influence of the Aberdeen colleges. These had a number of bursaries open to competition, and it was the version that counted more than anything else. At the beginning of the century the examination consisted solely of translation into Latin; later translation from

Latin and some Greek were added, and in the 1860's mathematics and English, but even then Latin was the most important subject and the version the most important part of it.

Outside the schools already mentioned we find in the early nineteenth century signs of an increasing provision for Greek teaching. At Pitsligo in 1812 Homer and Xenophon were read, and at Irvine Academy in 1823 the boys had read several prose authors and were able to translate readily from the first six books of the *Iliad*.[1] In 1835 there was provision for teaching Greek in twenty-three schools in all, and by the middle of the century all schools of any importance and some lesser ones taught the language.[2]

Perhaps the most remarkable feature of nineteenth-century Scottish education, and one not without its relevance to our subject, was the development of the parish schools in the counties of Aberdeen, Banff and Moray resulting from the Dick bequest. In 1828 James Dick left a sum of well over £100,000 for the benefit of the parish schoolmasters in these three counties. The schools which benefited by the bequest attracted men of high scholastic quality, and by 1873 nearly all of the parish schoolmasters in the counties concerned were university graduates.[3] Parish schools had always been grammar schools in the sense that their masters were generally qualified to teach Latin and sometimes did teach some, in addition to the elementary education which was their main business. The Dick bequest had the effect of increasing the amount of Latin and Greek taught at the schools which were affected by it; the masters, being themselves university men and appointed to their posts after a severe examination in university subjects, made it their business to prepare their boys for entry to the university. A bursary at Aberdeen was the aim of every clever boy in the three counties, and the parish schools, supplemented sometimes by a short period at Aberdeen Grammar School, provided the necessary classical training. In 1833 elementary Latin was taught to a few pupils in two-thirds of the Dick bequest schools.[1] As the effects of the bequest made themselves felt, the position of Latin greatly improved, and a fair amount of Greek came to be taught. In 1865 6·7 per cent of the pupils in these schools learned Latin and 1·5 per cent Greek; the corresponding figures for the rest of the country—4 per cent and 0·5 per cent—show the superiority of the Dick bequest schools.[2] As an example of one of these schools where the classics flourished we may mention that in the remote Banffshire village of Tomintoul, where in 1862 eighteen pupils were learning Latin and seven Greek, and where it was said that Liddell and Scott was 'as familiar a sight to the pupils spelling their way through an English book as to the gilded youth of Eton and Harrow'.[3]

In 1864 the English Schools Inquiry Commission sent one of their members to investigate the Scottish schools. His report was enthusiastic. According to him the wealth of the Scottish people had not outstripped their civilisation, and there was more humanity and refinement in the average middle-class Scotsman than in his English counterpart. The Scottish teachers were masters of their craft as few English teachers were.

> In front of this eager animated throng there stands the master, gaunt, muscular and time-worn, poorly clad, and plain in manner and speech, but with the dignity of a ruler in his gesture, and the fire of an enthusiast in his eye.... The whole scene is one of vigorous action and masterly force, forming the greatest possible contrast with the monotonous, unmethodical, ill-seconded working of the English teacher.[4]

This flattering picture needs to be supplemented by the report on Burgh and Middle-Class Schools of the Commission on Schools in Scotland appointed in the same year as the English Schools Inquiry Commission. This shows that education in Scotland was to some extent, though less no doubt than in England, affected by the spirit of utilitarianism. The classics were not universally popular. At Montrose Academy they were evidently not a favourite study; at Brechin they were in a decaying state and at Dollar they were regarded with apathy.[5] Parents looked on education as a means to an immediate end, and their object was to get their sons placed in some remunerative job. In the north-east the classics were popular because they paid; there was little commerce, there were bursaries to be won at Aberdeen and, thanks to the Dick bequest, there were good prospects in school teaching.[1]

The Commissioners mentioned six schools as particularly noted for their classical teaching, the two Edinburgh schools we have already mentioned, three at Aberdeen and Trinity College, Glen-almond, an Episcopalian foundation on the model of the English public schools. Of the Aberdeen schools the best known was the grammar school in New Aberdeen, where Melvin had taught and which still adhered to his methods. Here the commissioners noted the narrow range of reading, and described the teaching as characterised by 'scholarlike minuteness, simplicity and quietness of manner'.[2] At Edinburgh High School there was much wider reading, and the highest form was engaged on advanced authors such as Plautus, Lucretius and Tacitus in Latin, and Thucydides, Plato and the tragedians in Greek.[3] There was a similar range of reading at Edinburgh Academy, a school which could 'stand comparison with the English public schools in point of scholarship and spirit'.[4] This was the only school where much verse-composition was done, though even here it was not compulsory.[5]

Thus by the mid-Victorian period education in Scotland had come closer to that in England in that the position of Greek had noticeably improved and the range of Latin reading had been extended. There were, however, still differences between the two countries. Methods of teaching were different; in Scotland there was little learning by heart and little verse-composition and, especially in the schools under Aberdeen influence, there was a great deal of translation into Latin prose. There was nothing in Scotland equal to the advanced classical teaching given by the best English schools, and indeed this was hardly to be expected when the normal age for going to the university was still a year or two lower than in England. There was, however, a good average level of teaching; less stimulus perhaps to the brilliant boy than in England, but less wastage in the case of the less gifted. Classical teaching was more widely diffused, and in the parish schools of the north-east Latin and Greek were available to a class which in England would hardly have come by such an education.

For most of the nineteenth century the arts curriculum in the universities continued with little change. In the first half of the century Latin and Greek normally occupied the first two years, logic and mathematics being added in the second year, while the third year was occupied by moral philosophy and the fourth by natural philosophy.[1] The Aberdeen colleges were peculiar in that they included chemistry or, at Marischal College, civil and natural history, in the second-year course, reversed the normal order of moral and natural philosophy and postponed logic to the final years, adding rhetoric.[2] In 1863 the commission established as a result of the Scottish Universities Act of 1858 laid down regulations for all the universities. These required attendance as before at classes in Humanity, Greek, Mathematics, Logic, Moral and Natural Philosophy, and added English Literature; the ordinary four-year course was to include two years of the classical languages, but students could be exempted from the lower classes if qualified for higher work. Provision was made for an examination for Honours in various subjects, including classics, for those who had satisfied the requirements for graduation.[3] A further development took place in 1892, when as a result of the Scottish Universities Act of 1889 the old rigid scheme came to an end. Candidates for a degree were still required to attend classes in seven subjects, but there was more freedom of choice, and only one ancient language was required.[4] Thus for most of the nineteenth century the arts course remained a general one, involving some Latin and Greek and a number of other subjects. The Honours examinations established in 1863 were additional to the ordinary course and did not prove popular, at any rate in the two southern universities; at

Glasgow from 1864 to 1893 about 12 per cent of the graduates took Honours, and the figures for Edinburgh were very similar.[1]

The oldest university, St Andrews, had been small and unimportant in the eighteenth century. In the nineteenth it remained small, but its classical departments flourished, thanks to a series of Oxford-educated Scots who occupied the Greek and Latin chairs in the latter half of the century. J. C. Shairp, a cultured man of letters who was for a time professor of poetry at Oxford, was appointed professor of Humanity in 1861, and was remembered for his 'acute and suggestive expositions of Horace, vigorous and impressive criticisms of Lucretius, delicate, keenly appreciative and altogether masterly prelections on Virgil'.[2] In 1859 W. Y. Sellar had been appointed to the professorship of Greek, to be followed in 1863 by Lewis Campbell, the editor of Plato and Sophocles, who held the post until 1893, when he was succeeded by John Burnet. Thanks to the work of these scholars St Andrews in the later nineteenth century was noted for its classics, and when provision was made for graduation in Honours a remarkably large proportion of St Andrews students entered for Classical Honours.[3]

At Aberdeen some attempt had been made in the eighteenth century to increase the amount of classics done. In 1753, when King's College drew up a new scheme of study, the university authorities received a good deal of correspondence pointing out the importance of the classics and the harm done by their neglect. It was therefore resolved that classics should be taught to the higher years, though the subject was to be treated 'from the more literary and philosophic point of view'.[4] In practice this extension of classical teaching did not amount to much. At King's College in 1826 the third and fourth years attended the second humanity class with the second year, and in both this and the first class the amount of work done was small.[5] The first class did nothing but read Horace for two hours a week, while the second class, meeting three hours a week, read extracts from other authors. The Royal Commission of 1826 considered these classes 'altogether unfit for accomplishing the object which should be contemplated'.[1]

At Marischal College regular Latin classes were started in 1826, when James Melvin took up teaching at the College in addition to his work at the Grammar School. Until then some Latin had been taught to the second-year students by the professor of Natural and Civil history, and Latin texts were read in the Moral Philosophy class.[2] In 1841, when it was decided to have a professor of humanity, it was generally expected that Melvin would be appointed. Instead the chair went to J. S. Blackie, a young man who had studied in Germany and come back full of ideas for improving the standard of the Scottish universities. He set about his task with vigour and ingenuity, but in 1852 he moved to Edinburgh, and not long afterwards, with the union of the two Aberdeen universities, Marischal College ceased to be a home of classical studies.

At King's College the outstanding classical teacher in the second half of the century was W. D. Geddes, professor of Greek for thirty years from 1855. Geddes was a scholar of real distinction and an excellent teacher who did much to promote the study of Greek in the north-east. He 'taught us a great deal of Greek', writes one of his pupils, 'and he impressed us with much of his own enthusiasm for Greek; one could never forget with what rapt ecstasy he spoke, in a quavering falsetto, about the ancient Athenians'.[3] Among pupils of his who won distinction as Greek scholars were R. A. Neil, James Adam and John Strachan.

At Glasgow the professors in the early part of the century had to cope single-handed with enormous classes; in the years 1826–36 the numbers in Greek varied between 440 and 311 and in Humanity between 267 and 191,[4] and in Greek most of the class would be mere boys with no previous knowledge of the language. As the century progressed the task was eased by the appointment of assistants, and the average age and standard of attainment advanced, though in 1875, when Jebb went to Glasgow, the junior

Greek class still contained a large number of beginners and few who had done Greek for more than a year before entering the university.[1] In spite of the somewhat daunting conditions with which they were faced the Glasgow professors did distinguished work, not only as teachers of their large ordinary classes, but also in encouraging a higher scholarship in the 'private' or Honours classes. Glasgow was peculiar among the universities in having an Honours examination before 1863. Under regulations of 1826 candidates could obtain Honours in Classics and Mental Philosophy or in Natural Philosophy and Mathematics, in addition to satis-fying the minimum requirements in the obligatory subjects. So far as Classics were concerned a candidate for the highest Honours had to offer in Latin twelve books of the *Aeneid*, a decade of Livy (or nine speeches of Cicero), two comedies and three satires of Persius, and in Greek all Thucydides or Herodotus, all Sophocles or Aeschylus (or seven plays of Euripides or Aristophanes) and Aristotle's *Poetics* (or Longinus or Dionysius of Halicarnassus *De Compositione*). For 'honorary distinction' a smaller amount of reading was required, while the minimum for graduation was in Latin three books of Livy, three of the *Aeneid* and two of Horace's *Odes* and in Greek the Gospels and three books of Homer.[2]

The professor of Humanity from 1815 to 1831 was Josiah Walker, a former customs inspector appointed to the chair at the age of fifty-four, who has been described as 'an undistinguished dilettante'.[3] From 1831 to the end of the century the professor-ship was held successively by the two Ramsays, William and his nephew George, both well known outside their university for their contributions to classical studies. William Ramsay was an effective and stimulating teacher. 'His alert figure and sunny expression, his bright eye, his resonant enunciation, his precise and perspicuous language, his scholarship and wealth of illustration impressed his students and commanded their attention, and his energy and moral force bore them along and stimulated their minds and awakened their imagination.'[4]

In Greek John Young was succeeded in 1821 by D. K. Sandford, a man of vigorous personality and an able teacher, who, according to Archbishop Tait, one of his pupils, 'possessed in a wonderful degree the power of quickening into life the latent intellect of his pupils'.[1] From 1838 to 1875 the Greek chair was occupied by E. L. Lushington, Tennyson's brother-in-law. Scholarly and reserved, quiet in voice and gentle in manner, he lacked his colleague Ramsay's stimulating qualities, but none the less exercised a remarkable fascination over his classes.[2] His inaugural lecture was long remembered. 'It was a lecture which not only contained a most just and impressive survey and estimate of Greek literature, but was surcharged with the new thought and imaginative feeling pervading the remarkable Cambridge set to which he belonged...some of whom (and he certainly) looked on Coleridge then as their master.'[3] Lushington brought from Trinity not only an admiration for Coleridge but also the Cambridge belief in verbal accuracy. His lectures were severely linguistic, and he seldom moved outside the narrow limits he set himself.[4] At first he was little appreciated except by the best students, but as time went on the number of those who profited by his fine scholarship increased, and towards the end of his professorship he was universally regarded with reverence and affection.[5]

Lushington was succeeded by another Cambridge man, R. C. Jebb, who spent a fruitful period of fourteen years at Glasgow before returning to Cambridge. Like his predecessor, Jebb taught his ordinary classes by putting them on to translate and his Honours class by expounding the authors in lectures; like Lushington he won admiration by his idiomatic English translations of Greek, but whereas Lushington apparently confined himself to the exposition of texts, Jebb added lectures on Greek literature and Greek antiquities.[6] He was a methodical teacher who kept his classes under control and knew just how much he could require of his students, and to many of them he gave 'an idea from which we can never escape of what a scholar can be'.[1] To succeed Jebb Glasgow chose a young Oxford man of twenty-three, Gilbert Murray, who was to be the leading Hellenist of his generation and who, like Jebb, was to leave Scotland for the professorship in his own university.

At Edinburgh at the end of the eighteenth century the Humanity class was a 'scene of unchecked idleness and disrespectful mirth'.[2] Discipline was no doubt restored by Alexander Christison, professor from 1806 to 1820, who as a master at the High School had been distinguished, according to Lord Cockburn, by 'constant and indiscriminate harshness'.[3] Christison was succeeded by a more genial character, James Pillans, who has already been mentioned in this chapter as Rector of the High School. He varied the usual round of class-work with lectures on such subjects as universal grammar and the origin of language, the Twelve Tables, the manuscripts of the classics, the *Odes* of Horace and the history of literature and science among the Romans.[4] He taught his pupils to admire goodness, beauty and truth, and in his hands the Humanity class became 'a class of practical ethics'.[5] Pillans was succeeded in 1863 by W. Y. Sellar, whose great gifts as an expounder of Latin literature have become known outside the lecture room through his admirable books on the Roman poets.

For most of the first half of the century the Greek professor at Edinburgh was George Dunbar, compiler of Greek–English and English–Greek lexica. He held three classes; the first was the elementary one for beginners; to the second, in addition to work on books and composition, he gave lectures on Greek institutions and Greek philosophy; in the third class the more advanced authors were read, and there were exercises in composition, including translation into Greek verse.[6] Dunbar is described as a 'stern, rigid and conscientious instructor'.[7] Very different in character was his successor J. S. Blackie, who moved to Edinburgh and Greek from Aberdeen and Latin in 1852. A picturesque figure in plaid and broad-brimmed hat, abounding in energy and unorthodox in his methods, he inspired a good deal of enthusiasm and affection, but tended to neglect both the discipline of regular class-work and the niceties of scholarship. He disliked wasting time on minute grammatical points, and when faced with a difficult passage might decide to leave it alone and pass on.[1] A fluent lecturer and writer on a variety of subjects, he was, especially in his later years, inclined to let his outside interests encroach on his professorial work. 'His interest was diverted to so many questions of general importance that he overflowed with these at times into devious prologues to Xenophon and Thucydides', and became 'somewhat too independent of the conditions imposed by the class-room and the class hours.' 'His mind running on Gaelic, on the Celtic chair, on the crofters, on Goethe, on John Knox, on the Apostle Paul, would suddenly revolt at the overtrodden track of grammatical precision, and rush for a space with reinvigorating eagerness down some tempting vista.'[2]

Until the middle of the century academic contacts between Scotland and England were limited by differences of religion. Subscription to the Thirty-nine Articles was a condition of matriculation at Oxford and of graduation at Cambridge, while most of the college fellowships were open only to Anglican clergy; in Scotland all professors were required to subscribe to the Westminster confession. The latter provision did not prevent Sandford, William Ramsay and Lushington, all of whom were Episcopalians and graduates of English universities, from holding professorships at Glasgow.[3] But it debarred from such posts those in Anglican orders, or scrupulous men like Thomas Mitchell, the editor of Aristophanes, who had lost his fellowship at Cambridge through his refusal to take Orders and was prevented by the necessity of subscription from taking a professorship in Scotland.[4] With the abolition of religious tests in the Scottish universities there was no longer any barrier to the appointment of Englishmen or of Scotsmen who, like Lewis Campbell, had taken Anglican Orders.

By the latter part of the nineteenth century contact between the Scottish and the English universities was much closer than it had been at the beginning of the century. As Scotsmen in the sixteenth and seventeenth centuries had gone to the continent to complete their education, so in the nineteenth they often proceeded from a Scottish university to an English. In the eighteenth century the Snell exhibition had brought Glasgow men to Balliol at a time when Oxford had little of value to offer them. With the development of honours schools in the nineteenth century the prestige of the English universities increased, and more Scots went south to compete for the prizes of richer universities than their own. Many of them made their mark in the classical schools of Oxford and, less often, Cambridge. Some remained in the English universities, like D. B. Monro and J. A. Stewart at Oxford and James Adam and R. A. Neil at Cambridge. Others, like William Ramsay, Lewis Campbell, Sellar and Burnet, returned to teach in the Scottish universities. By the end of the nineteenth century Scotsmen were making a notable contribution to classical studies both in their own country and in England.

CHAPTER XIII

TRINITY COLLEGE, DUBLIN

The history of classical studies in Trinity College, Dublin, differs in some respects from that which we find in other British universities. Like the Scottish universities, Dublin retained in essentials down to the end of the nineteenth century its four-year arts course, but unlike them it provided a classical course which continued throughout the undergraduate career and was not confined to the first two years. In the eighteenth century the Dublin undergraduate was subjected to a course of classical reading which was probably a good deal more thorough than that provided in any other British university, and though throughout our period the college avoided the specialisation characteristic of Oxford and Cambridge, it developed in the later nineteenth century a school of classics which could stand comparison with those of the English universities.[1]

At the foundation of Trinity College in 1591 there were only four fellows, and yet, we are told, 'the tongues and arts were very exactly taught to all the students', and Aristotle was read in the original Greek.[2] In the college statutes of 1629 we find the undergraduate course consisting of two years of logic followed by Physiology (or Natural Philosophy) and Psychology with Ethics, while Mathematics and Politics were assigned to the Bachelors. All undergraduates were to compose a Latin theme or version once every week, there were to be regular declamations, and a special lecturer was to instruct all classes in Greek and Hebrew, 'si commode fieri potest'.[3] According to the University statutes of the same period candidates for the Master's degree must be able to prelect in Greek on a portion of the first book of the *Odyssey*.[4] The Laudian statutes of 1637 are more precise on the question of Greek teaching; all classes are to receive lectures in Greek three times a week, the two freshmen years from the junior Greek lecturer and the two Sophister years and Bachelors from the senior lecturer (who was later, in 1761, to develop into a professor of Greek).[1] The college evidently took the linguistic side of its work seriously. In 1659 it was laid down that no student should be admitted to the Bachelor's degree without a certificate of proficiency in Greek, and as early as the seventeenth century there were regular examinations in Greek and Latin as well as in other subjects, and classical merit was encouraged by the awarding of scholarships as the result of examination on the books read in college.[2]

While 'the tongues' had no doubt been originally taught mainly as ancillary to 'the arts', by the early eighteenth century the classics were being studied from the literary point of view and irrespective of their bearing on the traditional university subjects. The course of reading prescribed in 1736 was as follows. In the first year the undergraduate read in Latin Sallust, the whole of the *Aeneid* and Terence, and in Greek Dugard's Lucian, the first twelve books of the *Iliad*, *Hero and Leander* and some Theocritus; in the second year, Juvenal, Caesar, Justin, Horace, the second half of the *Iliad* and the first eight books of the *Odyssey*, the *Enchiridion* of Epictetus and the *Tabula* of Cebes; in the third year the *Georgics*, Cicero's *De Officiis* (or Pliny's Letters), Velleius Paterculus and the first third of Livy, the remainder of the *Odyssey*, some more Lucian and the *Cyropaedia*; in the fourth year the remainder of Livy, Suetonius and Tacitus, three plays of Sophocles, the speeches of Demosthenes and Aeschines on the Crown, the *Philippics* of Demosthenes and Longinus.[3]

In 1759 the list was revised. In that year the Dublin schoolmasters asked for advice on the books to be read at school, and the University drew up a list, which included some which until then had been read at college, such as Justin, the first six books of the *Aeneid*, Theocritus, Musaeus and Dugard's Lucian. These were accordingly removed from the university course, as were Velleius Paterculus and Suetonius, the *Odyssey*, Epictetus and the *Tabula* of Cebes. In their place were added five speeches of Cicero, more of Demosthenes, two plays of Euripides, twelve of Plutarch's *Lives* and the *Anabasis* and *Memorabilia*.[1]

In 1793 a new course was adopted. In Latin the second half of the *Aeneid* and the *Georgics*, the *Odes* and *Epodes* and four books of Livy were read in the first year; in the second, two more books of Livy, Caesar's *Civil War* and the *Satires* and *Epistles* of Horace; in the third, Juvenal and Persius, speeches of Cicero and selections from Quintilian; and in the fourth, Tacitus *Germania*, *Histories* and *Annals* and Plautus and Terence. In Greek the first year was occupied with *Iliad* XII to XXIV, Herodotus and Minor Poets, the second with two of Plutarch's *Lives*, the *Cyropaedia* and *Memorabilia*, and three dialogues of Plato; the third with Lucian and Greek oratory and the fourth with Thucydides, Sophocles, Euripides and Longinus. This course of reading went on, as before, concurrently with the course in 'the arts'. In this Euclid now shared the first year with logic, and Locke had found his way into the second year; the third year was occupied with Astronomy, Gravity and Mechanics, Hydrostatics and Pneumatics and Optics; while the fourth year studied text books on Natural Law and Revealed Religion, Locke on Government and Cicero's *De Officiis*.[2] It should be added that the course for the Master's degree had not lapsed, as it had in the English universities. Normally only scholars resided, but they attended lectures, including those of the professor of Greek, and were expected to read the more advanced classical authors whom they had not read as undergraduates.[3]

As has already been indicated, the Trinity College classical course was closely related to what was read in the schools. Dublin, unlike the English universities, ensured a more or less uniform standard of attainment on the part of its students by an entrance examination on prescribed classical texts. An examination of an informal nature was in existence in the first half of the eighteenth century. This was regularised in 1759.[4] From 1793 to the middle of the nineteenth century the books prescribed were the *Eclogues* and *Aeneid* I to VI, three plays of Terence, Horace, four satires of

Juvenal and Sallust; the first eight books of the *Iliad*, Murphy's Lucian, three books of the *Cyropaedia*, the Gospels and Acts in Greek, Epictetus *Enchiridion* and the *Tabula* of Cebes.[1] The last two books were later removed from the list, and in 1849 Terence, Juvenal and Xenophon were dropped, the amount of Virgil and Homer slightly reduced and Euripides *Hecuba* and three books of Livy added.[2] Though the Royal Commission on Endowed Schools in Ireland of 1855 criticised the schools for arranging their curriculum with a view to the Dublin entrance course and devoting too much time to the dead languages, the system at any rate ensured that Trinity College did not, as did Oxford and Cambridge, have to deal with students of widely differing classical attainments.[3]

Prizes were given from 1732 for good work in terminal examinations, and from 1793 for distinction in classics, including Latin prose- and verse-composition, to the two higher classes.[4] The Berkeley medals, founded in 1752, were awarded to Bachelors after examination and attendance at special lectures by the professor of Greek. Advanced lectures in classics were introduced in 1800,[5] but Honours courses date from 1833, when the degree course was reorganised. There was still a compulsory course for all, including mathematics, physics, logic and ethics, and, as before, Latin and Greek throughout the four undergraduate years, but there were also additional lectures for Honours candidates.

The classical course varied from time to time; that for 1853 may serve as an example. The first year's reading consisted of dialogues from Stock's Lucian, two volumes of Stock's Demosthenes, two books of Livy and the *Pro Archia*, *Pro Milone* and *Catilines* of Cicero, while candidates for Honours also read Lucian *On Writing History*, two further books of Livy, Aeschines and Demosthenes on the Crown, three of Cicero's *Philippics* and one book of *De Oratore*. In the second year the minimum course was Plato's *Apology* and *Crito*, one book of Herodotus, three of the *Iliad*, Cicero's *De Amicitia* and *De Senectute*, Tacitus *Agricola* and *Germania* and the *Georgics*; the additional course for Honours was the

Phaedo, two books of the *Tusculans*, one of Thucydides, two of the *Annals*, four of the *Odyssey* and four of the *Aeneid*. In the third year the pass man read the *Oedipus Tyrannus*, the *Medea*, and the *Septem*, two plays of Terence, eight satires of Juvenal and the *Odes* and *Epodes* of Horace; the Honours man read in addition the *Oedipus Coloneus*, the *Prometheus* and the *Knights*, two further plays of Terence, Persius and the *Ars Poetica*. The books for the final year were Aristotle's *Ethics* I to III, Cicero *De Officiis* I, Xenophon *Memorabilia* I and II, Horace *Satires* and *Epistles*, Thucydides VII and Lucretius I, to which the Honours man added books VI to IX of the *Ethics*, books II and III of *De Officiis*, books III and IV of the *Memorabilia* and *Annals* III to V. Examinations were held on the books read each term, while at the end of the fourth year came the Moderatorship, or Final Honours Examination, for which the books in 1853 were Aristotle's *Rhetoric* and *Poetics*, the *Eumenides* and *Frogs*, Pindar *Pythians*, Thucydides VII, Lucretius III and IV, *Annals* VI to XVI, Horace *Epistles* II and *Ars Poetica*.[1]

Considering that he had to study his other subjects as well, the reading of the Dublin Classical Honours man was extensive and varied. That for the ordinary degree is impressive both by modern standards and by comparison with contemporary Oxford and Cambridge, where the amount required was considerably less. But it may be doubted whether all the students left college with a thorough knowledge of their books. For though examinations for honours were partly written, those for pass students were oral, apart from Latin composition. The numbers involved were large, the time was inadequate for thorough questioning and it was easy for weak students to pass.[2]

By the end of the century the old system had to some extent been relaxed. It had proved impossible to maintain the exclusively classical entrance course; new subjects had come in and the amount of Greek and Latin required had been greatly reduced. The four-year arts course survived in essentials, but Greek and Latin were now compulsory only in the first two years. The course for

Classical Honours was much as it had been since its inception, with a wide variety of reading in addition to that of the ordinary course. Questions on Ancient History and Geography, Grammar and Literature were included, as was composition in Greek and Latin, both prose and verse.

Though the Dublin system ensured that all graduates were well read in the classics, it was not until the later nineteenth century that Trinity College became famous for its classical scholarship. The reason for this was that until then fellowships were awarded mainly for mathematics. The seventeenth-century statutes laid down that there should be a four-day examination consisting of Logic and Mathematics; Natural and Moral Philosophy; Languages and Humane Literature; and Latin theme and verse. With a fidelity to statute unknown in contemporary Oxford and Cambridge, Trinity College continued this examination until the mid-nineteenth century. At that time, apart from Latin composition, which was written, the examination was entirely oral, and the classical part of it was, as the whole examination had once been, conducted in Latin.[1] Examination in classics tended to be perfunctory, and what really counted was mathematics and natural philosophy.[2] Though scholarships were given entirely for classical learning, this was of little use for a fellowship, and the temptation was to let it rust after the scholarship was won. There were always some fellows who kept up their classics, and gave good service as teachers, for example Thomas Stack, professor of Greek from 1855 to 1866, whose heart, we are told, was 'thoroughly in the work of classical teaching as he understood it'.[3] But the old system, though it bred men of wide learning and culture, produced none who could be counted as outstanding classical scholars.

In 1855 alterations were made in the fellowship examinations which opened the way to that flowering of classical scholarship which marks Dublin of the later nineteenth century. The examination remained a general one, including mathematics, classics and philosophy, but its regulations were now more favourable to the classical scholar and it became possible to obtain a fellowship without strength in mathematics.[1] In 1863 the first such fellow was elected. He was followed in the next year by J. P. Mahaffy, whose earliest interest, however, was philosophy rather than classics, and in 1867 by Arthur Palmer, a skilful emendator of Latin texts, whose election is said to have inaugurated the triumph of pure scholarship at Dublin.[2] But the most influential figure in the Dublin Classical School was R. Y. Tyrrell, who was appointed fellow in 1868, professor of Latin in 1871 and of Greek in 1880, when Palmer succeeded to the Latin chair.[3] Tyrrell's interests were primarily literary; his strength lay in felicitous translation from and into Greek and Latin, and his graceful English renderings, we are told, filled the note-books of his admiring pupils.[4] He was a lively and stimulating teacher. His lectures were 'of the nature of a joint investigation with his pupils guided by a commanding and penetrating mind'. They were apt to be somewhat desultory, but they 'created a real, not a mere examination interest in the subjects he taught'. He brought into Dublin classical studies 'a new spirit whereby a fresh and vivid feeling for literature in general and for classical antiquity in particular was awakened, even if some loss of old world erudition was thereby sustained'.[5] His work was ably carried on by his pupil Purser, fellow from 1881, who was appointed to the chair of Latin in 1898.

Purser, like Palmer before him, specialised in Latin, but other Dublin scholars were marked by a capacity to distinguish themselves in divers fields of study. J. K. Ingram, professor of Greek from 1866 to 1877, was mathematician, philosopher and economist as well as classical scholar. Mahaffy wrote with distinction on a wide variety of subjects. Tyrrell held successively the professorships of Latin, Greek, and Ancient History; J. B. Bury was both professor of Greek and professor of Modern History, editor of Pindar and historian of the later Roman Empire. This versatility was a happy legacy from the old tradition of a wide general education.

CHAPTER XIV

CONCLUSION

Why do we study the classics? If a schoolmaster of the sixteenth century could have been asked this question he would hardly have understood it. Controversy over the advantages and disadvantages of a classical education belongs to a later age, when it was possible to envisage some alternative. This was hardly the case in the sixteenth century. There was certainly some opposition to the introduction of Greek and to humanist methods in Latin, but it came from the ignorant and prejudiced. The best minds of the day welcomed and encouraged humanism. Its opponents, the 'Trojans' of Oxford and their like, did not represent an alternative type of education so much as the same type in a lower form.

As long as all the best works of learning were in Latin or Greek there was clearly good reason for the study of these languages. But it might well be asked why they were studied as they were, why so much time was devoted to the reading of the poets and the imitation of the classical elegances of style. The answer would be that, as Erasmus put it, the knowledge of words is essential for the knowledge of things, and that the best way of acquiring a knowledge of a language is by reading good authors. The authors to be read first were those whose style was best and who would attract the reader by the charms of their subject.[1] The charms of Terence, Ovid and the *Eclogues* are not so easily appreciated by the young today, but we should not underestimate their appeal in an age which was not provided with copious and easy reading matter in the vernacular. Moreover, it would have been argued, there were valuable moral lessons to be learned from ancient literature, not only in the works of the professed philosophers and moralists, but also in writers whose object to us today seems to have been merely to entertain, but who could be made to yield moral lessons to an age determined to find them. There was no disposition, in the English scholastic world, to set up paganism in opposition to Christianity. The ideal was a combination of good literature and religion, the *pietas literata* of the Northern Renaissance.

Finally it should be remembered that humanist education was hardly new, for, as was pointed out at the beginning of this work, it was essentially the education of the ancient world. In an age which accepted almost without question the authority of the ancients there was nothing surprising in the adoption of methods supported by the best ancient authority on education, Quintilian. The object of the humanist movement was to return to the sources, to drink, as Cicero had put it, from the springs rather than from the rivulets that flowed from them. As the source of Christianity was to be found in the Scriptures and of philosophy in Plato and Aristotle, so for language and literature one must return to the best writers of Greece and Rome, to those authors who had been recognised as classical by the judgment of antiquity.

By the eighteenth century much had changed. We have seen in earlier chapters how the vernacular languages, instead of fading away as some humanists hoped, grew in strength and prestige, while Latin became, in the ordinary sense of the word, a dead language. We have seen too how the repute of the ancients declined with the rise of experimental science and of the new philosophy of Descartes and Locke. In the eighteenth century it was generally agreed that, though with the progress of knowledge the philosophy of the ancients had been superseded, this was not the case with their literature.

> In epic poetry [wrote Hugh Blair], Homer and Virgil, to this day, stand not within many degrees of any rival. Orators such as Cicero and Demosthenes we have none. In history, notwithstanding some defects ...it may be safely asserted, that we have no such historical narration, so elegant, so picturesque, so animated, and so interesting as that of Herodotus, Thucydides, Xenophon, Livy, Tacitus, and Sallust. Al-

though the conduct of the drama may be admitted to have received some improvements, yet for poetry and sentiment we have nothing to equal Sophocles and Euripides; nor any dialogue in comedy, that comes up to the correct, graceful and elegant simplicity of Terence. We have no such love elegies as those of Tibullus; no such pastorals as some of Theocritus's; and for lyric poetry, Horace stands quite unrivalled.[1]

Thus the classics were valued mainly for the training in taste and literary style which they provided. They were also still valued for their moral lessons. According to Swift, 'The books read at school and college are full of incitements to virtue, and discouragements from vice, drawn from the wisest reasons, the strongest motives, and the most influencing examples. Thus young minds are filled with an inclination to good and an abhorrence of evil, both of which increase in them, according to the advances they make in literature.'[2] Homer and Virgil, the Earl of Chatham wrote to his nephew, 'are not only the two greatest poets, but they contain the finest lessons for your age to imbibe: lessons of honour, courage, disinterestedness, love of truth, command of temper, gentleness of behaviour, humanity and in one word, virtue in its true signification'.[3]

While Plato and Aristotle were unduly ignored and depreciated, the moralists of later antiquity and the Roman satirists were held in high honour. Bishop Burnet, in his *Discourse of the Pastoral Care*, which was often reprinted in the eighteenth century, recommended the clergy to read 'Tully's Offices', a work which would 'give the Mind a noble Sett', the Roman satirists, who 'contribute wonderfully to give a man a detestation of Vice,' and above all Epictetus and Marcus Aurelius, whose works 'contain such Instructions, that one cannot read them too often nor repass them too frequently in his thoughts'.[4] Swift, who held that the inferiority of the heathen to the Christian world lay not in its moral teaching but in the lack of a divine sanction to support it, urged the young clergy to study the writings of the ancients, 'by the reading of which you will soon discover your Mind and Thoughts

169

to be enlarged, your Imagination extended and refined, your Judgment directed, your Admiration lessened and your Fortitude increased'.[1]

In the nineteenth century men's attitude to the classics changed further, and new arguments were used to justify a classical education. Some of these were of only temporary validity, such as the argument that the classics was the only subject which men knew how to teach and for which teachers were available; others were trivial and unworthy, such as the snobbish argument, which finds expression in some lectures given by Andrew Amos in 1846 to the boys of the City of London School *On the Advantages of a Classical Education as an Auxiliary to a Commercial Education.* In these he stressed the utility of the classics as enabling one 'to maintain with comfort and respectability the station of a gentleman', and warned his audience of the embarrassment they might incur if they betrayed their ignorance of the classics in the company of gentlemen, and of ladies too, for ladies particularly admired in men the intellectual attainments from which they were excluded.[2] In the nineteenth century the classics were no doubt regarded as the mark of a gentleman, but this was an accidental phenomenon resulting from the decay of the local grammar schools and the rise of the Public Schools. The creators of the Victorian Public School did not consciously devise an education for a governing class; they continued and adapted what had originally been the universal type of education, and because their schools were better than anything else available they attracted those who were or wished to become gentlemen.

Of the literary merits of the ancients the Victorians spoke with rather less confidence than the men of the eighteenth century. According to John Stuart Mill, the ancients were pre-eminent as regards perfection of form, whereas the moderns were superior in substance.[3] Others would have put the claims of ancient literature higher, but few would have maintained that it had an exclusive claim on one's attention. The typical cultured man of the nineteenth century, Tennyson, for example, or Matthew Arnold, was familiar with Dante, Shakespeare and Goethe, as well as Homer, Sophocles and Virgil. The ancients shared the throne with others, and whatever might still be said about the classics serving as models, there was no doubt that modern literature as a whole had deserted the ancients, and such classical influences as there were in modern literary works were the result of the taste of individuals rather than of a recognised tradition.

Much of the old confidence in the moral value of the classics was now lost.[1] Men ceased to respond to the old exhortations to virtue and heroism, and some of the inspiring works on which earlier generations had been nurtured dropped out of school and university reading. With the growth of the historic sense and the wider reading that was now encouraged there came a new consciousness of the differences between paganism and Christianity. 'No more forcible contrast', writes Dr Arnold's biographer, 'could have been drawn between the value of Christianity and of heathenism than the manner in which, for example, after reading in the earlier part of the lesson one of the scripture descriptions of the Gentile world, "Now", he said, as he opened the Satires of Horace, "we shall see what it was like."'[2] So far from looking to Tully's Offices and Juvenal to supplement the teaching of the Christian revelation, the clergy might be more inclined to defend a classical education on the grounds that by revealing the vices of the pagan world it led to a keener appreciation of Christianity.[3] There were also those who, faced with the contrast between paganism and Christianity, preferred the former, and embraced a Hellenism which meant for them a welcome freedom from moral restraints, while with the secularisation of the universities there grew up a new type of scholar schooled in the discipline of research to be indifferent to the lessons of antiquity whether moral or immoral.

Perhaps the firmest nineteenth-century believer in the moral value of the classics was one who was brought up and lived his life outside the world of church, school and university. John Stuart Mill had inherited from his father an eighteenth-century admiration for the wisdom of the ancients, and though he professed to regard the education of the English schools and universities 'with sentiments little short of utter abhorrence', he had no wish to banish the classics, and in his Rectorial Address to St Andrews University he vindicated, as he himself put it, 'the high educational value alike of the old classic and the new scientific studies, on even stronger grounds than are urged by most of their advocates'.[1]

In any course of instruction which aims at forming great minds, he wrote in 1836, ancient literature should fill a large part 'because it brings before us the thoughts and actions of many great minds ...and these related and exhibited in a manner tenfold more impressive, tenfold more calculated to call forth high aspirations, than in any modern literature'.[2] Later in life, in his St Andrews address, he spoke of the 'wisdom of life' and the 'maxims of singular good sense and penetration' to be found in ancient literature. The ancient world, he considered, had particular value for the modern world because it was unlike it without being too remote. By looking at facts through the eyes of other peoples the modern man could divest himself of preconceived notions, and so bring his opinions closer to facts. Classical antiquity provided examples of individual greatness to counteract the mediocrity of modern society and examples of patriotism and service to the state to counteract its selfishness, while the rigorous dialectic of the Platonic dialogues was a valuable corrective to modern looseness of thought.[3]

This sense of the difference between the ancient and the modern world was something new, the product of the historical sense of the nineteenth century and the passing of time which has loosened the bond which bound men to classical antiquity. It was also the result of an increased knowledge of Greece, for the Greeks are more remote from us than the Romans, and it was the Greeks that the Victorians had chiefly in mind when they spoke of the value of the classics. It was the Athenian democracy to which Mill's admiration was directed; it was Hellenism to which Matthew Arnold looked to correct the exaggerated Hebraism of his own day. The classics were now seen in their historical setting. They were the record of a civilisation whose importance for human history and whose achievements in the sphere of literature and thought gave it an especial claim on the attention of the educated man. 'Expel Greek and Latin from your schools', wrote Thomas Arnold in 1834, 'and you confine the views of the existing generation to themselves and their immediate predecessors; you will cut off so many centuries of the world's experience.'[1] 'The object of education', wrote his son Matthew in 1868, 'is to enable man to know himself and the world.... To know himself, a man must know the capabilities and performances of the human spirit; the value of the humanities, of *Alterthumswissenschaft*, the science of antiquity, is that it affords for this purpose an unsurpassed source of light and stimulus.'[2] The importance of the civilisations of Greece and Rome in the history of Western Europe was undeniable, whether one thought of them, like Gladstone, from the Christian point of view as providing a *praeparatio evangelica*,[3] or like Mill, from the secular point of view as having given birth to the ideas of political and intellectual freedom, or whether, like Matthew Arnold, one thought of Hellenism and Hebraism, intellectual and moral culture, as the two elements to be combined in a complete and harmonious humanity.

At the same time, though the importance of the classics was generally recognised,[4] there could be no return to the classicism, predominantly Latin in tone, of the eighteenth century. According to Thomas Mozley, writing in 1882, 'the poetry, the philosophy, the politics of the country have left the old classical models. The lines of thought have ceased to be classical.'[5] This was the case even with those whose formal education was exclusively classical. As Cardinal Newman said, 'the drift and meaning of a branch of knowledge varies with the company in which it is introduced to the student'.[1] The Victorian undergraduate would inevitably be open to many other influences besides those of the classics, would read Coleridge and Goethe, Carlyle and Mill, as well as Plato and Aristotle, and these would contribute to his outlook on life and to the way in which he regarded the classics. Moreover the ancient world had ceased to be a unity and had broken up into distinct periods and personalities. It is hardly possible to speak any more of classical influence without further definition. Historical study brought a new consciousness of the different character of different periods in the thousand years or so of ancient civilisation, and wider reading revealed the variety of ancient literature. Ancient philosophy ranged from Anaximander to Epictetus, ancient poetry from Sappho to Statius. Different men saw different aspects of the ancient world; the lessons which Nietzsche drew from Greece were very different from those drawn by Mill or Jowett.

Finally, the nineteenth century saw the fading away of the old rhetorical tradition. The ideal which inspired the ancient schools of grammar and rhetoric was that of the perfect orator, and the idea which inspired their teaching was that eloquence could be taught. The ancient methods, if not the ancient ideals, passed to the humanist schools; men were taught to write according to rules, to develop a theme in the recognised manner and to adorn it with elegant figures of speech and apt similes and examples. This was how for generations Englishmen received their literary training; they received it in a language not their own, and perhaps one of the indirect advantages of classical education in the past was that it saved Englishmen from being taught to write their own language and so left our literature relatively untouched by the deadening influence of ancient rhetoric. However that may be, the old rhetoric gave place in the nineteenth century to the new linguistic discipline that resulted from careful and accurate translation from and into the ancient languages. A classical education was now valued as a training in accuracy and precision, excellent qualities, but different from that copiousness and elegance of style which had been the aim of the older type of teaching.

Thus classical education was gradually transformed. The change was obscured by the continuity of our educational system and by the conservatism of the schoolroom, but it took place none the less. To put the matter in its simplest terms, with the passing of the centuries mankind moved gradually further away from the ancient world. Men ceased to use Latin, and their minds ceased to be formed by the Latin classics. In teaching the emphasis shifted from writing to reading. Men no longer read Latin in order to write it, and they wrote it now mainly in order to understand the language and appreciate the style of its writers. The ancient authors were read no longer as the accepted models of style, the teachers of morality and the authorities in science, but rather as representatives of a past civilisation which had a strong but not an exclusive claim on the interest and admiration of the modern world.

If Mill was right in his belief that one of the merits of a classical education was that it provided a corrective to the faults and weaknesses of his own day, this argument applies with no less force today than in the mid-Victorian period. There may be more public spirit now than there was then, but mediocrity and loose thinking are always with us; the Hebraism which Arnold attacked may have passed away, but whether there is more Hellenism than in his day is doubtful. In other respects we have moved still further from the ancient world. In literature and the arts we have seen a startling break with tradition, and above all the technological revolution which we are witnessing is transforming our lives and insensibly affecting our outlook, encouraging us to live in the present, judging everything by the standard of technical efficiency and assuming that the latest is always the best. Descartes compared the study of antiquity to foreign travel; it was useful, he said, to know something of the manners of different nations, but when too much time was spent in travelling, men became strangers to their own country, 'and the overcurious in the customs of the past are generally ignorant of those of the present'.[1] Today there is little danger of living in the past; men are more likely never to enlarge their minds by that form of foreign travel which we know as the study of the classics. Though the ancient writers are no longer regarded as models in literature or authorities in science, they are still classical in the sense that they can provide a standard by which we can judge our own age. We may decide that we have nothing to learn from them, but it is impossible even to reach this conclusion without hearing what they have to say.

It might of course be maintained that, granted the desirability of some study of the past, there are other periods as suitable for this purpose as those of ancient Greece and Rome. Certainly the old idea of the primacy of the classics has been gravely weakened, and the organisation of learning today would suggest that all ages, civilisations and literatures were of more or less equal value. Nor are there many today who would accept the old view that all was dark from the fall of Rome to the age when, in Pope's words, Erasmus 'stemm'd the wild torrent of a barbarous age', and even if this view were accepted it might be argued that since the time of Erasmus mankind had learned as much as it needed from the ancients and had incorporated it in modern literature and learning. But these considerations are not strong enough to shake the view that, if there is any period of human history on which our study of the past can profitably be concentrated, it is that in which the civilisations of Greece and Rome flourished. It was this period which saw the development of philosophy, of drama and of historiography, of democratic government and of the political oratory and political theorising that went with democracy. And if we owe our religion to Judea rather than to Greece or Rome, we should remember that its basic documents are in Greek and that its theology was formulated by men brought up in the Greco-Roman culture of the Empire.

Moreover the very fact that for so long men looked back to the ancients as their masters provides a ground for continuing to study them. Pope's advice to 'trace the Muses upward to their spring' is still relevant. For many centuries after the fall of Rome the ancient world lived on; politically it had passed away, but intellectually it survived. Virgil was Dante's guide; Aristotle to him was 'master of them that know'. What we call the Renaissance was only the most complete of a series of such movements in which intellectual advance came from a return to the sources of civilisation, and the recovery of the classics at the Renaissance gave them a hold over men's minds which only gradually weakened. Any study of European literature and thought down to at least the eighteenth century needs to begin with Greece and Rome, and the study of the classics helps to unite the modern man not only with the men of the ancient world but with all those who in later centuries learned from them.

It may be said that a sufficient knowledge of the literature and thought of antiquity can be obtained through translation, but to admit this would be to abandon that training in verbal accuracy which the nineteenth century made so important a part of classical education and which we can ill afford to lose. For if in the last century superficiality and inaccuracy needed to be counteracted by a slow and careful linguistic training, this is no less the case today when new media of communication have been developed which require even less attention on the part of the receiver than popular journalism. This side of classical education is one whose value is perhaps better appreciated by teachers than by their pupils, and it has sometimes been derided as a dry pedantry which kills the spirit of the ancient authors by making them mere vehicles for grammatical discipline. Yet the traditional methods of classical teaching are not in themselves conducive to grammatical pedantry, for the constant practice of translation from and into the ancient languages saves much grammatical explanation and should reveal rather than obscure the mind and imagination of the authors so handled.

Finally, it is sometimes said that the classics involve so great an expenditure of time that they can only be regarded as an educational luxury, and that while such an education may have been well enough suited to the leisured gentleman of the past, it has no place in the busy world of today. But if the acquisition of Greek and Latin is necessarily a slow process, it brings with it certain incidental advantages. A child taught Latin at an early age needs little instruction in the correct use of English, and an acquaintance with ancient poetry can save much laborious explanation of classical allusions in modern works of literature. Plato and Aristotle provide a well tried introduction to philosophy, and as a training in historical study Thucydides and Tacitus have the advantage of being at once primary sources and works of literary distinction. Indeed, so far from being a luxury, a classical education might be considered as remarkably economical in that, in addition to what is peculiar to itself, it includes much of what can be obtained from the study of other subjects. It cannot of course claim to include science, for the days are long past when Aristotle was sufficient authority for the knowledge of nature, and the science of today is based for the most part on methods unknown to the ancient world. To argue the claims of the classics does not mean to deny or depreciate those of science, and there is much to be said for Mill's view that these two branches of learning should be combined together instead of being regarded as rival alternatives, though such a programme would be hard to realise today when modern history, languages and literatures, which Mill would have excluded from the ordinary curriculum, have won so large a place in our school and university education.

But it is no part of this work to enter upon the educational problems of the present day. It will be enough to have suggested that the classics have not lost their relevance and that there should still be a place for them in our education. If the reasons which justified the humanist education of the sixteenth century have lost much of their validity, this is no ground for rejecting the classical education which derives from it. Continuity does not necessarily mean stagnation, and a system which was devised for one age can with modifications be made to suit the needs of a different age, provided that it is based on what is of permanent value. To the classical teacher today, the schoolmaster cramped by the exigencies of a crowded timetable, or the university teacher looking enviously at the crowded lecture rooms of his colleagues in other departments, these pages may seem like the record of a vanished golden age; yet they may also suggest some reflections which are not entirely gloomy. Though the old prestige of the classics has departed, they are no longer subject to the criticism which is commonly directed against the established or the odium which attaches to the compulsory. If the high standard reached in the major schools of the nineteenth century has hardly been maintained, it is unlikely that the classics are anywhere today taught with so little profit as they were in some of the lesser schools a hundred years ago. Finally the classics survived, in spite of all the adverse influences of the nineteenth century. It is not difficult to imagine English education taking a different path if, let us say, Dr Arnold had devoted his energies to evolving a new type of education instead of revivifying the old. But he did not, and the fact that neither he nor the many other Victorians of high ability who devoted themselves to education lost faith in the classics is a testimony to their vitality.

NOTES

PAGE 5

1 1509 is the traditional date for the foundation of St Paul's, but the school was not fully established until 1512.

2 To save further reference, the sources for the statutes and other educational documents used in this chapter are given here.

ALDENHAM. Ordinances, 1599. *Victoria County History, Hertfordshire*, vol. II, pp. 83–4 (summary).

BANGOR, FRIARS. Statutes, 1598. H. Barber and H. Lewis, *History of Friars School, Bangor* (1901), pp. 139–57; L. S. Knight, *Welsh Independent Grammar Schools to 1600* (Newtown, 1926), pp. 94–105.

BLACKBURN. Statutes, 1597. G. A. Stocks, *Records of Blackburn School* (Chetham Society, New Series, vol. 66) (1909), pp. 72–5.

BURY ST EDMUNDS. Statutes, 1550. *Victoria County History, Suffolk*, vol. II, pp. 313–15 (summary). The statutes are printed in full, in an English translation, in *Original Statutes of King Edward VI Grammar School, Bury St Edmunds* (Bury, 1878).

CAMBERWELL. Statutes, 1615. N. Carlisle, *Concise Description of the Endowed Grammar Schools in England and Wales* (2 vols. 1818), vol. II, p. 560.

CANTERBURY, KING'S SCHOOL. Statutes, 1541. A. F. Leach, *Educational Charters and Documents* (Cambridge, 1911), pp. 464–8.

CUCKFIELD. Curriculum, 1528 (copied from Eton). *Etoniana*, 19 July 1911.

DURHAM. Statutes, 1593. *Victoria County History, Durham*, vol. I, pp. 377–8.

EAST RETFORD. Statutes, 1552. Carlisle, *op. cit.* vol. II, pp. 282–4.

ETON. Time-table, 1528 (see Cuckfield above); Time-table, 1530 (Leach, *op. cit.* p. 451); Malim's *Consuetudinarinm*, 1560 (*Etoniana*, 6 December 1905; summarised in H. C. Maxwell-Lyte, *History of Eton College* (1899), pp. 149–50).

GUISBOROUGH. Statutes, 1561. T. W. Baldwin, *William Shakspere's small Latine & lesse Greeke* (Urbana, 2 vols. 1944), vol. I, pp. 430–1.

HARROW. Statutes, 1590. *The Commemoration of the Tercentenary of Harrow School* (1871), pp. xxvi–xxviii.

HAWKSHEAD. Statutes, 1588. Carlisle, *op. cit.* vol. I, pp. 656–61.

HEXHAM. Ordinances, 1600. *A History of Northumberland* (Northumberland County History Committee), 1893–1909, vol. III, pp. 214–15.

IPSWICH. Wolsey's letter to the masters, 1528. J. Strype, *Ecclesiastical Memorials...* (1822), vol. I, pt. ii, pp. 139–43. Ordinances, 1571; I. E. Gray and W. E. Potter, *Ipswich School* (1950), pp. 39–41.

KIRKBY STEPHEN. Statutes, 1566. Carlisle, *op. cit.* vol. II, p. 717.

MANCHESTER. Statutes, 1525. A. A. Mumford, *Manchester Grammar School* (1919), pp. 473–83.

NORWICH. Statutes, 1566. H. W. Saunders, *History of the Norwich Grammar School* (Norwich, 1932), pp. 144–8.

OAKHAM and UPPINGHAM. Statutes, 1625. Carlisle, *op. cit.* vol. II, p. 325.

RIVINGTON. Statutes, *c.* 1570. Margaret M. Kay, *The History of Rivington and Blackrod Grammar School* (Manchester, 1931), pp. 163–89.

RUTHIN. Statutes, 1595. R. Newcome, *Memoir of Gabriel Goodman* (Ruthin, 1825), Appendix F. English version in Knight, *op. cit.* pp. 113–22.

ST BEES. Statutes, 1583. Carlisle, *op. cit.* vol. I, pp. 156–8.

ST PAUL'S. Statutes, 1518. J. H. Lupton, *Life of Dean Colet* (1909), pp. 271–84.

SANDWICH, SIR ROGER MANWOOD'S. Statutes, 1580. Carlisle, *op. cit.* vol. I, pp. 605–6.

SHREWSBURY. Ordinances, 1578. *Baker's History of the College of St John the Evangelist, Cambridge,* ed. J. E. B. Mayor (Cambridge, 2 vols. 1869), pp. 409–13.

SOUTHWARK, ST SAVIOUR'S. Statutes, 1562. *Victoria County History, Surrey,* vol. II, p. 177.

TIDESWELL. Statutes, 1560. *Victoria County History, Derbyshire,* vol. II, p. 248.

WESTMINSTER. Statutes, *c.* 1570. Leach, *op. cit.* pp. 506–18. (For the date see Baldwin, *op. cit.* vol. I, pp. 380–1.)

WINCHESTER. Time-table, 1530. Leach, *op. cit.* pp. 448–50.

WITTON. Statutes, 1558. Carlisle, *op. cit.* vol. I. p. 131.

PAGE 6

1 C. S. Lewis, *English Literature in the Sixteenth Century excluding Drama* (1954), p. 160.

2 D. L. Clark, *John Milton at St Paul's School* (1948), pp. 101–2.

3 See Lupton, *Life of Dean Colet,* p. 76.

4 *Erasmi Epistolae* (ed. P. S. Allen, 1906–47), 230 (vol. I, p. 470); 258 (vol. I, p. 508). Cf. Erasmus, *Opera* (1703), vol. I, 521.

5 The eight-form system was, as Strype suggested (*Ecclesiastical Memorials* (1822), vol. I, p. 181), taken from St Paul's. That the programme of reading was also is only a conjecture, though a probable one (Baldwin, *William Shakspere's small Latine & lesse Greeke,* vol. I, p. 118). In Erasmus's Colloquy *Pietas Puerilis* the schoolboy Gaspar, who has been brought up by Colet, and who is believed to be based on Thomas Lupset, reads only the chaste poets,

and if there is any indecent passage in what he reads passes over it as Ulysses passed the Sirens.

6 Juvencus, Prudentius and Palingenius at St Saviour's, Southwark; Mantuanus, Palingenius, Buchanan, Sedulius and Prudentius at St Bees; Mantuanus at Canterbury; Buchanan at Rivington; Mantuanus and Palingenius at Durham and Hexham; Palingenius at Aldenham. The statutes of Witton, while borrowing Colet's formula about 'Christian authors that wrote their wisdom with clean and chaste Latin', specify only pagan authors.

PAGE 7

1 Charles Hoole in the seventeenth century states that Mantuan's *Eclogues* were read in most schools (*A New Discovery of the Old Art of Teaching Schoole* (ed. 1913), p. 65).

2 Stanbridge (1463–1510) and Whittington (*fl.* 1520) both published a number of grammatical works in the early sixteenth century. Stanbridge after teaching at Magdalen College School, Oxford, moved to Banbury. His teaching there had a considerable reputation, as can be seen from the statutes of Manchester Grammar School in which the master is directed to teach grammar 'after the school use, manner and form of the school of Banbury in Oxfordshire'.

3 R. Ascham, *Scholemaster* (ed. Arber, 1927), pp. 27–8.

PAGE 8

1 Strype, *Stow's Survey* (1710), vol. I, bk. I, p. 124. For medieval practice see William Fitzstephen, *Vita S. Thomae*, prologus 8: 'Pueri diversarum scholarum versibus inter se conrixantur; aut de principiis artis grammaticae vel regulis praeteritorum vel supinorum contendunt.'

2 According to Hoole, writing in 1659, the Aesop then generally in use was 'a mere Rapsodie of some fragments' of translations by Erasmus and his contemporaries (*New Discovery*, p. 61). *Sententiae Pueriles*, a collection of simple moral maxims for beginners made by Leonhard Culmann in 1544, is recommended by Brinsley, *Ludus Literarius* (ed. 1917), p. 142.

PAGE 9

1 Bury, East Retford, Witton, Bangor, Rivington, Westminster, Harrow, Durham, Ruthin, Aldenham.

2 Vives is found at Eton (1560), Norwich, Rivington, Westminster and Ruthin. At Ruthin it is his *Introductio ad Sapientiam* that is specified, and it may be that 'Vives' in other documents means this work rather than the *Colloquies*. The ordinances of Shrewsbury mention 'two litle books of Dialogues drawen oute of Tulleys Offices and Ludovicus Vives by Mr Thomas Ashton' (headmaster 1561–71).

3 Rivington, Westminster and Sandwich. Little is heard of this work after the sixteenth century (though Hoole, *New Discovery*, p. 69, recommends it), but the appearance of a fourteenth English edition in 1715 attests its continued popularity.

4 *Carmen de Moribus*, Ipswich, 1528 (no doubt used elsewhere owing to its inclusion in Lily's grammar). *Christiani Hominis Institutum*, St Paul's and Witton. *De Moribus in Mensa*, Eton (1530), Blackburn. *De Quattuor Virtutibus*, Bury, Bangor and Harrow.

5 Erasmus, *Opera* (1703), vol. I, 521.

6 Erasmus, *De Pueris...Liberaliter Instituendis* (*Opera*, vol. I, 510). Statutes of Kirkby Stephen school, Westmorland.

PAGE 10

1 It is only in the closely related statutes of Bury and Bangor that we find any mention of Plautus.

2 For Roman practice see Eugraphius, *Commentum Andriae*, prologus. For English practice, Robert Laneham, quoted in Strype, *Stow's Survey* (1720), vol. I, bk. ii, p. 121: 'I went to School, forsooth, both at *Polles* [St Paul's] and also at *St Antonies*; was in the fifth Forme, past *Esops* Fables, red *Terence, Vos istaec intro auferte*: [the first line of the *Andria*] And began with my Virgil; *Tityre tu patulae.*'

3 H. C. Maxwell-Lyte, *History of Eton College*, pp. 118, 159.

4 A similar provision (Statutes, 24) did not prevent the Christmas plays at Trinity College, Cambridge, from dying out. In the early eighteenth century they were no longer in use (E. Miller, *Account of the University of Cambridge...* (1717), p. 119).

5 *Epistolae*, Cuckfield, Rivington, Hexham. *Fasti*, Ipswich. *Letters from Pontus*, Aldenham.

PAGE 11

1 The *Georgics* are, however, mentioned in the statutes of Bury and Bangor as alternatives to the *Eclogues*.

2 At Aldenham Lucan and Seneca's tragedies, and at Hexham Lucan, are prescribed as alternatives to more familiar authors.

3 At Norwich and St Saviour's, Southwark.

4 *Acts of the Privy Council*, 21 April 1582; Strype, *Annals*, vol. III, pt. i, pp. 224-5.

PAGE 12

1 So the statutes of East Retford recommend Cicero's *Letters* 'for the familiar phrase of the same'.

2 Erasmus, *Opera*, vol. I, 521.

PAGE 13

1 Justin, Eton (1560), Westminster, St Bees, Ruthin, Southwark, Aldenham. Valerius Maximus, Eton (1560), Norwich, Southwark.

2 J. Brinsley, *Ludus Literarius* (ed. 1917), p. 41.

PAGE 14

1 Manchester, Cuckfield, Canterbury, Bury, Rivington, Bangor, Ipswich (1571), Shrewsbury, Harrow, Ruthin. At Ruthin it is laid down that the lower three forms should speak English and the upper three Latin. This appears to be due less to a desire to make things easier than to the necessity of practising Welsh-speaking boys in English as well as Latin; those in the upper forms were to be punished for speaking English, those in the lower for speaking Welsh.

2 R. Ascham, *Scholemaster* (ed. Arber), pp. 28–9.

3 Similar provisions at Bury, Bangor and Harrow. The vocabulary given at the beginning of Stanbridge's *Vulgaria* (1519) corresponds roughly with the first half of the list in the Rivington statutes.

PAGE 15

1 R. Ascham, *Scholemaster* (ed. Arber), p. 25. Brinsley, *Ludus Literarius*, p. 148, echoes Ascham's criticisms. Whittington's *Vulgaria* along with that of Stanbridge (1519) was reprinted by the Early English Text Society in 1932 (ed. Beatrice White).

2 *De Conscribendis Epistolis* is found at Eton (1530), Bury, Bangor, Rivington and Harrow. Other books in use were Hegedorff's *Methodus Conscribendi Epistolas* (1537), and Macropedius, *Methodus de Conscribendis Epistolis*, both of which Brinsley (*Ludus Literarius*, p. 168) considered of little use.

3 Erasmus, *De Conscribendis Epistolis*, 7 (*Opera*, vol. 1, 350).

PAGE 16

1 Brinsley, *Ludus Literarius* (ed. 1917), p. 184. Cf. the Westminster statutes: 'Duo aut tres a ludimagistro assignati de proposito themate declament idque publice in aula coram universa collegii frequentia pulsata prius campana.'

2 *Ad Herennium*, Bury, Norwich, Durham. Quintilian, Bury, Norwich, Rivington. Aphthonius, Sandwich, Rivington, Norwich, Blackburn. Cf. Brinsley, *Ludus Literarius*, p. 172.

3 King's School, Canterbury.

4 Erasmus, *De Copia*, vol. 1, 33 (*Opera*, vol. 1, 23–30).

PAGE 17

1 Brinsley, *Ludus Literarius*, p. 191.

2 One of the methods advocated by Brinsley, *Ludus Literarius*, p. 107.

3 John Stockwood, *Progymnasma Scholasticum* (1597), pp. 413–49. Stockwood also shows how a single hexameter line can be turned 104 different ways keeping the same words (pp. 458–63).

4 See M. F. J. McDonnell, *History of St Paul's School* (1909), pp. 45–7.

PAGE 18

1 T. Warton, *Life of Sir Thomas Pope* (1772), p. 227. Maxwell-Lyte, *History of Eton College*, p. 105. The references to Greek in Horman's *Vulgaria* have been taken to show that the language was taught in the late fifteenth century at Eton and Winchester, of which schools Horman was successively headmaster (Eton, 1485–94, Winchester, 1494–1502) (A. F. Leach, *History of Winchester College* (1899), pp. 227–9). They do not in fact provide valid evidence. The *Vulgaria* are in part based on Horman's experience as a teacher, but he explains in his preface that much of his old material has been lost and that he has added to it. A. A. Tilley (*English Hist. Rev.* vol. LIII (1938), pp. 452–3), following M. R. James, regards the *Vulgaria* as evidence for the teaching of Greek at Eton at the time of its publication (1519). We have Pope's evidence that it was taught about then, but Horman does not give very strong confirmation, and some of his references to Greek suggest the university rather than the school, e.g. 'He hath founded a reder in Greke for a c. ducatts a year. Profitenti Graece annua centena constituit' and 'I shall rede openly a lectur of greke if so be that honest wages be assigned out for the yere. Publice Graece profitebor modo honestum salarium sive honesta annua mihi constituant.'

2 Warton, *Life of Sir Thomas Pope*, p. 227.

3 Norwich, Rivington, Bangor, Shrewsbury. The Rivington statutes were probably not completed until after 1570 (see M. M. Kay, *History of Rivington and Blackrod Grammar School*, p. 31 n.), but may well reflect the practice of the school since its foundation in 1566. Similarly the Shrewsbury Ordinances are dated 1578, but they are based on the curriculum under Thomas Ashton, headmaster 1561–71. Andrew Downes the Greek scholar entered the school in 1562.

4 Erasmus, *Opera*, vol. I, 521. Sir Thomas Elyot held that a child should learn Greek and Latin at the same time, or should begin with Greek (*Governour*, bk. I, ch. x).

5 In the method used by Bonner at Rotherham in the early seventeenth century, which, according to Hoole, was the same as that used by most schoolmasters, Greek books were construed into Latin (Hoole, *New Discovery*, pp. 298–304). For English as an alternative to Latin see Brinsley, *Ludus Literarius*, pp. 223, 239.

PAGE 19

1 Cebes, Norwich and Rivington; Aesop, Norwich and Bangor; Lucian, Norwich and Westminster.

2 The *Cyropaedia* is specified at Shrewsbury. Xenophon is also found at Ruthin; Demosthenes at Westminster, Harrow, Durham and Blackburn; Isocrates at Bangor, Rivington, Shrewsbury (*Ad Demonicum*), Harrow, Durham, Ruthin, Blackburn; Homer at Norwich, Westminster, Durham, Ruthin, Blackburn; Hesiod at Norwich, Harrow, Durham, Blackburn.

3 Norwich and Rivington.

4 Theognis was regarded as useful for Greek verse-composition (Brinsley, *Ludus Literarius*, pp. 240, 242).

5 This is almost certainly the case with 'Basills Epistells', one of which was printed in Clenardus (compare the ordinances of Hexham school, which mention 'Basil's Epistles at the end of Clenardus's grammar'), and might also apply to Theocritus and Pindar. I suggest that in the passage of the statutes transcribed as 'Pindarus, *Olnithrace*, *Demostenes* Oracions', the word 'Olnithrace' should be emended to Olympia. The editor takes it to refer to Demosthenes's *Olynthiacs*.

6 Erasmus, *Opera*, vol. 1, 934. See Brinsley, *Ludus Literarius*, pp. 242–3.

7 Cf. the statutes of Ely Cathedral School (1544, revised under Elizabeth): 'Hos pueros volumus impensis ecclesiae nostrae ali donec mediocrem Latinae grammaticae notitiam adepti fuerint et Latine loqui et Graece scribere didicerint.' *Cathedrals Commission Report* (1854), p. 161.

8 Orations, epistles and verses in Latin and Greek at Hawkshead. Epistles, themes, orations and verses in Latin and Greek at Durham. Variations, double translations, disputations, verses, epistles, themes and declamations in Latin and Greek at Blackburn. The Rivington statutes mention the exercise of turning Greek into Latin and Latin into Greek, which would correspond to translating Latin into English and then re-translating.

9 Camberwell, Oakham and Uppingham.

PAGE 20

1 Brinsley, *Ludus Literarius*, p. 242.

2 Erasmus, *Opera*, vol. 1, 923. On the occasion of Edward VI's visit to Winchester in 1552 forty-three boys wrote Latin verses, one Greek verses (A. F. Leach, *History of Winchester College* (1899), p. 281). The publication of a collection of Greek epigrams by John Stockwood of Tonbridge School (*Progymnasma Scholasticum*, 1597) suggests an interest in Greek verse-composition, though as the epigrams are accompanied by a number of Latin elegiac versions the intention may have been rather to help with Latin verse-writing. The fact that the Greek is printed with an interlinear transliteration in Roman

characters 'ne lectionis difficultas iuniores a legendo deterreret' suggests that Greek teaching was still rather imperfect.

PAGE 21

1 Erasmus, *Opera*, vol. I, 521.

PAGE 22

1 *Ibid.* 522.
2 *Erasmi Epistolae* (ed. P. S. Allen), no. 185 (vol. I, p. 415).
3 *Statutes of the Colleges of Oxford* (1853), vol. II, Statutes of Corpus Christi College, cap. 21.

PAGE 23

1 T. Fowler, *The History of Corpus Christi College* (Oxford, 1893), pp. 87–8.
2 *Erasmi Epistolae* (ed. Allen), no. 907 (vol. III, p. 463).
3 J. A. Gee, *Life and Works of Thomas Lupset*, pp. 96–7.
4 *Erasmi Epistolae* (ed. Allen), vol. III, p. 508; H. C. Maxwell-Lyte, *History of the University of Oxford to 1530* (1886), p. 439.

PAGE 24

1 J. Jortin, *Life of Erasmus*, vol. II, pp. 662–7; *Erasmi Epistolae* (ed. Allen), no. 948 (vol. III, pp. 546–7).
2 *Ibid.* no. 948 (vol. III, pp. 546–7.)
3 *Ibid.* no. 233 (vol. I, p. 473).
4 J. B. Mullinger, *The University of Cambridge* (3 vols. Cambridge, 1873–1911), vol. I, p. 518.
5 *Ibid.* vol. I, pp. 529–37. In a further oration Croke encouraged his students to persevere.
6 J. Strype, *Life of Sir Thomas Smith* (1820), pp. 13–14. Strype says that Smith read 'Socrates and Euripides' for philosophy and morality. As elsewhere he describes Smith as a 'great Platonist' (p. 159), I assume that by Socrates he means Plato.

PAGE 25

1 R. Ascham, *Works* (ed. Giles), vol. I, p. 26.
2 Mullinger, *The University of Cambridge*, vol. II, pp. 54–7; J. Strype, *Life of Sir John Cheke* (1821), pp. 14–19, *Life of Sir Thomas Smith* (1820), pp. 10–13.
3 Ascham, *Works*, vol. I, pp. 26–7. According to Cheke, Gardiner's edict resulted in an unprecedented number of defections from the Greek class. *Joannis Cheki Angli de Pronuntiatione Graecae potissimum Linguae Disputationes* (Basle, 1555), p. 104. See pp. 18–21 for the text of Gardiner's edict.

PAGE 26

1 Ascham, *Works*, vol. I, pp. 26–7. Smith's letter, written in August 1542, was printed in Paris in 1568, with the title *De Recta et Emendata Linguae Graecae Pronuntiatione*. The correspondence of Cheke and Gardiner is to be found in the work cited in the previous note.

2 Mullinger, *The University of Cambridge*, vol. II, pp. 59–63.

3 Ascham, *Works*, vol. II, pt. 2, pp. 67–8.

4 *Ibid.* vol. I, pt. 2, pp. 220, 226; Epistle to Sir W. Cecil prefixed to Wilson's translation of Demosthenes's *Olynthiacs*, quoted in Arber's edition of Ascham's *Scholemaster*, p. 6.

5 Ascham, *Works*, vol. I, pt. 2, p. 221.

6 Quoted in Arber's edition of Ascham's *Scholemaster*, p. 7.

PAGE 27

1 *Ibid.*; Ascham, *Works*, vol. I, pt. 2, p. 226.

2 Ascham, *Scholemaster* (ed. Arber), p. 129.

3 Ascham, *Works*, vol. II, pt. 2, p. 67.

4 Edward Grant, *Oratio de Vita et Obitu Rogeri Aschami*, in Ascham's *Works*, vol. III, p. 315. Ascham lectured privately on Thucydides, Herodotus, Demosthenes and Isocrates, and also expounded, whether publicly or privately, various philosophers, orators and poets (*ibid.* p. 313). *Epistola de Vita et Obitu Nicolai Carri*, by Bartholomew Dodington, printed with Carr's Latin version of Demosthenes's *Olynthiacs* and *Philippics* (1571).

5 Bacon, *Advancement of Learning*. *Works*, ed. by J. Spedding, R. L. Ellis and D. D. Heath (14 vols. 1857–74), vol. III, p. 284.

6 Ascham, *Works*, vol. I, pp. 189–90.

PAGE 28

1 Ascham, *Scholemaster* (ed. Arber), p. 136.

2 *Statutes of the Colleges of Oxford*, vol. II, Statutes of Cardinal College, pp. 127–8; C. E. Mallet, *History of the University of Oxford* (1924–7), vol. I, p. 440.

3 A. à Wood, *Athenae Oxonienses* (1813), vol. I, 546–7.

4 Anthony Walker, *Life of John Bois*, in F. Peck, *Desiderata Curiosa* (1779), p. 328.

5 *Baker's History of the College of St John the Evangelist, Cambridge*, ed. Mayor (2 vols. 1869), vol. I, p. 171. (Baker refers to a MS. life of Bois, presumably that printed by Peck.) Mullinger, *The University of Cambridge*, vol. II, pp. 419–20.

PAGE 29

1 Peck, *Desiderata Curiosa*, p. 329. The statutes of St John's specifically state that the Greek lecturer must give his pupils something to write in Greek or

translate into Greek. *Documents relating to the University and Colleges of Cambridge* (1852), vol. III, St John's Statutes, cap. xvii.

2 Peck, *Desiderata Curiosa*, pp. 328–9; *Baker's History of the College of St John...*, vol. I, p. 180.

3 Peck, *Desiderata Curiosa*, p. 331.

4 À Wood, *Athenae Oxonienses*, vol. II, 13. The two orations delivered by Rainolds as Greek reader in 1576 and published in 1587 are moral exhortations, adorned with copious classical illustrations.

5 See I. Bywater, *Four Centuries of Greek Learning in England* (1919), p. 13.

PAGE 30

1 Ascham, *Works*, vol. I, pt. 2, p. 353.

2 Quoted in *D.N.B. s.v.* Henry Cuffe.

PAGE 31

1 Mullinger, *The University of Cambridge*, vol. I, pp. 629–30.

2 *Ibid.* vol. II, pp. 109–11; C. E. Mallet, *History of the University of Oxford* (1924–7), vol. II, pp. 84–5.

3 Mallet, *History of the University of Oxford*, vol. II, p. 120.

4 Bartholomew Dodington, professor of Greek at Cambridge from 1562 to 1585, often lectured to empty benches. Mullinger, *The University of Cambridge*, vol. II, p. 426, n. 4.

PAGE 32

1 Mallet, *History of the University of Oxford*, vol. II, pp. 4–6; *Statutes of the Colleges of Oxford*, vol. II, Statutes of Brasenose College, cap. xi.

2 Mullinger, *The University of Cambridge*, vol. I, pp. 459, 623; *Documents Relating to the University and Colleges of Cambridge* (3 vols. 1852), vol. III, p. 201; *Early Statutes of the College of St John*, ed. J. E. B. Mayor (Cambridge, 1859), p. 250.

3 Mullinger, *The University of Cambridge*, vol. I, p. 630; Mallet, *History of the University of Oxford*, vol. II, pp. 62–3.

4 Mallet, *History of the University of Oxford*, vol. II. pp. 157, 159–60; *Statutes of the Colleges of Oxford*, vol. III, Statutes of St John's College, cap. 24.

PAGE 33

1 Mullinger, *The University of Cambridge*, vol. II, pp. 595–9.

2 Peck, *Desiderata Curiosa*, p. 329.

PAGE 34

1 W. M. Warlow, *History of the Charities of William Jones* (Bristol, 1899), p. 358; Carlisle, *Concise Description of the Endowed Grammar Schools*, vol. I,

p. 418. Cf. the statutes of Newport (Salop) (1656), Woodbridge (1662) and Wigan (1664) (Carlisle, *op. cit.* vol. II, pp. 359, 540; vol. I, pp. 728–9).

2 Newport (Salop) (Carlisle, *op. cit.* vol. II, 359); Wigan (*ibid.* vol. I, p. 730); Southampton (*Victoria County History, Hampshire,* vol. II, p. 390). A. K. Cook, *About Winchester College,* p. 302; Dryden, *Works* (1893), vol. XVIII, p. 100. Cf. G. F. Russell Barker, *Memoir of Richard Busby* (1895), p. 93.

3 William Lilly, *History of his Life and Times* (1715), p. 6; *Life of Adam Martindale* (Chetham Society, vol. IV, 1845), p. 15.

4 Archbishop Holgate was a pioneer in the introduction of Hebrew into the schools. At his school at Old Malton, Yorks (1546) the Master was to 'have understanding' in Latin, Greek and Hebrew, and at his later foundation of East Retford (1552) the Master was to teach Hebrew grammar 'if he be expert in the same' (Carlisle, *Concise Description of the Endowed Grammar Schools,* vol. II, pp. 284, 858). For Hebrew at Westminster see Leach, *Educational Charters and Documents,* p. 513; at Merchant Taylors', C. M. Clode, *Memorials of the Guild of Merchant Taylors* (privately printed, 1875), p. 408; at St Paul's, Strype, *Stow's Survey of London* (1710), vol. I, bk. i, p. 164; at Ashby de la Zouch, Lilly, *History of his Life and Times,* p. 5; at Rotherham, Hoole, *New Discovery* (ed. 1913), pp. 191–5, 302; see also Foster Watson, *English Grammar Schools to 1660* (Cambridge, 1908), p. 529.

PAGE 35

1 Hoole, *New Discovery,* p. 194.

2 Milton's *Works* (Columbia edition), vol. III, p. 302.

3 *Autobiography and Correspondence of Sir Simonds D'Ewes,* ed. J. O. Halliwell [-Phillipps] (2 vols. 1845), vol. I, p. 102; William Lilly, *History of his Life and Times,* p. 6.

4 See the account of Westminster school *c.* 1630 quoted in F. H. Forshall, *Westminster School* (1884), pp. 415–17; T. Sargeaunt, *Annals of Westminster School* (1898), pp. 279–82; and Russell Barker, *Memoir of Richard Busby,* pp. 77–81. Lord Halifax when at Westminster was noted for his extemporary epigrams (Johnson, *Lives of the Poets* (World's Classics edition), vol. I, p. 391).

PAGE 36

1 Evelyn, *Diary,* 13 May 1661.

2 John Hacket, *Scrinia Reserata: A Memorial Offer'd to the Great Deservings of John Williams, D.D.* (1693), p. 45.

3 Johnson, *Lives of the Poets* (World's Classics edition), vol. I, p. 302.

4 Maittaire, quoted in G. F. Russell Barker, *Memoir of Richard Busby,* p. 45.

5 Henry Felton, *A Dissertation on Reading the Classics...* (1718), pp. 41–2. Examples of Greek texts without Latin translations printed *in usum scholae*

Westmonasteriensis are ΑΝΘΟΛΟΓΙΑ ΔΕΥΤΕΡΑ *sive Graecorum epigrammatum florilegium novum*, 1667; Aeschylus, *Choephori* with the *Electra* plays of Sophocles and Euripides, 1729; ἐκ τῶν περὶ ΣΩΚΡΑΤΟΥΣ (selections from Plato and Xenophon), 1760.

PAGE 37

1 Sargeaunt, *Annals of Westminster School*, pp. 119–20; M. L. Clarke, *Greek Studies in England, 1700–1830* (1945), pp. 224–5. Philip Henry, a pupil of Busby, was 'very ready and exact in the greek accents' (*An Account of the Life and Death of Mr Philip Henry* (1797), p. 6).

2 Dryden, Dedication to *The Rival Ladies*, *Dramatic Works* (1882), vol. II, p. 136.

3 Note prefixed to Dryden's translation of Persius's third satire, *Works* (1887), vol. XIII, p. 232.

4 *Autobiography of Sir John Bramston*, ed. Lord Braybrooke (Camden Society, 1845), p. 101; à Wood, *Athenae Oxonienses* (1813), vol. III, p. 214.

PAGE 38

1 D. Masson, *Life of Milton* (7 vols. 1859–94), vol. III, pp. 253–4.

PAGE 39

1 Hoole, *New Discovery*, pp. 196, 198, 207.

2 For particulars of these and other works referred to by Hoole see the notes in E. T. Campagnac's edition of *New Discovery* (1913).

3 Hoole, *New Discovery*, pp. 183–5.

PAGE 40

1 *Ibid.* pp. 157–60.

2 *Ibid.* pp. 186–8.

3 But see the brief account of the school *c.* 1679 quoted in *Victoria County History, Buckinghamshire*, vol. II, p. 198.

4 A. K. Cook, *About Winchester College* (1917), pp. 301–4.

PAGE 41

1 'Orders of the School concerning the Removing out of one Form into another' in *The School's Probation...for the use of Merchant-Tailors School in London*, 1652 (see also pp. 8–15); D. L. Clark, *John Milton at St Paul's School*, pp. 110–13 (summarised in F. J. McDonnell, *History of St Paul's School*, pp. 265–6).

PAGE 42

1 But Terence was back again in the St Paul's curriculum in the early eighteenth century (McDonnell, *History of St Paul's School*, pp. 289–90).

2 If Apolli' (*sic*), which appears in the Westminster curriculum of *c*. 1630, is to be interpreted as Apollodorus.

3 Dionysius Periegetes was used in the Anglesey school of Beaumaris in 1783 (John Williams, *David Hughes and his Free Grammar School at Beaumaris* (ed. 1933), p. 17).

4 For 'Heathen Gods' see John Clarke, *Essay upon...Grammar Schools* (1720), p. 39. *An Historical Account of the Heathen Gods...* by William King was published in 1710 for use at Westminster and other schools.

5 Milton, *Works* (Columbia edition), vol. xii, p. 16.

PAGE 43

1 The Royal Recommendation is printed at the front of the Cambridge edition of 1666. See also *Museum Criticum*, vol. ii, p. 690.

2 Quoted W. A. L. Vincent, *The State and School Education 1640–1660 in England and Wales*, p. 16.

3 *The Journal of George Fox* (ed. by J. L. Nickolls, 1952), p. 333.

PAGE 44

1 J. A. Comenius, *Great Didactic* (ed. M. W. Keatinge, 1896), pp. 383–400.

2 Milton, *Of Education*, in *Milton's Prose* (World's Classics), pp. 147–9.

3 J. Locke, *On Education*, §§ 147, 164, 165, 170–1, 174, 195.

PAGE 45

1 Busby, though a royalist, seems to have satisfied the authorities of his loyalty to the Commonwealth. J. M. Gray, *History of the Perse School, Cambridge* (Cambridge, 1921), p. 50, supposes that William Dell, as chairman of the trustees of the school, put his views into practice there. But he quotes no evidence that there was any change in the curriculum.

PAGE 46

1 J. Ruskin, *Praeterita*, ed. E. T. Cook and A. Wedderburn (39 vols. 1903–12), vol. xxxv, p. 192; H. L. Thompson, *Christ Church* (College Histories) (1900), p. 217. According to a writer of 1851, the continuance of the Latin services 'only increases the inattention of the undergraduates who are compelled to be present' (Ward and Heywood, *Oxford University Statutes*, vol. ii, p. xviii).

PAGE 47

1 Henry Montagu Butler, an accomplished composer in Latin, was slow and embarrassed in his attempts to speak the language with a parish priest in the Tyrol (E. Graham, *The Harrow Life of Henry Montagu Butler* (1920), p. xxx).

2 John Clarke, *Essay upon...Grammar Schools* (1720), p. 43.

3 Bishop Watson's father, master of Heversham school in the early part of the eighteenth century, insisted on Latin conversation, and Watson once heard

an old man who had been his father's pupil say to a fellow labourer, 'Frangam tibi caput' (*Anecdotes of the Life of Bishop Watson* (1817), p. 6).

4 Boswell, *Life of Johnson*, ed. G. B. Hill and L. F. Powell (6 vols. Oxford, 1934–40), vol. I, pp. 99–100; Carlisle, *Concise Description of the Endowed Grammar Schools*, vol. I, p. 737, vol. II, p. 651; Foster Watson, *The English Grammar Schools to 1660*, p. 346. Clarke's *Select Colloquies of Erasmus* reached a twenty-third edition in 1800.

5 John Clarke, *Essay upon…Grammar Schools*, p. 115.

PAGE 48

1 *Ibid.* pp. 48, 65, 79.

2 John Clarke, *Dissertation upon the Usefulness of Translations of Classic Authors* (1734). Clarke published a number of literal translations of Latin writers.

3 Lester Bradner, *Musae Anglicanae* (1940), pp. 226 f. A second series of Westminster compositions, *Lusus Alteri Westmonasterienses*, began in 1863.

PAGE 49

1 J. S. Harford, *Life of T. Burgess* (1840), pp. 4–5.

2 In 1787 an ex-waiter, 'very illiterate', was appointed to the mastership (Carlisle, *Concise Description of the Endowed Grammar Schools* (2 vols. 1820), vol. I, p. 755).

3 *D.N.B. s.v.* James Upton.

PAGE 50

1 Thomas Zouch, *Works*, vol. II, pp. 11–12, 17.

2 William Field, *Memoirs of the Life, Writings and Opinions of Samuel Parr* (2 vols. 1828), vol. I, pp. 74, 77–8.

3 Samuel Parr, *Works* (8 vols. 1828), vol. I, p. 212.

4 The sources for school curricula used in the following paragraphs are given here:

APPLEBY PARVA, 1802–18. Carlisle, *Concise Description of the Endowed Grammar Schools*, vol. I, pp. 737–8.

BEAUMARIS, 1783. John Williams, *David Hughes and his Free Grammar School at Beaumaris* (1933), p. 17.

CANTERBURY, KING'S SCHOOL, 1749. C. E. Woodruff and H. J. Cape, *Schola Regia Cantuariensis* (1908), p. 173.

CHESTERFIELD, early eighteenth century. J. W. Adamson, *Short History of Education* (Cambridge, 1919), p. 193; 1818, Carlisle, *op. cit.* vol. I, p. 216.

CHRIST'S HOSPITAL, 1792–1800. Leigh Hunt, *Autobiography* (World's Classics, ed. 1928), pp. 88, 97.

COVENTRY, 1818. Carlisle, *op. cit.* vol. II, p. 651.

Eton, 1766. *Etoniana*, 3 July and 30 November 1906; summarised in Maxwell-Lyte, *History of Eton College*, pp. 319–26.

Halifax, *c.* 1730. Carlisle, *op. cit.* vol. II, pp. 813–14.

Heversham, 1818. Carlisle, *op. cit.* vol. II, p. 707.

Dr Johnson's scheme for a grammar school, *c.* 1736. Boswell, *Life of Johnson* (ed. Hill and Powell), vol. I, pp. 99–100.

Louth, 1818. Carlisle, *op. cit.* vol. I, pp. 828–31.

Monmouth, 1816. W. M. Warlow, *History of the Charities of William Jones*, pp. 184–5.

Rugby, under James, headmaster 1775–94. Butler, *Life and Letters of Dr Samuel Butler* (2 vols. 1896), vol. I, pp. 25–30; W. H. D. Rouse, *History of Rugby School* (1898), pp. 137–41.

St Paul's, 1702, 1704, 1710. McDonnell, *History of St Paul's School*, pp. 288–91.

Sandwich, Sir Roger Manwood's, 1818. Carlisle, *op. cit.* vol. I, p. 615.

Southwell, 1789–96. H. Fynes Clinton, *Literary Remains* (1854), pp. 4–6.

Wakefield, under John Clarke, headmaster 1751–9. Thomas Zouch, *Works*, vol. II, pp. 11–12.

Westminster, 1796–9. H. Fynes Clinton, *op. cit.* pp. 6–7.

Winchester, 1825–30. Roundell Palmer, *Memorials* (2 vols. in 4, 1896–8), vol. I, pp. 100–1.

PAGE 51

1 Maxwell-Lyte, *History of Eton College*, p. 539.

2 See George Pryme, *Autobiographic Recollections* (Cambridge, 1870), p. 25.

3 Hoole's edition, however, was reprinted in 1722, and Stirling's in 1734.

4 Aesop in Greek and Latin was printed for use at Eton in 1682, 1709, 1755, 1769, 1783, 1799, but the full account of the Eton curriculum in 1766 makes no mention of the reading of the Latin Aesop. It is also missing from King's School, Canterbury, 1749, and from all early nineteenth-century curricula known to me. But H. Clarke's *Select Fables of Aesop, with a Literal English Translation* reached a tenth edition in 1789.

5 Found at St Paul's 1704 and 1710, Halifax, Canterbury, Eton, Rugby, Beaumaris, Chesterfield 1818, Louth, Sandwich, Appleby Parva. A selection from Phaedrus was published *in usum scholae Carthusianae* in 1789.

6 *Evangelia seu Excerpta quaedam ex novo Testamento secundum Latinam Sebast. Castellionis versionem in usum classium inferiorum scholae Etonensis* (1766 and 1821).

7 Eutropius, St Paul's 1702 and 1710, Johnson's scheme, Monmouth, Chesterfield 1818, Coventry, Appleby Parva. Cornelius Nepos, Halifax, Johnson's scheme, Canterbury, Eton, Beaumaris, Monmouth, Louth, Heversham, Appleby Parva. Justin, Canterbury, Johnson's scheme, Beaumaris. Q. Curtius,

St Paul's 1704 and 1710. John Clarke published literal translations of Justin, Florus, Eutropius, and Nepos.

8 Sallust at Beaumaris, Southwell, Westminster, Chesterfield 1818, Louth, Appleby Parva; missing at Halifax, Canterbury, Eton and in Johnson's scheme.

9 *Selecta ex Cicerone Livio Tacito Velleio Plinio* (Eton, 1766). Known as *Scriptores Romani* in later editions, 1791, 1809, 1858.

10 A collection of Latin epigrams in use at Eton in the seventeenth century (fourth edition, 1689) was reprinted in 1703, 1711 and 1715. In 1766 the sixth form was required to learn by heart passages from this.

PAGE 52

1 John Clarke, commending his scheme for teaching Latin by the use of literal translations, points out that Latin translations are recognised as necessary for learning Greek (*Dissertation upon the Usefulness of Translations of Classic Authors,* in Clarke's *Introduction to the making of Latin* (ed. 1787), pp. 286–7). Burton's *Pentalogia* without the Latin was out of print at the end of the eighteenth century (Butler, *Life of Samuel Butler,* vol. I, p. 28).

2 J. H. Overton and E. Wordsworth, *Christopher Wordsworth, Bishop of Lincoln* (1888), p. 17.

3 See Clarke, *Greek Studies in England, 1700–1830,* pp. 15–16.

4 The Greek Testament, missing from Eton, is found at King's School, Canterbury, as a first reading-book, followed by Lucian. A collection of funeral orations from Thucydides, Plato (*Menexenus*) and Lysias was in use at Eton in 1766 and was reprinted there *erudiendae iuventutis gratia* in 1798. It was also used at Westminster. The edition of Aeschines *In Ctesiphontem* and Demosthenes *De Corona* by Foulkes and Freind (1715) was designed *in usum scholae Etonensis,* but it does not appear in the curriculum of 1766.

PAGE 53

1 Aristophanes is found at Chesterfield and Wakefield.

2 John Clarke, *Essay upon...Grammar Schools,* pp. 96–9.

3 Maxwell-Lyte, *History of Eton College,* p. 391.

PAGE 54

1 *Greyfriar* II (1890–5), p. 6, quoted by G. N. Ray, *Thackeray, The Uses of Adversity* (1955), p. 96.

2 Thomas Arnold, *Miscellaneous Works* (1845), p. 352; A. P. Stanley, *Life of Arnold* (10th ed. 1877), vol. I, p. 128.

3 Charles Wordsworth, *Annals of My Early Life* (1891), p. 18; *Life and Correspondence of John Duke, Lord Coleridge* (1904), p. 39. See Morley's *Life of Gladstone* (1903), vol. I, pp. 42–3 for Gladstone's reading at Eton in the 1830's.

PAGE 55

1 *Edinburgh Review*, vol. LI (1830), p. 68; *Public Schools Commission Report*, vol. I, p. 88.

2 W. S. Walker, *Poetical Remains* (1852), p. ix; A. D. Coleridge, *Eton in the Forties* (1896), pp. 20–1.

3 W. R. W. Stephens, *Life and Letters of Walter Farquhar Hook* (1878), vol. I, p. 343; Roundell Palmer, *Memorials*, vol. I, pp. 102–3.

4 Norman Wymer, *Dr Arnold of Rugby* (1953), p. 29.

5 *Autobiography and Letters of Charles Merivale* (1899), pp. 48–9. As regards Lucan Merivale was following the example of his uncle Henry Drury who as a boy had repeated the whole of the *Pharsalia* while on a walk from Harrow to Eton. Benjamin Jowett could repeat the greater part of Virgil and Sophocles as well as a good deal of Aeschylus when a boy at St Paul's in the 1830's (E. Abbott and L. Campbell, *Life and Letters of Benjamin Jowett* (2 vols. Oxford, 1897), vol. I, p. 35).

6 *Stories from the Dictionary* or *Pantheon* and Kennet's *Roma Antiqua* were used at Canterbury; *Pantheon* at Eton. *Historia Antiqua or Ancient History To be rendered into Latin*, designed for either private reading or translating into Latin school exercises, reached an eighth edition in 1791.

PAGE 56

1 Sense, however, might precede Nonsense, at at Louth in 1818.

2 This was the requirement in 1766. By 1830 it was reduced to twenty lines of elegiacs and five or six stanzas of lyrics (*Edinburgh Review*, vol. LI (1830), p. 68).

3 *Musae Etonenses* (1755), vol. I, preface.

4 Leslie Stephen, *Life of Sir James Fitzjames Stephen* (1895), p. 81.

5 Lady Holland, *Memoir of Sydney Smith* (ed. 1855), vol. I, p. 7.

6 *Edinburgh Review*, vol. LIII (1831), p. 71. The latter exercise had, however, been given up by 1831 (*A Letter to the Editor of the Edinburgh Review...respecting Westminster School* (1831), p. 12).

7 A. F. Leach, *History of Warwick School* (1906), p. 162. Whewell found it necessary to argue in 1845 that the writing of Latin verse ought to come after the writing of Latin prose and not be made a primary part of classical culture (*Of a Liberal Education*, p. 91).

PAGE 57

1 *Works of Sir William Jones* (13 vols. 1807), vol. I, pp. 49–50; Byron, *Letters and Journals*, ed. Prothero, vol. v, p. 453.

2 *Edinburgh Review*, vol. LI (1830), p. 73.

3 H. L. Thompson, *Henry George Liddell* (1899), pp. 11, 14.

4 Byron, *Childe Harold's Pilgrimage*, Canto IV, lxxv–lxxvii; Connop Thirlwall,

Letters to a Friend (1881), pp. 224–5; *Alfred, Lord Tennyson, A Memoir* by his Son (1899), p. 13. Cf. A. D. Coleridge, *Eton in the Forties*, p. 21.

5 Maxwell-Lyte, *History of Eton College*, p. 393.

PAGE 58

1 C. A. Wilkinson, *Reminiscences of Eton* (1888), pp. 50–1; *Public Schools Commission Report*, vol. I, p. 88.

2 *Life and Letters of Charles Darwin*, ed. Sir F. Darwin (3 vols. 1887), vol. I, p. 32.

3 Leigh Hunt, *Autobiography* (World's Classics edition), p. 100; Frederick Harrison, *Autobiographic Memoirs* (2 vols. 1911), vol. I, p. 62.

4 W. S. Walker, *Poetical Remains*, p. xvi; Isaac Williams, *Autobiography* (1892), p. 5.

5 *Edinburgh Review*, vol. LI (1830), p. 74.

6 Isaac Williams, *Autobiography*, p. 6; E. S. Purcell, *Life of Cardinal Manning* (2 vols. 1896), vol. I, p. 19. Cf. *Quart. Rev.* vol. LXIX (1842), pp. 440–1.

PAGE 59

1 E. Graham, *Harrow Life of Henry Montagu Butler* (1920), p. 310; C. S. Calverley, *Literary Remains* (1885), pp. 17–18.

2 B. H. Kennedy, *Between Whiles*, quoted *Classical Review*, vol. III (1889), p. 226; Memoir of T. S. Evans, prefixed to his *Latin and Greek Verse*, ed. J. Waite (Cambridge, 1893), pp. iii–iv. Oscar Browning composed his first Latin verses at Eton (Alcaics) in his head as he walked up the Slough Road (Browning, *Memories of Sixty Years*, p. 20).

3 G. A. Denison, *Notes of my Life* (1878), p. 38.

4 Maxwell-Lyte, *History of Eton College*, p. 441; Goldwin Smith, *Reminiscences* (New York, 1911), p. 36.

5 *Life and Letters of Charles Darwin*, vol. I, p. 32; H. C. Adams, *Wykehamica* (1878), p. 350.

PAGE 60

1 *Edinburgh Review*, vol. LI (1830), pp. 65–80; *Quart. Rev.* vol. XLIV (1831), p. 122.

2 Thomas Mozley, *Reminiscences, Chiefly of Towns, Villages and Schools* (2 vols. 1885), vol. I, p. 386; *Public Schools Commission Report*, vol. III, p. 120.

PAGE 61

1 *Oxford University Statutes*, ed. by G. R. M. Ward and J. Heywood (2 vols. 1845–51), vol. I, pp. 19–24.

2 John Potenger, who entered Corpus Christi College in 1664, 'did not immediately enter upon logick and philosophy, but was kept for a full year to

the reading of classical authors, and making of theams in prose and verse'. If grammar and rhetoric are interpreted as meaning the study of the classics, this was in accordance with the university statutes, but one gets the impression from his account that his case was exceptional, owing to his youth at the time of entry (*Reminiscences of Oxford by Oxford Men*, ed. L. M. Quiller-Couch (Oxford Historical Society, 1892), p. 54).

PAGE 62

1 Mallet, *History of the University of Oxford*, vol. II, pp. 257–9.
2 *Statutes of the Colleges of Oxford*, vol. III, Statutes of Pembroke College, cap. 15; D. Macleane, *History of Pembroke College, Oxford* (Oxford Historical Society, 1897), p. 188.
3 À Wood, *Athenae Oxonienses*, vol. III, 410.
4 *Ibid.* 918. Wood records of Henry Stubbs of Christ Church that as an undergraduate during the Commonwealth he and some others used to discourse in the public schools very fluently in the Greek tongue. 'But since the king's restoration we have had no such matters' (*ibid.* 1068).
5 *De Graecis Illustribus Linguae Graecae Literarumque Humaniorum Instauratoribus*, published posthumously in 1742. The preface (pp. i and xxxiii) states that this work was delivered as lectures at Oxford.
6 Archbishop Williams, who took his B.A. in 1601, attended Downes's lectures as a Bachelor in accordance with the statutes, but this was then exceptional (Hacket, *Scrinia Reserata*, p. 10).

PAGE 63

1 Isaac Barrow, *Theological Works*, ed. A. Napier (9 vols. Cambridge, 1859), vol. IX, p. 36; see also P. H. Osmond, *Isaac Barrow* (1944), p. 37.
2 Barrow, *Theological Works*, vol. IX, p. 133.
3 *Ibid.* pp. 133–5; Osmond, *Isaac Barrow*, pp. 43–5.

PAGE 64

1 Barrow, *Theological Works*, vol. IX, p. 140.
2 *Baker's History of the College of St John...Cambridge*, ed. J. E. B. Mayor, pp. 598–9. Downes also gave private lectures in his house, but these D'Ewes did not attend owing to the expense. His lectures on Demosthenes, *De Pace* were reprinted in Dobson's *Demosthenes*, vol. V.
3 Barrow, *Theological Works*, vol. IX, pp. 141–2.
4 His notes on Demosthenes, *On the Symmories* and *On the Liberty of the Rhodians* were published in Dobson's *Demosthenes*, vol. V.
5 *Museum Criticum*, vol. II, p. 681. Duport also lectured on Theocritus. Barrow, *Theological Works*, vol. IX, p. 160.

PAGE 65

1 *Ibid.* p. 141.

2 *Ibid.* pp. 156–7.

3 *Ibid.* pp. 160–9.

PAGE 66

1 *Ibid.* p. 202.

2 Bradner, *Musae Anglicanae*, p. 206.

3 Mullinger, *The University of Cambridge*, vol. III, p. 368.

4 T. Fowler, *History of Corpus Christi College* (Oxford Historical Society), pp. 239, 248.

PAGE 67

1 Edmund Miller, *Account of the University of Cambridge* (1717), pp. 105–6.

2 John Jebb, *Remarks upon the Present Mode of Education in the University of Cambridge* (3rd ed. 1773), p. 20 n.; *Oxford University Statutes*, ed. Ward and Heywood, vol. II, p. 34.

3 Thomas Rutherforth in 1748 used English for his lectures on mechanics, optics, hydrostatics and astronomy at St John's, Cambridge (*A System of Natural Philosophy...*, 1748). John Randolph, Professor of Divinity at Oxford, 1783–99, used Latin for his inaugural lecture, but English for his course to Divinity students (Randolph, *A Course of Lectures...*, 1869).

4 Herbert Marsh, *Course of Lectures...*, pt. I, 1809, pp. 1–2. The statutes of the Oxford lectureship in Anglo-Saxon (1795) directed that the lectures should be in the vulgar tongue (*Oxford University Statutes*, ed. Ward and Heywood, vol. II, pp. 26–7).

PAGE 69

1 J. W. Clark, *Endowments of the University of Cambridge* (1904), pp. 371–2.

2 J. S. Watson, *Life of Richard Porson* (1861), p. 32; Samuel Parr, *Works* (8 vols. 1828), vol. VIII, p. 332.

3 *Cambridge University Calendar* (1803), p. 26.

PAGE 70

1 Daniel Waterland, *Advice to a Young Student* (2nd ed. 1730), ('drawn up above twenty years ago by a University Tutor for the private use of his own Pupils'), pp. 7–8, 18–27.

2 Robert Greene, 'Ἐγκυκλοπαιδεία *or A Method of Instructing Pupils* (1707), p. 8.

3 John Clarke, *Essay upon Study* (2nd ed. 1737), pp. 137–8.

4 Christopher Wordsworth, *Scholae Academicae* (Cambridge, 1877), pp. 354–5.

5 John Jebb, *Proposal for the Establishment of Public Examinations in the University of Cambridge* (1774), pp. 27–8, 33.

PAGE 71

1 Richard Lloyd, *Memoir of the Reverend Thomas Lloyd, M.A.* (1830), pp. 28, 38, 39.
2 Christopher Wordsworth, *Social Life at the English Universities in the Eighteenth Century* (Cambridge, 1874), pp. 576–7.
3 James Hurdis, *Vindication of the University of Oxford* (n.d., privately printed), p. 17; P. Duigenan, *Lachrymae Academicae* (1777), p. 155 n.

PAGE 72

1 Hurdis, *Vindication of the University of Oxford*, pp. 14–16, 18.
2 J. S. Harford, *Life of T. Burgess* (1840), p. 89.
3 Jeremy Bentham, *Works* (11 vols. 1838–43), vol. x, p. 37; Gibbon, *Autobiography* (World's Classics edition, 1907), p. 42; *Reminiscences of Oxford by Oxford Men* (Oxford Historical Society), p. 214.
4 Harford, *Life of Burgess*, p. 9; *Life and Correspondence of Robert Southey* (6 vols. 1849–50), vol. i, p. 215.
5 Sir William Jones, *Works*, i, p. 57.
6 *Correspondence of Thomas Gray* (ed. P. Toynbee and L. Whibley, 3 vols. Oxford, 1935), p. 33; H. Fynes Clinton, *Literary Remains*, p. 230.

PAGE 73

1 According to John Jebb, in Cambridge of 1773, except for the Chancellor's Medals and Members' Prizes, classical merit was altogether disregarded (*Remarks upon the present mode of education in the University of Cambridge*, 3rd ed. p. 10).

PAGE 74

1 According to the Digest of the Report on Schools of the Charity Commissioners (1842) there were 714 grammar schools. The Schools Inquiry Commission of 1868 counted 782 in addition to the nine so-called public schools. These figures include Wales.
2 This did not exclude the teaching of other subjects as extras or to boys not on the foundation. More freedom was allowed under the Grammar Schools Act of 1840, and even before then it had been possible to revise school foundations by private Act of Parliament.

PAGE 76

1 Coleridge, *Biographia Literaria* (Everyman edition), p. 3.

PAGE 77

1 Carlisle, *Concise Description of the Endowed Grammar Schools*, vol. ii, p. 389; Butler, *Life and Letters of Dr Samuel Butler* (2 vols. 1896), vol. i, pp. 196–7,

252–3. Tacitus was also read at some lesser schools at this time (Carlisle, *op. cit.* vol. I, pp. 738, 829, vol. II, p. 707). In 1817 Butler was using Dalzel's *Collectanea Maiora* for Greek prose writers (Carlisle. *op. cit.* vol. II, p. 389). In 1829 Henry Drury of Harrow wrote to Butler: 'I have no doubt you have supplanted the old desultory method of reading [from extract books] by something solid and continuous' (Butler, *Life of Samuel Butler*, vol. I, p. 355).

2 At Eton some geography was taught from Pomponius Mela (reprinted for use at Eton as late as 1820) and ancient history was supposed to be acquired out of school.

3 Carlisle, *Concise Description of the Endowed Grammar Schools*, vol. I, p. 389.

4 For details see *Classical Review*, vol. III (1889), p. 226.

5 Carlisle, *Concise Description of the Endowed Grammar Schools*, vol. II, p. 388.

PAGE 78

1 T. S. Evans, quoted in Memoir prefixed to Evans's *Latin and Greek Verse*, p. v.

2 Butler, *Life of Samuel Butler*, vol. I, p. 253.

3 *Ibid.* vol. I, p. 211.

4 J. Morley, *Life of William Ewart Gladstone* (3 vols. 1903), vol. I, p. 62.

5 See D. S. Colman, *Sabrinae Corolla: The Classics at Shrewsbury School under Dr Butler and Dr Kennedy* (Shrewsbury, n.d.).

PAGE 79

1 Norman Wymer, *Dr Arnold of Rugby*, p. 31.

2 Stanley, *Life of Arnold*, vol. I, pp. 14, 118, 119, 128.

3 *Ibid.* vol. I, p. 120.

PAGE 80

1 *Ibid.* vol. I, pp. 124–5; Arnold, *Miscellaneous Works*, p. 347. Stanley gives a list of subjects set for themes by Arnold in Appendix B.

2 Stanley, *Life of Arnold*, vol. I, pp. 130–1, 352, 361, 374; Matthew Arnold, *Letters* (ed. G. W. E. Russell, 1895), vol. I, p. 204.

3 Arnold, *Miscellaneous Works* (1845), p. 346; A. H. Clough, *Remains* (2 vols. 1869), vol. I, p. 405. When Clough left Rugby in 1837 he had read the following (some books two or three times): all Thucydides except books VI and VII, the first six books of Herodotus, five plays of Sophocles, four of Aeschylus, four or five of Euripides, considerable portions of Aristophanes, nearly all the *Odyssey* and about a third of the *Iliad*, one or two dialogues of Plato, not quite all of Virgil, all Horace, a good deal of Livy and Tacitus, a considerable portion of Aristotle's *Rhetoric* and two or three books of the *Ethics*, 'besides of course other things' (Clough, *loc. cit.*).

4 Arnold, *Miscellaneous Works*, p. 351; Stanley, *Life of Arnold*, vol. I, pp. 128–9.

5 For Thackeray at Charterhouse see G. N. Ray, *Thackeray, The Uses of Adversity* (1955), ch. 3.

6 H. L. Thompson, *H. G. Liddell* (1899), p. 11. Thomas Mozley, however, who was at Charterhouse at about the same time, recalled reading several books of Thucydides (Thomas Mozley, *Reminiscences, chiefly of Towns, Villages and Schools*, vol 1, p. 394), but Liddell is probably more reliable on this point.

PAGE 81

1 McDonnell, *History of St Paul's School*, p. 398.

2 Abbott and Campbell, *Life and Letters of Benjamin Jowett*, vol. 1, p. 35.

3 H. A. Holden and F. Rendall (bracketed, 1845), Charles Evans (1847) and B. F. Westcott (1848).

4 *Life and Letters of Brooke Foss Westcott*, ed. A. Westcott (2 vols. 1903), vol. 1, pp. 26, 27. Cf. A. C. Benson, *Life of Edward White Benson* (2 vols. 1899), vol. 1, pp. 40–1.

PAGE 82

1 J. H. Evans was a brother of T. S. Evans, the composer of Latin and Greek verse.

2 James M. Wilson, *An Autobiography*, ed. E. T. K. and J. S. Wilson (1932), p. 29.

3 *Ibid.* p. 23. Ernest Pontifex in *The Way of all Flesh* was given Schömann's book as a leaving present by his headmaster.

PAGE 83

1 J. C. Thirlwall, *Connop Thirlwall* (1936), p. 1.

2 Roundell Palmer, *Memorials*, vol. 1, p. 64; W. C. Green, *Memories of Eton and King's* (1905), p. 15; Oscar Browning, *Memories of Sixty Years* (1910), p. 11; *Life and Letters of Rowland Williams*, by his wife (2 vols. 1874), vol. 1, p. 4; Horatio Brown, *John Addington Symonds, A Biography* (1903), p. 18.

3 J. Conington, *Miscellaneous Writings* (2 vols. 1872), vol. 1, p. x.

4 Palmer, *Memorials*, vol. 1, p. 64; Iris Morgan, *Memoirs of Henry Arthur Morgan* (1927), p. 57.

5 G. O. Trevelyan, *Life and Letters of Lord Macaulay* (2 vols. 1878), vol. 1, p. 41; Herbert Paul, *Life of J. A. Froude* (1905), p. 10.

6 Frederick Harrison, *Autobiographic Memoirs*, vol. 1, pp. 28–9.

PAGE 84

1 H. P. Liddon, *Life of E. B. Pusey* (4 vols. 1893–7), vol. 1, pp. 9–10.

2 Lonsdale Ragg, *Memoir of Dean Wickham* (1911), p. 6.

PAGE 85

1 *Schools Inquiry Commission Report*, vol. VII, p. 306.

2 *Ibid.* vol. 1, p. 131. The other 7% were in abeyance.

PAGE 86

1 See Clarke, *Greek Studies in England 1700–1830*, p. 22. But Hertford Grammar School, mentioned there as a school where there was no demand for Greek, had recovered as a classical school by the 1830's. See *Digest of Schools and Charities for Education* (1842), p. 39 and Lewis Turnor, *History of Hertford* (1830), p. 333.

2 *Schools Inquiry Commission Report*, vol. IX, p. 109.

3 *Ibid.* vol. VIII, pp. 32–3. These schools may, however, have been private rather than endowed schools.

4 *Ibid.* vol. VIII, p. 147. The commissioner was T. H. Green, who, fresh from Rugby and Balliol, no doubt had high standards. He is referring to Warwickshire and Staffordshire, excluding Birmingham.

5 *Ibid.* vol. VIII, p. 399; vol. IX, p. 174.

6 *Ibid.* vol. VII, p. 19.

PAGE 87

1 *Ibid.* vol. IX, p. 903; vol. XIX, pp. 169–70, 360.

2 *Ibid.* vol. IX, p. 904. One reason for the strength of the classics was that in a region remote from the universities men were often ordained on the strength of a grammar school education only, and stayed at school long enough to qualify for ordination.

3 *Ibid.* vol. IX, pp. 174, 642.

4 *Ibid.* vol. IX, p. 560.

PAGE 88

1 J. Morley, *Life of Richard Cobden* (1906), p. 893.

2 *Schools Inquiry Commission Report*, vol. I, p. 18.

3 *Ibid.* vol. VIII, p. 336. The better local grammar schools might in the case of promising boys serve as preparatory schools for the public schools. Cf. the remarks of the headmaster of Carlisle grammar school in the *Cathedral Commission Report* (1854), p. 737.

4 The system of open entrance scholarships dates in the main from after the Royal Commissions of 1850, but had been known before then. At Oxford Balliol was the pioneer. There, in the seven years from 1838, all the winners of open scholarships, except Sellar from Scotland, were public school men (Abbott and Campbell, *Life and Letters of Benjamin Jowett*, vol. I, p. 102).

PAGE 89

1 Maxwell-Lyte, *History of Eton College*, p. 543. By the 1860's themes were generally on a historical rather than a moral subject (*Public Schools Commission Report*, vol. III, p. 250).

2 *Public Schools Commission Report*, vol. III, p. 190; Oscar Browning, *Memories of Sixty Years*, p. 20. It was commonly held by nineteenth-century scholars that it was easy to express anything in Greek iambics. T. S. Evans asserted that there was no saying in any language or dialect which could not be readily and accurately reproduced in iambics (T. S. Evans, *Latin and Greek Verse*, p. vii). James Lonsdale used to say to his nephew 'Let us turn everything we meet into Greek iambics' (R. Duckworth, *Memoir of Rev. James Lonsdale* (1893), p. 204). J. M. Wilson when headmaster of Clifton once said to a young assistant master 'Can you turn this into Greek iambics: "To find four points such that the line joining any two of them is at right angles to the line joining the other two"?' The master had the answer ready the next morning (J. M. Wilson, *Autobiography*, p. 172).

3 *Public Schools Commission Report*, vol. I, p. 144.

4 Ragg, *Memoir of Dean Wickham*, pp. 38–42.

5 Roundell Palmer, *Memorials*, vol. I, p. 101; E. M. Watson, *Life of Bishop John Wordsworth* (1908), p. 14; Laura Ridding, *George Ridding* (1915), p. 92.

6 W. A. Fearon, *The Passing of Old Winchester* (1924), pp. 54–5; cf. p. 63.

PAGE 90

1 *Public Schools Commission Report*, vol. II, pp. 392–7; Sir Charles Oman, *Memories of Victorian Oxford* (1941), p. 55. A single year's reading may of course give a misleading impression.

2 E. Graham, *The Harrow Life of Henry Montagu Butler* (1920), pp. 303–4, 308; P. E. Matheson, *Life of Hastings Rashdall* (1928), p. 13; *Public Schools Commission Report*, vol. IV, p. 291. For Vaughan's teaching see E. W. Howson and G. T. Warner, *Harrow School* (1898), p. 109.

3 Graham, *The Harrow Life of Henry Montagu Butler*, p. 303.

4 *Ibid.* pp. 309, 372.

5 Quoted, D. S. Colman, *Sabrinae Corolla: The Classics at Shrewsbury School under Dr Butler and Dr Kennedy* (n.d.), pp. 10–11.

PAGE 91

1 *Public Schools Commission Report*, vol. IV, p. 291.

2 C. A. Bristed, *Five Years in an English University* (1852), p. 275.

3 Oman, *Memories of Victorian Oxford*, p. 55.

4 Colman, *Sabrinae Corolla*, p. 12.

5 Benjamin Hall Kennedy, *Between Whiles* (1877), pp. vii–viii.

6 *Memoirs of Archbishop Temple*, ed. E. G. Sandford (2 vols. 1906), vol. I, pp. 35, 87–8. Temple had himself read Lucretius at school at Blundell's, and had lectured on him at Balliol. It is interesting to find that the second Arch-

bishop Temple shared his father's love of Lucretius, and had read all the *De Rerum Natura* before he left Rugby (F. A. Iremonger, *William Temple* (1948), p. 16).

7 *Memoirs of Archbishop Temple*, vol. I, pp. 160, 166; *Public Schools Commission Report*, vol. IV, pp. 291–2. Guizot had been used by Arnold as a means of teaching French and history concurrently.

PAGE 92

1 *Public Schools Commission Report*, vol. II, pp. 440–51.

2 Private information.

3 *Public Schools Commission Report*, vol. I, p. 239; vol. IV, pp. 292, 299, 357.

4 W. R. Inge, *Vale* (1934), p. 1.

PAGE 93

1 *Schools Inquiry Commission Report*, vol. IV, p. 319.

2 F. W. Farrar (ed.), *Essays on a Liberal Education* (1867), pp. 206–7; R. Farrar, *Life of Frederick William Farrar* (1904), p. 103.

3 Howard Staunton, *The Great Schools of England* (1869), p. 265 n. Bosworth Smith, the historian of Carthage, is said to have been one of the first classical tutors at Harrow to 'break away from the tyranny of Latin verses' (Lady Grogan, *Reginald Bosworth Smith* (1909), p. 113).

PAGE 94

1 *Life and Letters of Brooke Foss Westcott*, ed. A. Westcott, vol. I, p. 194.

PAGE 95

1 *Public Schools Commission Report*, vol. I, p. 28.

2 *Schools Inquiry Commission Report*, vol. I, p. 25.

3 *Ibid.* vol. I, pp. 26–7, 84–8.

PAGE 96

1 *Ibid.* vol. VII, p. 279.

PAGE 97

1 *D.N.B. s.v.* L. R. Farnell; L. R. Farnell, *An Oxonian Looks Back* (1934), p. 24.

PAGE 98

1 Ward and Heywood, *Oxford University Statutes*, vol. II, p. 33.

2 What appears to be the only surviving account of an examination of this period is that of Daniel Wilson's examination for the M.A. degree. (This examination was abolished in 1807.) Wilson 'took up' Thucydides and

Herodotus in Greek, and in Latin all the classical authors. The examination was entirely oral and included translation into Latin at sight, translation from Livy, with questions, from Thucydides and Xenophon (not Herodotus, although he had been taken up) and questions on physics (Josiah Bateman, *Life of Daniel Wilson* (2 vols. 1860), vol. I, pp. 66–7).

PAGE 99

1 Ward and Heywood, *Oxford University Statutes*, vol. II, p. 62.

2 *Ibid.* vol. II, p. 166.

3 Charles Hole, *Life of the Rev. William Whitmarsh Phelps* (2 vols. Reading, 1871), vol. I, pp. 230, 244; *Memoirs of Archbishop Temple*, vol. II, pp. 429–32.

4 V. A. Huber, *English Universities* (2 vols. in 3, 1843), vol. II, pt. ii, p. 524. According to James Pycroft's *Collegian's Guide* (1845), however, one could obtain a first class even though one's Greek was barely grammatical (2nd ed. p. 29).

5 Huber, *English Universities*, vol. II, pt. ii, p. 524; *Hints to Students in reading for Classical Honours in the University of Oxford*, by a Class Man, 2nd ed. 1843, p. 40; Pycroft, *Collegian's Guide*, p. 29.

6 E. Copleston, *Reply to the Calumnies of the Edinburgh Review* (1810), pp. 140–2. In 1811 Sir William Hamilton took up, besides the books ordinarily taken up by candidates for a first class, the whole of Aristotle and Cicero (J. Veitch, *Memoir of Sir William Hamilton* (1869), p. 42). Gladstone in 1830 had to construe, besides the *Rhetoric* and *Ethics* of Aristotle, from Plato's *Phaedo*, Herodotus, Thucydides, the *Odyssey*, the *Wasps* and Persius (Morley, *Life of Gladstone*, vol. I, p. 78).

PAGE 100

1 *Hints to Students . . .*, pp. iv, 16; Pycroft, *Collegian's Guide*, p. 300. According to the *Oxford University Commission Report* (1852), p. 62, two or three dialogues of Plato were usually included. See also Huber, *English Universities*, vol. II, pt. ii, p. 523, where Cicero's philosophical works are given as an alternative to Plato.

2 The list in Huber adds Polybius I, II and VI.

3 *Oxford University Commission Report*, p. 62. The author of *Hints to Students in reading for Classical Honours* does not recommend Lucretius as a book to be 'taken up' (p. 29).

4 Stopford A. Brooke, *Life and Letters of Frederick W. Robertson* (2 vols. 1865), vol. II, p. 208.

5 Bristed, *Five Years in an English University*, p. 138. Cf. H. Fynes Clinton, *Literary Remains*, p. 229, where Clinton, writing in 1825, observes that Plato, among a number of authors, is not studied at Oxford. But the Oxford under-

graduate reading for a first in Pycroft's *Collegian's Guide* has read a number of books which he does not take up (pp. 301, 303).

6 *Oxford University Commission Report*, p. 62.

7 *Anthologia Oxoniensis* (ed. W. Linwood, 1846), preface, p. vii.

PAGE 101

1 A. H. Clough, *Remains*, vol. I, p. 76; *Oxford University Commission Report*, p. 62.

2 J. Veitch, *Memoir of Sir William Hamilton*, p. 30.

3 *Quarterly Review*, vol. LXI (1838), p. 218.

4 M. Pattison, *Essays* (2 vols. 1899), vol. I, pp. 463–5.

5 Clough, *Remains*, vol. I, p. 82; R. W. Church, *The Oxford Movement* (1891), p. 130; Stopford Brooke, *Life and Letters of F. W. Robertson*, vol. I, p. 39.

PAGE 102

1 F. Meyrick, *Memoirs of Life at Oxford* (1905), p. 112. Cf. G. D. Boyle, *Recollections* (1895), p. 105. 'He would commence a lecture on Aristotle in the usual way, but would end with, perhaps, the Athanasian creed or the beauties of Gothic architecture.'

2 Clough, *Remains*, vol. I, p. 82; Samuel Clark, *Memorials* (1878), p. 135.

3 Abbott and Campbell, *Life of Benjamin Jowett*, vol. I, p. 132.

4 *Letters and Verses of A. P. Stanley* (ed. R. E. Prothero, 1895), pp. 26–7. But Mark Pattison, who took his degree in 1836, says that those who took up Livy were expected to know something of Niebuhr (*Memoirs* (1885), p. 151).

5 W. A. Knight, *Principal Shairp and his Friends* (Edinburgh, 1888), p. 36.

PAGE 103

1 Pattison, *Essays*, vol. I, p. 480.

2 T. J. Hogg, *Life of Shelley* (1858), vol. I, p. 258; Stanley, *Life of Arnold*, vol. I, p. 347. But Archdeacon Phelps, a Corpus man of a few years later, expressed high appreciation of his college lectures (Hole, *Life of the Rev. William Whitmarsh Phelps*, vol. I, p. 110).

3 *Oxford University Commission, Evidence*, p. 12. Cf. Charles Wordsworth, *Annals of my Early Life*, p. 39; Mark Pattison, *Memoirs*, p. 64.

4 *Letters and Verses of A. P. Stanley*, p. 26; Clough, *Remains*, vol. I, p. 406.

5 Quoted in R. H. Coon, *William Warde Fowler* (Oxford, 1934), p. 3.

6 Abbott and Campbell, *Life of Benjamin Jowett*, vol. I, pp. 105–6.

PAGE 104

1 A. H. Wratislaw, *Observations on the Cambridge System*, pp. 13–14.

2 Charles Merivale, *Autobiography and Letters* (1899), p. 76; J. W. Donaldson, *Classical Scholarship and Classical Learning* (Cambridge, 1856), p. 73.

3 *Cambridge University Calendar* (1824), p. 151.

PAGE 105

1 Bristed, *Five Years in an English University*, pp. 184–6.
2 D. A. Winstanley, *Early Victorian Cambridge* (Cambridge, 1940), p. 71.
3 See R. Burn in *The Student's Guide to the University of Cambridge* (1863), pp. 137–8.
4 In 1815 few other colleges had examinations (Winstanley, *Early Victorian Cambridge*, p. 155). By 1829 there were examinations at Corpus (J. P. T. Bury, *The College of Corpus Christi. . ., a history from 1822 to 1952* (Cambridge, 1952), p. 31).

PAGE 106

1 [J. M. F. Wright], *Alma Mater, or Seven Years at the University of Cambridge* (2 vols. 1827), vol. I, pp. 126, 163, 184, 194, 206, 225. In the third year, according to Wright, 'the classical lecturer takes leave of us' (vol. II, p. 23). But he gives the text of a paper for Senior Sophs (third year) set by Dobree on Homer, *Iliad* VI–VIII (vol. I, p. 295). See also Huber, *English Universities*, vol. II, pt. ii, p. 531, and Bury, *The College of Corpus Christi. . .from 1822 to 1952*, p. 31 (no examination in classics after the first year at Corpus in 1829).
2 *Alma Mater*, vol. I, pp. 230, 240, 295; George Pryme, *Autobiographic Recollections* (Cambridge, 1870), p. 90.
3 Trevelyan, *Life and Letters of Lord Macaulay* (2 vols. 1878), vol. I, p. 84; Macaulay, *Works* (1871), vol. VIII, p. 594. B. H. Kennedy, *Between Whiles* (1877), quoted *Classical Review*, vol. III (1889), p. 227.
4 J. E. B. Mayor, Preface to *First Greek Reader* (1905 reprint), p. 26.

PAGE 107

1 W. E. Heitland, *After Many Years* (1926), pp. 129–30.

PAGE 108

1 *Alma Mater*, vol. I, pp. 127–41.
2 *Memoir of the Rev. Professor Scholefield* by his Widow (1855), pp. 324–5; W. C. Green, *Memories of Eton and King's* (1905), p. 76; Bristed, *Five Years in an English University*, p. 128.
3 John Willis Clark, *Old Friends at Cambridge* (1900), pp. 306–7.
4 Sir J. Frederick Maurice, *Life of Frederick Denison Maurice* (2 vols. 1884), vol. I, pp. 52–3.
5 *Ibid.* vol. I, p. 54.
6 T. Mozley, *Reminiscences, Chiefly of Oriel College and the Oxford Movement* (2 vols. 1882), vol. I, p. 44. Sterling's friend Frank Edgeworth was 'learned in Plato' (Carlyle, *Life of Sterling* (World's Classics edition, 1907), p. 135).
7 Stanley, *Life of Arnold*, vol. I, p. 16.

PAGE 109

1 Connop Thirlwall, *Letters Literary and Theological* (1881), pp. 91–2; J. W. Donaldson, *Classical Scholarship and Classical Learning* (1856), pp. 141–2. Rowland Williams was lecturing on Plato and Aristotle at King's in the 1840's (*Life and Letters of Rowland Williams* (1874), vol. I, pp. 107–8).

2 C. A. Bristed, the American who studied at Trinity in the 1840's, and has left an interesting account of Cambridge classical studies, was advised by his tutor to work five or six hours a day for six months on composition if he wanted to get a first. *Five Years in an English University* (1852), p. 170.

3 C. R. Kennedy, *Classical Education Reformed* (1837), p. 50; J. E. B. Mayor, *First Greek Reader* (1905 reprint), p. 27.

4 *Memoir of Bishop Cotton*, edited by Mrs Cotton (1871), p. 6.

5 Bristed, *Five Years in an English University*, pp. 143, 159, 259, 276, 320–6.

PAGE 110

1 Conington, *Miscellaneous Writings* (2 vols. 1872), vol. I, p. xviii.

PAGE 112

1 Mark Pattison, *Memoirs* (1885), p. 237.

2 *Oxford University Commission, Evidence*, p. 130. Sir William Hamilton (*Discussions on Philosophy...* (1866), p. 749) calculated that in 1847, of the college teachers *in literis humanioribus*, more than half had not taken a first class. But in view of Oxford's habit of denying a first to many of her most gifted sons, the calculation is not perhaps of much significance.

PAGE 113

1 Ward and Heywood, *Oxford University Statutes*, vol. II, p. 294.

2 *Oxford University Commission Report*, p. 66; A. S. Farrar, *Hints to Students in reading for Classical Honours in the University of Oxford*, 2nd ed. (1856), pp. 5–6; Montagu Burrows, *Pass and Class* (1861), p. 65.

3 Burrows, *Pass and Class*, p. 66.

4 *Ibid.* pp. 97, 99, 120.

PAGE 114

1 *Ibid.* p. 97.

2 J. E. Thorold Rogers, *Education in Oxford* (1861), p. 39.

3 Ward and Heywood, *Oxford University Statutes*, vol. II, p. 289; *Oxford University Commission Report*, p. 66.

4 Pattison, *Memoirs*, p. 303.

5 L. R. Farnell, *An Oxonian Looks Back* (1934), pp. 38–41; Thorold Rogers, *Education in Oxford*, pp. 131–2.

PAGE 115

1 Burrows, *Pass and Class*, pp. 50–1.
2 Thorold Rogers, *Education in Oxford*, pp. 60–1, 103.
3 Burrows, *Pass and Class*, p. 60.
4 L. Ragg, *Memoir of Dean Wickham* (1911), pp. 54–60; E. W. Watson, *Life of Bishop John Wordsworth* (1915), p. 21.
5 Farnell, *An Oxonian Looks Back*, p. 37.
6 Abbott and Campbell, *Life and Letters of Benjamin Jowett*, vol. II, p. 133.
7 A. E. Housman came away from the one lecture of Jowett's he attended disgusted by his disregard for the niceties of scholarship (A. S. F. Gow, *A. E. Housman* (1936), p. 5).

PAGE 116

1 *D.N.B. s.v.* John Conington.
2 Abbott and Campbell, *Life of Benjamin Jowett*, vol. I, p. 249.
3 Pattison, *Memoirs*, pp. 249–52.
4 Horatio F. Brown, *John Addington Symonds, A Biography* (1903), pp. 68–73, 78–86, 129–33; R. L. Nettleship, Memoir of T. H. Green prefixed to his *Works*, vol. III, p. xviii. See also the memoir of Conington by H. J. S. Smith in Conington's *Miscellaneous Works*, vol. I and Henry Nettleship in *D.N.B. s.v.* Conington.
5 E. W. Watson, *Life of Bishop John Wordsworth*, p. 50.

PAGE 117

1 Bywater in *D.N.B. s.v.* Nettleship.
2 *Journal of Philology*, vol. XXXIV (1915–18), p. 1.
3 W. W. Jackson, *Ingram Bywater* (2 parts, Oxford, 1917–19), pp. 95, 137.
4 *J. Philology*, vol. XXXIV (1915–18), pp. 2–3. Cf. Jackson, *Ingram Bywater*, pp. 67–8.
5 H. Nettleship, *Lectures and Essays*, first series (Oxford, 1885), pp. 1–2.

PAGE 118

1 *Ibid.* second series (Oxford, 1895), pp. xv, xxiii–xxiv.
2 *Ibid.* p. xxvi.
3 Abbott and Campbell, *Life of Benjamin Jowett*, vol. I, p. 261.
4 Frederick Harrison, *Autobiographic Memoirs* (2 vols. 1911), vol. I, pp. 83–6.
5 Burrows, *Pass and Class*, p. 121; Nettleship, *Lectures and Essays*, second series, p. 183.

PAGE 119

1 Ernest Barker, *Age and Youth* (1953), p. 319.
2 Pattison, *Essays* (1889), vol. I, p. 474.

3 R. H. Coon, *William Warde Fowler* (1934), p. 27.

4 T. H. Green, *Works*, ed. R. L. Nettleship (3 vols. 1885–8), vol. III, p. xxxiii; *D.N.B. s.v.* W. L. Newman.

5 P. E. Matheson, in J. W. Mackail, *James Leigh Strachan-Davidson* (1925), p. 39.

PAGE 120

1 H. F. Pelham, *Essays*, ed. F. Haverfield (Oxford, 1911), pp. xi–xiii.

2 H. L. Thompson, *Henry George Liddell* (1899), p. 140.

3 Farnell, *An Oxonian Looks Back*, pp. 76–7.

4 *Classical Review*, vol. I (1887), p. 22.

5 Farnell, *An Oxonian Looks Back*, p. 116; Percy Gardner, *Autobiographica* (1933), p. 59, *Oxford at the Crossroads* (1889), pp. viii, 40.

PAGE 121

1 These reforms were approved in 1849 and came into effect in 1851.

2 *Student's Guide to the University of Cambridge* (1863), p. 17. In the three years 1842–4 the average number of those taking the Classical Tripos was 31 and of those taking the Mathematical 118. In the three years 1861–3 the corresponding figures were 57 and 93.

3 J. W. Donaldson, *Classical Scholarship and Classical Learning*, p. 224.

4 *Cambridge University Commission, Evidence*, p. 287. The suggestion came from W. H. Thompson, who, according to Merivale, 'had a sad contempt for Latin verse making', *J. Philology*, vol. XV (1886), p. 307. Cf. G. Peacock, *Observations on the Statutes of the University of Cambridge* (1841), pp. 157–9.

5 See W. Whewell, *Of a Liberal Education* (1850), pt. 2, p. 26.

6 *Cambridge University Commission, Evidence*, p. 288.

7 *Ibid.* p. 279.

PAGE 122

1 *Student's Guide to the University of Cambridge* (1874), p. 28. The authors were Plato, Aristotle, Cicero's philosophical works, Lucretius and Quintilian. In 1874 the books set were the *Philebus*, the *Gorgias* and the *Phaedrus*, Aristotle's *Rhetoric*, the *Academica* of Cicero and a book of Lucretius (W. Leaf, *Some Chapters of Autobiography* (1932), p. 103). To the choice of the *Academica* we owe Reid's valuable edition.

2 *Student's Guide* (1874), pp. 169–70.

3 From 1882 to 1895 there was a compulsory section of Part II consisting of prose-composition and unseen. The new Section A (literature and criticism) included proses and unseens until 1904.

PAGE 123

1 Wratislaw, *Observations on the Cambridge System*, p. 30.
2 D'Arcy Wentworth Thompson, *Wayside Thoughts* (1868), pp. 95–6. Pembroke is thinly disguised as St Ignavia.
3 See the Evidence from colleges in *Cambridge University Commission*, pp. 306f., and for St John's, p. 284.
4 E. Graham, *Harrow Life of Henry Montagu Butler* (1920), p. xxxivn.
5 Heitland, *After Many Years*, p. 128.
6 R. St J. Parry, *Henry Jackson* (1926), pp. 19, 25. Coaching was, however, not entirely superseded even for Trinity men. Walter Leaf in the 1870's found it necessary to go to Paley for tuition (Leaf, *Some Chapters of Autobiography*, p. 60).
7 Heitland, *After Many Years*, p. 139.

PAGE 124

1 J. W. Clark, *Old Friends at Cambridge* (1900), p. 307. Cf. Bristed, *Five Years at an English University*, pp. 129–30.
2 Heitland, *After Many Years*, p. 131.
3 *D.N.B.* second supplement, *s.v.* R. C. Jebb.
4 Memoir prefixed to J. E. B. Mayor, *Twelve Cambridge Sermons*, ed. H. F. Stewart (1911), p. xliv.

PAGE 125

1 M. R. James, *Eton and King's* (1926), p. 181.
2 Parry, *Henry Jackson*, pp. 37–9, 42–3; J. d'E. E. Firth, *Rendall of Winchester* (1954), p. 23.
3 Parry, *Henry Jackson*, pp. 38–9.
4 Leaf, *Some Chapters of Autobiography*, p. 102; F. M. Cornford, *The Republic of Plato* (1941), p. ix. Finding mistakes in Jowett was, it should be said, an amusement not unknown in Oxford.

PAGE 126

1 P. Gardner, *Autobiographica* (1933), p. 51; E. V. Lucas, *The Colvins and their Friends* (1928), p. 29.
2 J. D. Duff in *Life and Letters of Sir R. C. Jebb* (1907), p. 93; R. Y. Tyrrell in *Proceedings of the British Academy* (1905–6), p. 445.
3 Memoir prefixed to A. W. Verrall, *Collected Literary Essays*, ed. M. A. Bayfield and J. D. Duff (Cambridge, 1913), pp. xxxvii–xxxix.

PAGE 127

1 Greats bred philosophers and historians. It kept its philosophers, but its historians might move on to the new school of Modern History. The fact

that Oxford in the later nineteenth century produced a flourishing school of Modern History whereas Cambridge did not was one result of the different character of Greats and the Classical Tripos.

PAGE 128

1 *Student's Guide to the University of Durham* (1880), p. 40. The first year examination, however, included three books of the *Ethics*, a logic paper and papers on Greek and Roman history, and the Final examination included Latin verse-composition and a critical paper. Jowett, who acted as external examiner for two years, considered that the standard of the Durham examination was fair; a first class at Durham was about as good as a second at Oxford (*Durham University Commission, Evidence* (1863), p. 91).

2 Memoir prefixed to Evans, *Latin and Greek Verse*, p. xxxvii. For Edwards see C. E. Whiting, *The University of Durham* (1933), p. 94. James Lonsdale was a tutor at Durham from 1851. 'No one knows...', wrote a pupil, 'how good and kind he was to me. He used to weep over my Latin prose, and by that means made me take pains' (R. Duckworth, *Memoir of Rev. James Lonsdale* (1893), p. 38).

3 E. D. Stone, *Herbert Kynaston* (1912), p. xxiii. This Herbert Kynaston, formerly Snow, is to be distinguished from the Herbert Kynaston who was High Master of St Paul's.

PAGE 129

1 H. H. Bellot, *University College, London, 1826–1926* (1929), p. 79.

2 In 1839 the prescribed books were Homer, Aeschylus (four plays), Sophocles (three), Aristophanes (three), Euripides (four), Polybius I and VI, Thucydides, Herodotus, Plato (three dialogues), Aristotle, *Ethics* and *Poetics*, Aeschines and Demosthenes, *On the Crown* and Demosthenes, *Midias*; Virgil, Horace, Juvenal (six satires) and Persius (two), Plautus (three plays) and Terence (three), Lucretius V and VI, Cicero, *De Natura Deorum, Tusculans, De Officiis, De Oratore* and *Letters,* Tacitus, *Annals* and *Histories.* There were two papers on Greek and two on Latin books (*London University Examinations,* 1839).

PAGE 130

1 F. J. C. Hearnshaw, *Centenary History of King's College, London* (1929), pp. 136, 181; *Royal Commission on a University for London, 1889, Minutes of Evidence,* p. 30.

2 *Royal Commission on a University for London, 1889, Minutes of Evidence,* p. 173. An early example was A. S. Wilkins, the editor of Cicero, who went up to St John's College, Cambridge, from University College in 1864.

3 Key was joint headmaster of University College School from 1831 to 1842 and from 1842 sole headmaster, combining this post with a professorship of

comparative grammar. He was perhaps more effective as a schoolmaster than as a professor (Bellot, *University College, London*, p. 92).

PAGE 131

1 *Ibid.* pp. 93–4.
2 *Ibid.* p. 257.
3 *Ibid.* p. 326.
4 A. S. F. Gow, *A. E. Housman* (Cambridge, 1936), p. 17.
5 Edwin Arnold in R. Farrar, *Life of Frederick William Farrar* (1904), p. 27.

PAGE 132

1 H. B. Charlton, *Portrait of a University* (Manchester, 1951), p. 28.

PAGE 134

1 The following are the sources for school curricula referred to in this chapter:
   ABERDEEN GRAMMAR SCHOOL, 1553, 1659, 1700, 1796, H. F. M. Simpson, *Bon Record* (1906), pp. 80–1, 98–100, 164–5, 178–9.
   DUMFRIES, 1751–74, George Chapman, *Treatise on Education* (ed. 1790), pp. 175–92.
   EDINBURGH HIGH SCHOOL, 1598, W. Steven, *History of the High School of Edinburgh* (1849), Appendix, p. 25; 1614, T. McCrie, *Life of Andrew Melville* (2 vols. 1824), vol. II, p. 508, Steven, *op. cit.* Appendix, pp. 29–30; 1644, G. Chalmers, *Life of Thomas Ruddiman* (1794), pp. 88–90, Steven, *op. cit.* pp. 57–8.
   GLASGOW HIGH SCHOOL, *c.* 1570, James Grant, *History of the Burgh Schools of Scotland* (1876), pp. 336–8; 1685, *ibid.* p. 338n.; 1786, J. Cleland and T. Muir, *The History of the High School of Glasgow* (Glasgow, 1878), p. 24.
2 James Melville, *Autobiography and Diary* (ed. 1842), p. 17.

PAGE 135

1 See Chalmers, *Life of Ruddiman*, pp. 21, 62. Also p. 383 for a list of grammar books by Scotsmen.
2 Claudian was recommended by a committee of Edinburgh professors for reading at Edinburgh High School in 1710, but there is no evidence that the recommendation was carried into effect (Steven, *History of the High School of Edinburgh*, Appendix, p. 36).
3 The committee referred to in the previous note made it clear that they did not wish to replace Cato (*ibid.* p. 35).
4 Glasgow, *c.* 1570 (Corderius, Erasmus and Castalio); Edinburgh, 1598 (Corderius); Edinburgh, 1614 (Corderius and Erasmus); Edinburgh, 1644 (Corderius); Glasgow, 1685 (Corderius and Erasmus); Aberdeen, 1700 (Corderius and Erasmus); Dumfries, 1751–74 (Corderius); Glasgow, 1786

NOTES

(Corderius). Castalio's *Sacred Dialogues* was one of the books sold by Ruddiman in the 1730's (Chalmers, *Life of Thomas Ruddiman*, p. 142 n.). At Aberdeen in 1659 it was laid down that a *Colloquium* of Erasmus should be acted before the visitors.

5 Aberdeen, 1659; Glasgow, 1685; Aberdeen, 1700. Cf. Steven, *History of the High School of Edinburgh*, Appendix, p. 35.
6 Glasgow, *c.* 1570; Edinburgh, 1578 (on Sundays); Edinburgh, 1640; Aberdeen, 1659; Glasgow, 1685 (also Buchanan's *Epigrams* and his Latin plays *Jephtha* and *Baptistes*); Aberdeen, 1700. The Edinburgh professors in 1710 disclaimed any intention 'to thrust out of schools Buchanan's immortal Paraphrase on the Psalms, which...can never be too much read or studied in Christian schools' (Steven, *History of the High School of Edinburgh*, Appendix, pp. 34-5).
7 Glasgow, *c.* 1570; Edinburgh, 1614 (themes and epistles); Aberdeen, 1659; Glasgow, 1685.

PAGE 136

1 John Strong, *History of Secondary Education in Scotland* (1909), pp. 89-90; cf. *Scottish Universities Commission (1826), Evidence*, vol. III (St Andrews), 1837, p. 222.
2 James Melville, *Autobiography and Diary*, p. 39. The statutes of Aberdeen grammar school, 1553, contain the clause 'loquantur omnes Latine, Grece, Hebraice, Gallice, Hybernice, nunquam vernacule, saltem cum his qui Latine noscunt'. This is somewhat slender evidence for the teaching of Greek. The last words suggest that Latin was the only real alternative to the vernacular.
3 Steven, *History of the High School of Edinburgh*, Appendix, pp. 8-10.
4 Grant, *Burgh Schools of Scotland*, p. 331.
5 *Ibid.* p. 332.
6 McCrie, *Life of Andrew Melville*, vol. II, pp. 413, 508. Steven, *History of the High School of Edinburgh*, pp. 29-30, quotes the last word as Thergius.

PAGE 137

1 Strong, *History of Secondary Education in Scotland*, p. 156.
2 *Scottish Universities Commission (1826), Evidence*, vol. III (St Andrews), 1837, pp. 222-3. Dr R. G. Cant informs me that it is by no means certain that the document originates from St Andrews. That prohibitions such as this had some ground is shown by some remarks of Alexander Jaffray, who in 1631 went from school to the university, 'where, passing the first class, having made the manner to learn some Greek in Banchory, I entered to my logics' (quoted, I. J. Simpson, *Education in Aberdeenshire before 1872* (1947), pp. 40-1).
3 *Register of the Privy Council of Scotland*, vol. III (3rd series), p. 450; Strong, *History of Secondary Education in Scotland*, p. 156; Sir A. Grant, *Story of the*

215

University of Edinburgh (2 vols. 1884), vol. I, pp. 267–8; John Burnet, *Essays and Addresses* (1929), p. 79; *Scottish Universities Commission (1826), Evidence*, vol. III (St Andrews), 1837, p. 220.

4 Steven, *History of the High School of Edinburgh*, pp. 103–4, 119–21; Grant, *Story of the University of Edinburgh*, vol. II, p. 324.

5 Grant, *Burgh Schools of Scotland*, p. 333; Simpson, *Education in Aberdeenshire before 1872*, p. 41; *Burgh Schools Commission Report (1868)*, vol. I, pp. 3–4. There are a number of records of masters being appointed able to teach Greek, but this does not necessarily mean that Greek was taught.

PAGE 138

1 Chalmers, *Life of Ruddiman*, p. 133; Adam Dickinson, preface to William Pyper's *Gradus ad Parnassum* (1813).

2 G. Chapman, *Treatise on Education*, p. 203.

PAGE 139

1 Lord Cockburn, *Memorials of his Time* (ed. H. A. Cockburn, 1909), p. 19.

2 Chalmers, *Life of Ruddiman*, p. 148.

3 Chapman, *Treatise on Education*, p. 204.

PAGE 140

1 James Melville, *Autobiography and Diary* (1842), p. 49.

2 *Ibid.* pp. 53–4.

PAGE 141

1 A. Morgan, *Scottish University Studies* (1933), p. 65.

2 Melville, *Autobiography and Diary*, pp. 24, 30. One of the regents taught the Greek alphabet and simple 'declintiones', but no more.

3 R. G. Cant, *The University of St Andrews* (1946), p. 48; McCrie, *Life of Andrew Melville*, vol. II, pp. 357–8.

4 Melville, *Autobiography and Diary*, p. 123.

5 J. M. Bulloch, *A History of the University of Aberdeen* (1895), pp. 79–80; Morgan, *Scottish University Studies*, p. 66. It is said that when James V visited Aberdeen in 1541 orations were delivered in Greek as well as in other languages (Bulloch, *op. cit.* p. 60), but in view of other evidence about the introduction of Greek to Scotland some scepticism seems justified.

6 R. S. Rait, *The Universities of Aberdeen* (Aberdeen, 1895), p. 255.

7 Grant, *Story of the University of Edinburgh*, vol. I, p. 148.

8 J. Coutts, *History of the University of Glasgow* (Glasgow, 1909), p. 109. At both universities the Greek course included translation to and from Greek, while at Glasgow those who had the faculty might compose verses. That Greek verse-composition was an accomplishment not unknown in seven-

teenth-century Glasgow is shown by the fact that when King James visited the city in 1617 one of the regents recited Greek verses in his honour (*ibid.* p. 86).

PAGE 142

1 Rait, *Universities of Aberdeen*, pp. 153, 284. King's College read one speech of Isocrates, one of Demosthenes and one book of Homer, Marischal College one of Isocrates, two of Demosthenes and some portion of Homer. King's College added 'Basilius Magnus his epistle' (no doubt that in Clenardus's grammar) and 'some of Nonni Paraphrasis'.

2 Grant, *Story of the University of Edinburgh*, vol. I, pp. 189–90, 263.

3 Coutts, *History of the University of Glasgow*, pp. 108, 155.

4 Cant, *The University of St Andrews*, p. 67. St Salvator's followed suit.

5 *Fasti Aberdonenses* (Spalding Club, 1854), p. 448. In the same year it was announced that the professor of Humanity besides teaching a Humanity class as was done in other universities would give an hour twice a week for the benefit of all the students (*Abstract of some statutes and orders of King's College in Old Aberdeen* (1753), p. 11).

6 *Fasti Academiae Mariscallanae Aberdonensis* (New Spalding Club, 1889–98), vol. II, p. 63.

PAGE 143

1 Strong, *History of Secondary Education in Scotland*, p. 152 n. The rule had been reasserted by the Commissioners appointed by the General Assembly at their visitation in 1642 (Coutts, *History of the University of Glasgow*, p. 108).

2 J. D. Mackie, *The University of Glasgow* (Glasgow, 1954), pp. 159–60, 234–5.

3 Grant, *Story of the University of Edinburgh*, vol. I, pp. 289–90.

4 *Ibid.* vol. II, p. 44.

5 Coutts, *History of the University of Glasgow*, p. 188. Thomas Reid, *Works* (ed. 1863), vol. II, p. 734.

6 Grant, *Story of the University of Edinburgh*, vol. I, p. 266.

7 *Ibid.* p. 267; *Scottish Universities Commission (1826), Report (1830)*, p. 125; Reid, *Works*, vol. II, p. 734.

PAGE 144

1 A. Dalzel, *History of the University of Edinburgh* (2 vols. Edinburgh, 1862), vol. I (Memoir), p. 9.

2 J. Veitch, *Memoir of Sir William Hamilton* (1869), p. 20 (quoting Thomas Hamilton, *Cyril Thornton*).

3 Dalzel, *History of the University of Edinburgh*, vol. I, p. 49.

PAGE 145

1 Lord Cockburn, *Memorials of his Time*, p. 18.

PAGE 146

1 *Scottish Universities Commission Report* (*1830*), p. 26.
2 Sir William Hamilton, *Discussions on Philosophy* (ed. 1866), p. 350.
3 *Ibid.*

PAGE 147

1 Lord Cockburn, *Memorials of his Time*, p. 4.
2 Steven, *History of the High School of Edinburgh*, p. 178.
3 *Ibid.* pp. 184–90. *Memoir of James Pillans*, by an old student (1869), pp. 20–2. The volume of verse was severely criticised by the *Quarterly Review*, and Pillans himself admitted that its publication was premature.
4 Steven, *History of the High School of Edinburgh*, pp. 292–6.
5 Cockburn, *Memorials of his Time*, p. 388.
6 Scott, *Journal*, 25 June 1828.

PAGE 148

1 *Commission on Schools in Scotland, Report on Burgh and Middle Class Schools* (*1868*), vol. II, p. 194.
2 W. A. Knight, *Principal Shairp and his Friends* (Edinburgh, 1888), p. 9; Memoir prefixed to William Young Sellar, *Roman Poets of the Augustan Age. Horace and the Elegiac Poets* (Oxford, 1892), pp. xxiii–xxiv.
3 Grant, *Burgh Schools of Scotland*, p. 333; Simpson, *Bon Record*, pp. 208, 243.
4 Simpson, *Bon Record*, pp. 221–6.

PAGE 149

1 Simpson, *Education in Aberdeenshire before 1872*, p. 41; Grant, *Burgh Schools of Scotland*, p. 333.
2 Grant, *Burgh Schools of Scotland*, p. 334; Strong, *History of Secondary Education in Scotland*, p. 175.
3 Strong, *History of Secondary Education in Scotland*, p. 202.

PAGE 150

1 John Kerr, *Scottish Education* (1910), p. 282.
2 Simpson, *Education in Aberdeenshire before 1872*, pp. 37, 42.
3 Professor Laurie, quoted in William Barclay, *Schools and Schoolmasters of Banffshire* (Banff, 1925), p. 182.
4 *Schools Inquiry Commission, Report*, vol. VI, pp. 19, 52.
5 *Commission on Schools in Scotland, Report on Burgh Schools*, vol. II, pp. 29, 36, 106.

PAGE 151

1 *Ibid.* vol. I, pp. 115–16.
2 *Ibid.* vol. I, pp. 110–13; vol. II, p. 284.

3 *Ibid.* vol. II, p. 209.

4 *Ibid.* vol. II, p. 201.

5 *Ibid.* vol. I, p. 113. Of other schools Dumfries Academy, where thirteen pupils were learning Greek, was described as excellent, while the boys of Dundee High School were proverbial for their accuracy. *Ibid.* vol. II, pp. 56–7, 191.

PAGE 152

1 At Glasgow at the end of the eighteenth century there was in theory a five-year course with a single subject to each year. The order of subjects was Latin, Greek, Logic, Moral Philosophy, Natural Philosophy, and an examination in the previous year's subject qualified for entry to that of the following year (Thomas Reid, *Works* (1863), vol. II, p. 732). But it seems to have been usual to attend other classes at the same time as that to which the student officially belonged.

2 This order dated from 1755. See *Plan of Education in Marischal College* (1755). At the other universities rhetoric was included in the logic class.

3 *Scottish Universities Commission (1858), General Report (1863)*, pp. xxvii–xxviii. These arrangements were very similar to those proposed by the Commission of 1826, but not then put into effect.

4 These regulations were the belated result of the Royal Commission of 1876. In 1907 the universities acquired the right to frame their own courses.

PAGE 153

1 Coutts, *History of the University of Glasgow*, p. 437; Grant, *Story of the University of Edinburgh*, vol. II, p. 122.

2 Knight, *Principal Shairp and his Friends*, p. 195.

3 Burnet, *Essays and Addresses*, p. 82.

4 Bulloch, *A History of the University of Aberdeen*, pp. 152–3.

5 Similarly at St Andrews in 1826 it was common for third- and fourth-year students to continue attending the Senior (second) Latin and Greek classes (*Scottish Universities Commission (1826), Report (1830)*, p. 401).

PAGE 154

1 *Ibid.* pp. 318, 335.

2 *Ibid.* p. 350; Alexander Bain, *Autobiography* (1904), p. 72.

3 A. F. Murison, *Memoirs of Eighty-eight years* (Aberdeen, 1935), p. 70.

4 *Glasgow University Commission (1837), Report (1839)*, p. 71.

PAGE 155

1 *Scottish Universities Commission Report (1878)*, vol. III (Evidence, pt. II), p. 410.

2 *Glasgow University Commission (1837), Report (1839)*, p. 63.

3 C. J. Fordyce in *Fortuna Domus* (1952), p. 36.

4 David Murray, *Memories of the Old College at Glasgow* (Glasgow, 1927), p. 211.

1 R. T. Davidson and W. Benham, *Life of Archibald Campbell Tait* (2 vols. 1891), vol. I, p. 26.

2 Murray, *Memories of the Old College at Glasgow*, p. 198.

3 Sellar in Knight, *Principal Shairp and his Friends*, pp. 14-15.

4 Murray, *Memories of the Old College at Glasgow*, p. 200.

5 *Classical Review*, vol. VII (1893), p. 426.

6 Lady Jebb, *Life and Letters of R. C. Jebb* (Cambridge, 1907), pp. 186-92.

1 *Ibid.* pp. 186-8; Coutts, *History of the University of Glasgow*, p. 447.

2 Lord Cockburn, *Memorials of his own Time*, p. 17.

3 *Ibid.* p. 3.

4 *Memoir of James Pillans*, p. 29.

5 *Ibid.* p. 28; cf. Grant, *Story of the University of Edinburgh*, vol. II, pp. 321-2.

6 *Scottish Universities Commission (1826), Report (1830)*, pp. 123-5.

7 *Memoir of James Pillans*, p. 26.

1 A. M. Stoddart, *John Stuart Blackie* (2 vols. 1895), vol. II, p. 223.

2 *Ibid.* vol. I, p. 301; vol. II, p. 224.

3 Lushington, when asked by the Principal whether he had read the Westminster confession, replied 'The law requires that I shall subscribe, not that I shall read, the Confession of Faith' (Murray, *Memories of the Old College at Glasgow*, p. 204).

4 A. C. Tait and Robert Scott both considered applying for the Glasgow Greek professorship on Sandford's death (Davidson and Benham, *Life of Archibald Campbell Tait*, vol. I, p. 66; Butler, *Life and Letters of Dr Samuel Butler*, vol. II, p. 278). For Mitchell see *Classical Museum* (1846), vol. III, p. 215.

1 For a survey of classical education and scholarship at Trinity College Dublin see W. B. Stanford, *Classical Scholarship in Trinity College Dublin*, reprinted from *Hermathena*, vol. LVII (1941).

2 Life of James Ussher, in C. R. Elrington and J. H. Todd's edition of Ussher's *Works* (17 vols. Dublin, 1847), vol. I, p. 7 (quoting from Bernard, Ussher's first biographer).

3 The statutes are printed in J. P. Mahaffy, *An Epoch of Irish History* (1903), pp. 327-75. See especially sections 13 and 14.

4 J. M. Stubbs, *History of the University of Dublin from 1591 to 1800* (Dublin, 1889), pp. 44–5.

PAGE 161

1 *Ibid.* p. 139.
2 *Ibid.* pp. 91, 197–8, 323. Terminal examinations were prescribed by statute.
3 *Ibid.* pp. 199–200.

PAGE 162

1 *Ibid.* p. 205.
2 *Ibid.* pp. 257–8.
3 *Ibid.* p. 207; P. Duigenan, *Lachrymae Academicae* (Dublin, 1777), p. 65.
4 *Dublin University Commission (1851), Report (1853)*, p. 64; Stubbs, *History of the University of Dublin*, p. 204.

PAGE 163

1 Stubbs, *History of the University of Dublin*, p. 259.
2 *Dublin University Commission (1851), Report (1853)*, p. 64.
3 *Endowed Schools, Ireland, Commission Report (1858)*, pp. 204, 248.
4 Stubbs, *History of the University of Dublin*, pp. 198–9, 258.
5 *The Book of Trinity College Dublin, 1591–1891* (Dublin, 1892), p. 114.

PAGE 164

1 *Dublin University Commission (1851), Evidence*, pp. 213–15.
2 *Ibid. Evidence*, p. 337. In the 1840's the proportion of students who failed to get a degree was considerably higher at Oxford than at Dublin (*Oxford University Commission Report (1852)*, p. 61).

PAGE 165

1 *Dublin University Commission (1851), Evidence*, p. 107.
2 *Classical Review*, vol. 1 (1887), p. 115.
3 *Ibid.* p. 116.

PAGE 166

1 The scale of marks was altered more than once in the second half of the century. In 1863 the marks allotted to Classics, Mental and Moral Science and Hebrew together totalled 1650 and those to Mathematics and Science 1600. In 1870 the corresponding marks became 1250 each. At the end of the century they were 1400 (Classics 800, Hebrew 100, Mental and Moral Science 500) to 1300 (Mathematics 1000, Experimental Science 300).
2 *Classical Review*, vol. 1 (1887), p. 116.
3 The professorship of Latin was founded in 1870.

4 K. C. Bailey, *A History of Trinity College Dublin 1892–1945* (Dublin, 1947), p. 193; cf. *D.N.B. s.v.* R. Y. Tyrrell.

5 *Proceedings of the British Academy* (1915–16), pp. 533–4.

PAGE 167

1 Erasmus, *Works*, vol. I, 521.

PAGE 169

1 Hugh Blair, *Lectures on Rhetoric* (3 vols. 1813), vol. III, pp. 14–15.

2 Jonathan Swift, *Essay on Modern Education.*

3 *Correspondence of William Pitt, Earl of Chatham* (4 vols. 1838–40), vol. I, pp. 62–3. See also Clarke, *Greek Studies in England*, pp. 12–13.

4 Gilbert Burnet, *Discourse of the Pastoral Care*, ed. 1692, pp. 162–3. This book was one of those adopted by the S.P.C.K. as standard works for those in or contemplating Holy Orders. Another such work was Henry Owen's *Directions to Young Students in Divinity* (2nd ed. 1773) which similarly recommended the reading of Tully's *Offices*, Plutarch, Seneca, Epictetus, Marcus Aurelius, Juvenal and Xenophon's *Memorabilia*. (See W. K. L. Clarke, *Eighteenth Century Piety* (1944), pp. 22–3.)

PAGE 170

1 Jonathan Swift, *Letter to a Young Gentleman lately enter'd into Holy Orders* (1721).

2 A. Amos, *Four lectures on the Advantages of a Classical Education* (1846), pp. 18, 72–5.

3 J. S. Mill, *Inaugural Address at the University of St Andrews* (1867), p. 17.

PAGE 171

1 Cf. the remarks of the Royal Commission on Endowed Schools in Ireland. 'Notwithstanding the serious moral imperfections of various kinds which pervade most of the writings of antiquity...we think that a knowledge of the masterpieces of ancient literature is to be desired...' (*Report*, p. 203).

2 Stanley, *Life of Arnold*, vol. I, p. 133.

3 See Henry Sidgwick in *Essays on a Liberal Education* (1867), p. 104.

PAGE 172

1 J. S. Mill, *Dissertations* (3rd ed. 1875), vol. I, p. 193; *Autobiography* (1886), p. 307.

2 Mill, *Dissertations*, vol. I, p. 202.

3 *Ibid.* vol. I, p. 202; vol. II, pp. 518, 526, 528; vol. III, pp. 284–5; *Inaugural Address to St Andrews University*, pp. 13–17; *Autobiography*, p. 233.

PAGE 173

1 Thomas Arnold, *Miscellaneous Works* (1845), p. 349.

2 Matthew Arnold, *Higher Schools and Universities in Germany* (1882), p. 155.

3 See Morley, *Life of Gladstone*, vol. I, pp. 646–8.

4 In the latter half of the century one notices a certain loss of faith in classical education on the part of some who had enjoyed such an education. See Mark Pattison, *Essays*, vol. I, p. 432; Richard Congreve, preface to edition of Aristotle's *Politics* (1855); Henry Sidgwick in *Essays on a Liberal Education*. These criticisms were a natural reaction to the peculiar development of education in England, which made it possible for a time to go through school and university having learned virtually nothing except the classics. Things would have looked rather different in Scotland or Ireland.

5 T. Mozley, *Reminiscences, chiefly of Oriel College*, vol. II, p. 423.

PAGE 174

1 J. H. Newman, *On the Scope and Nature of University Education*, Discourse IV.

PAGE 176

1 R. Descartes, *Discourse on Method*, pt. I.

THEME WRITING IN
THE SEVENTEENTH CENTURY

The following examples of specimen themes from seventeenth-century school-books illustrate the old method of teaching composition.

John Clarke's *Formulae Oratoriae*, the fourth edition of which was published in 1632, gives examples of three themes in both long and short version. I quote the short version on the Horatian text *quo semel est imbuta recens, servabit odorem testa diu* (9th ed., 1664, pp. 169–70).

1. Propositio   Nemo potest illos dediscere mores, aut eam excutere vivendi rationem, ad quam ab ipsis olim incunabulis assuevit.

2. Ratio   Quoniam impetus ille primus, tenerae pueritiae inditus, tam magnam habet in universa hominum vita momentum, ut dediscat id sero, quod *quis* didicit diu.

3. Confirmatio   Quae enim longa annorum serie, frequentissima actionum iteratione acquiruntur, in alteram quasi naturam transeunt.

4. Similitudo   Quemadmodum enim avium pulli, et ferarum catuli, semel mansuefacti, semper manent cicures, etiam quando in grandiores evaserint: non dissimiliter quos didicerit mores puerilis aetas, eosdem etiam tum quando adoleverit, penitissime sibi infixos usque retinebit.

5. Exemplum   *Ovidio*, scribendis versibus a teneris annis dedito, tam familiaris ac pene naturalis facta est *Poetica* facilitas, ut illi per universam deinceps vitam, *sponte sua numeros carmen veniebat ad aptos.*—

6. Exempli accommodatio   Nec dissimiliter contigit in reliquis artibus, vivendique institutis, quin quibus est imbutus vitae, ac morum praeceptis a teneris annis, iisdem sese semper addicat senex.

7. Testimonium   —Ad quid enim aliud respexit *Cicero*, cum dixerit, '*Nullum* nos posse maius meliusve Reipublicae afferre munus, quam docendo et erudiendo juventutem?' Num *hoc* innuere illum non

putabimus, *viz.* quod *recta juventutis institutio* ad summum Reipublicae emolumentum conducat maxime?

8. Conclusio   Proinde siquis in votis habeat, *liberos* suos ad virtutem
formare, ac bonos mores; id imprimis operam det, ut virtutis atque
pietatis *odore*, ab ipsis statim fasciis intimius imbuantur; *quem*, ad
extremam usque senectutem redolebunt.
—*adeo in teneris assuescere multum est.*

The Winchester Latin Phrase-Book (*Scholae Wintoniensis Phrases
Latinae*, by Hugh Robinson, 1654; 11th ed., 1685), following
Aphthonius, distinguishes two kinds of theme, Gnome and Chreia,
the former being a precept such as *Festina lente* or *Inprimis venerare
Deum*, and the latter an apophthegm such as *mors omnibus communis*
or *labor improbus omnia vincit*. I quote the treatment of the Gnome
Festina lente (ed. 1670, pp. 396–7).

1. Propositio   Damnosa est in gerendis rebus nimia festinatio.
2. Ratio   Nihil enim consilio tam inimicum est, quam temeraria
negotii praecipitatio.
3. Confirmatio   Sine consilio autem quidquid fit, recte fieri non
potest.
4. Similitudo   Ut aestas frugibus, ita deliberandi spatium maturan-
dis negotiis necessarium.
5. Exemplum   Fabius Maximus, ut ferunt, Romanam cunctando
restituit rem.
6. Veterum Testimonium   Noverat enim verum esse vetus illud
verbum omnia fieri sat cito si sat bene.
7. Conclusio   Bene igitur videtur consulere, qui Lente monet
festinare.

The following is a specimen theme given (as a fourth-form
exercise) in the Merchant Taylors' Probation Book (1652). The
prose theme is followed by some elegiacs on the same subject,
illustrating Hoole's practice (see p. 40) of making his pupils ' comprise the sum of their Themes in a Distich, Tetrastich, Hexastich,
or more verses'. The theme is *Literae sunt hominis ornamentum.*

Socratem ferunt saepius juvenes admonuisse, ut se jugiter in speculo
intuerentur, ut, si formosi essent, digni ea specie fierent; sin autem

minus speciosi, eam deformitatem eruditione tegerent. Literarum enim studia (ut recte Cicero) adolescentiam alunt, senectutem oblectant, secundas res ornant, adversis perfugium ac solatium praebent, delectant domi, non impediunt foris, pernoctant nobiscum, peregrinantur, rusticantur. Cogitandum igitur est, quam multos ditârint, quam multos ad summam dignitatem auctoritatemque provexerint literae. Absque his si sit, homines in belluas, in truncos, in lapides, in monstra denique immania transformarentur. Atque hinc est, quod Aristippus dixerit melius longe mendicum fieri, quam indoctum; ille enim solis pecuniis, hic autem ipsissima caret humanitate. Junium igitur Syllanum bene nummatum, sed indoctum, auream pecudem appellavit Caesar; hominem autem doctrina ornatum, animalium pulcherrimum nominabat Socrates. Quemadmodum enim inter planetas Sol, inter stellas Lucifer, vel inter orbes Primum Mobile; sic etiam inter reliquorum hominum genus longe eminet eruditus, et omnes alios, multis (quod aiunt) parasangis, antecellit. E contrario vero indoctus, qui a Musis abhorret, est tanquam lapis super lapidem, qui tantum differt a doctis, quantum vivens a mortuis. Veneranda igitur doctrinae majestas, colenda eruditionis dignitas, summo studio, et ambabus ulnis amplectendae literae; sine quibus vita nihil aliud est quam vivi hominis sepultura.

Carmina in idem Thema

Hector Trojanis, Argivis saevus Achilles,
　　Caelicolisque decus Jupiter ipse suis.
Ornamenta viris sic Musae; ut pinguibus arvis
　　Sunt segetes, laetis vitibus uva decus.

The scheme used in the first two themes quoted is derived from Aphthonius; the third shows a freer treatment. No doubt the schoolboy started by following the traditional divisions, but outgrew them as he progressed. This, I take it, is the meaning of the sentence in the description of Eton *c.* 1670: 'At first they began with the parts of a theme, then threw them off' (*V.C.H., Bucks,* vol. II, p. 198).

INDEX

INDEX

Printed in Great Britain
by Amazon

45822213R00142